D0884371

07

THE
DEATH
OF INNOCENCE

Library
Oakland S.U.M.

ALSO BY SAM JANUS

A Sexual Profile of Men in Power

28107

THE
DEATH
OF INNOCENCE

HOW OUR CHILDREN
ARE ENDANGERED BY THE
NEW SEXUAL FREEDOM

Sam Janus, Ph.D.

Introduction by
Judianne Densen-Gerber, J.D., M.D.

WILLIAM MORROW AND COMPANY, INC.
New York   *1981*

Copyright © 1981 by Sam Janus

All rights reserved. No part of this book may be reproduced or
utilized in any form or by any means, electronic or mechanical, including photocopying, recording or by any information storage and
retrieval system, without permission in writing from the Publisher.
Inquiries should be addressed to William Morrow and Company, Inc.,
105 Madison Ave., New York, N. Y. 10016.

Library of Congress Cataloging in Publication Data

Janus, Sam, 1930–
    The death of innocence.

    Bibliography: p.
    Includes index.
        1. Sex customs—United States.   2. United States
—Moral conditions.   3. Children—United States—
Sexual behavior.   4. Youth—United States—Sexual
behavior.   I. Title.
HQ18.U5J35   306.7   81-164
ISBN 0-688-00136-X   AACR2

Printed in the United States of America

First Edition

1   2   3   4   5   6   7   8   9   10

BOOK DESIGN BY MICHAEL MAUCERI

ACKNOWLEDGMENTS

This book would not have been possible without the dedication and assistance of many people. To all of the brave, concerned human beings listed here, I give special thanks. Particular gratitude is due to the thousands who relived the trauma of personal loss in the death of their innocence. I fulfill now the pledge I made to them, that the world would know of and hopefully prevent these traumas for future generations.

Among the many psychiatrists, psychologists, and other mental health workers, special thanks to Dr. William Prendergast, Dr. Margaret McHugh, Drs. Irving and Toby Bieber, Dr. Virginia Sadock, Dr. Alan Jong, Dr. Simeon Feigen, Dr. Jules Bemporad, Dr. Edward Greenwood, Dr. James Comer, Dr. Henry Giaretto, Ms. Lucy Berliner, Mr. Bob Meltzer, Dr. Adele Hoffman, Dr. Elizabeth McAnarney, Dr. Dorothy Bracey, Dr. Louis Lieberman, Dr. Abraham Cohen, and especially Dr. Harold Greenwald.

And from among the nation's finest of law enforcement personnel, special gratitude to Sgt. Lloyd Martin and Sgt. Glen Sousa of the L.A.P.D., Captain Eimil of the S.F.P.D., Sgt. Jose Elique of the Port Authority Police, to Deputy Inspectors Dillon and Maher and Detective James Ross of the N.Y.P.D., and especially to Sgt. John Johnstone of the New York State Troopers.

Father Bruce Ritter, whose painstaking work in arousing the conscience of the world to the plight of children has been an inspiration to many, and his tireless efforts have their own reward.

A special word about Dr. Judianne Densen-Gerber, whose crusading spirit and limitless energy have often turned seeming failure into success in saving lives and shaking up America. She has become a beacon of hope to many of society's casualties.

A grateful thanks to Kathryn Randall and Ingrid Nelson for their dedication and tireless help in editing this manuscript. And to George Sharrard and Stanley Keyles for their valuable research assistance.

Also to my editors at Morrow, Pat Golbitz and Naomi Cutner, without whose energy and hard work this book would not have seen daylight.

And finally, a special and personal thanks to my wife, Cynthia, whose infinite patience and inspiration kept me working these many years on this painful but vital project.

CONTENTS

INTRODUCTION

Today's sexual revolution, which is perhaps better called the sexual holocaust, has radically altered the whole fabric of society. As a mother of four children, two girls and two boys, ranging in age from six to twenty, I find it difficult to know how to parent in these rapidly changing times. There seem to be almost no parameters of conduct, no limitations on behavior. Permissiveness is exalted. Those of us from past generations have no anchors to secure us.

Our parents had firm ideas of right and wrong. When we misbehaved, we may have felt hypocritical and a bit guilty, but at least we had value systems against which we could test ourselves. Today, with sexual freedom leading more often to license than to happiness, our children have become frightened, alienated, and isolated. They search for intimacy in immediate genital gratification rather than in sustained caring relationships. Perhaps they do not know how to care for themselves or each other because we, as parents, don't know how to care for them.

Good parenting has three major components. The first task is to provide at least a minimum amount of love and security for the child. This gives the child a foundation from which to venture forth into the world and basic inner resources of self-confidence to face the future. Love and security are also essential if the child is to mature sufficiently, if he or she is to be able to make future subject-to-subject relationships rather than treat everyone else as an object in the fulfillment of his or her own personal needs. The parent must begin this process by giving love free from exploitation.

One of the most frightening aspects of the recent politicizing for the right of pedophiles (persons who obtain sexual gratification from relationships with children) to use children sexually is their pro-incest rationalization. They claim that present-day children are so isolated from warm, touching family relationships that incest is better than no intimacy at all (*Psychology Today*, March, 1980; *Time* magazine, April, 1980). There are pro-pedophile, pro-incest movements in this country and throughout the world. These people are self-serving abusers of children.

The Rene Guyon Society based in California boasts 8,500 members who espouse the motto "Sex by eight or it's too late." The eastern equivalent, the North American Man/Boy Love Association (N.A.M.B.L.A.), presently active to my knowledge in eleven major cities in the Northeast and Midwest, advocates total abolition of the "age of consent" laws relating to sexual intercourse between adult and child (mostly man and boy). This group vigorously advocates such intimacy as healthy for the child. N.A.M.B.L.A. began in 1978 as a defense fund and social spokesman for several New England independent school-teachers who had been indicted in Massachusetts on the charge of sexually molesting (without force) several of their high school students.

The British equivalent, The Paedophiliac Information Exchange (P.I.E.), first surfaced in 1975 at the British Psychiatric Association meetings in Wales. They suggest four as the age of consent. Lest we moms and dads think that this is a powerless lunatic fringe, we should note that Denmark no longer has legal sanctions against nonforceful incest; Sweden defeated similar legislation by one vote; the British Royal Commission recommended in the summer of 1979 that all age of consent laws be abolished; and, closer to home, in the same year New Jersey almost lowered the age of consent to thirteen.

The United States has no national uniform policy protecting

our children—one is vitally necessary—nor do we have much in the way of legislation which makes possible sensible legal and psychiatric handling for children who are victims of inappropriate early sexualization and sexploitation (incest, rape, prostitution, and pornography). We need to be awakened, to be informed, and to respond.

Parenting's second task is to negotiate the system on behalf of the child; to obtain for the child the very best that the society has to offer. For example, while many parents deeply love their children, parental inadequacies, fears, or handicaps may prevent them from adequately caring for the health or educational needs of their young. In such instances, it is important for the community to aid and assist the parents with supportive services. Examples of this are the aid given to a middle-class family with a severely deformed child; the guidance given to an illiterate migrant family with a learning-disabled child; the information given to all of us about junk food and proper feeding of our young, or about the levels of radioactivity in the atmosphere.

Similar guidance by experts is extremely necessary in the area of sexuality, since so many of us in the parental generation were poorly instructed by our own parents, given few if any facts and some misinformation. One of the greatest dangers we now face is from so-called experts who are flooding the field with distortions.

A book like *Show Me*, which was written by a physician, purports to be a sex-hygiene text suitable and suggested for use by seven- to eight-year-olds. I am sure many parents wanting to do the right thing by their children buy *Show Me* in the mistaken belief that this is appropriate. I am distressed by the photographs in *Show Me* which show sexual intercourse occurring between young teenagers. This is particularly dangerous at a time when we have an epidemic of teenage venereal disease and pregnancy. Over one million babies were born to girls teenage or younger in 1978, 9,000 of whom were eleven or younger.

It is also clear from the text of *Show Me* that many of the couples engaging in sexual intercourse are not married. Our children will learn soon enough that sexual relations occur outside of matrimony. But when they are first presented with "the facts of life," such facts should be explained within the context of caring, love, and commitment. Human sexuality and its teaching should always incorporate *feeling* as well as mechanical facts.

Show Me portrays to the eight-year-old that labor is an excruciatingly painful experience—clearly a template destructive to natural childbirth at twenty-five. It also depicts fellatio. Are these questions asked by seven-year-olds, or once again are we destroying childhood by adultomorphizing our young? It is sad that though parents set out to help their children, they may harm them by such confused, inappropriate messages.

The third task of parenting is that parents must be role models for their children. The essence of childhood is to imitate and copy. Children learn primarily through identification with and admiration of the parenting figures. If the parent is an alcoholic, is drug addicted, or is sexually promiscuous, if the parent lies, steals, or has few values, the child will have nothing good with which to identify. Even during the rebellion of adolescence, the child needs a backboard of parental values and traditions against which to define him or herself. It is better for the parent to be wrong but firm than to be uncommitted and permissive.

The same is true of society at large. None of us can rear our young in isolation. We adults have expectations of society that are similar to those our children have of us. Society must provide us with healthy soil in which to nurture our young. Society must provide us with the information and tools to negotiate the world as it now assaults us. And, finally, there must be models and leaders within our communities who articulate "No-No's"—to show us right from wrong.

Dr. Janus in *The Death of Innocence* confronts us with the stark realities of modern-day living. It appears we are entering a modern-day era of Caligula, and we must resist together in one voice to ensure our children of their most basic right—the right to be a child. Thank you, Sam Janus, for a task well done.

JUDIANNE DENSEN-GERBER, J.D., M.D.

May, 1980
NEW YORK, N.Y.

Chapter 1

CHILDREN NO MORE

An explosion of news stories over the past year has focused public attention on a new phenomenon in our society: the prevalence of an active, open, and extensive sexuality among young middle-class children. A drastic drop in the age at which menstruation first occurs, a rising birth rate among nine-to fifteen-year-old girls (at a time when in every other age group the birth rate is falling), and the alarming increase in the incidence of venereal disease among preteenagers all suggest that we are undergoing a cultural upheaval that is changing the character of American experience. A basic tenet of modern developmental psychology always has been the belief that between infancy and adolescence, sexuality goes underground—becomes "latent"—in the interests of psychic and physical growth. It now appears that after thirty-five years of post-Freudian enlightened child-rearing, the so-called "latency period" is a thing of the past, and that our children are going straight from babyhood to puberty as fully sexual beings, with no intermission. The eroticization of childhood is becoming a fact of life in modern society.

Our adult view of children is changing as well; we seem to have abandoned our belief in childhood innocence, a trend reflected at its most shocking extreme in the exploitation of children by the commercial sex industry. The juvenile branch of this business has escalated over the past few years to the point where an estimated 300,000 children have been used by pornographers to service a burgeoning adult market. A further symptom of disturbance is what psychologists are calling an "epidemic" of incest among members of middle-class families. This development, in turn, is not unrelated to the record number of "baby pros" (child prostitutes) cruising our city streets, a high proportion of whom report that they left home to escape intolerable sexual pressures from fathers or from father figures, such as stepfathers or mothers' boyfriends. Pornography and incest exploit children; so does pederasty. We also are witnessing the mobilization of pederasts into politically active groups to defend their "right" to use children for sexual pleasure.

In June, 1977, Dr. Judianne Densen-Gerber, a New York psychiatrist and attorney, testified before a congressional subcommittee. She said, "I believe the American system hates its children." She was referring to the sexual abuse of children at the hands of pimps and pornographers, and she thus echoed the feelings of many experts. But her remark might just as well have referred to the million and a half runaways who leave the comfort and relative security of middle-class homes each year for a brutal life on the streets. And it could have referred to the unwed teenage mothers who give birth to 600,000 babies annually.

In this book we will examine the following issues: the recent and radical changes in the sexual behavior of middle-class, preadolescent children; the possible causes of what could be called the filtering down of the "sexual revolution" to our youngest; the forms this new childhood sexuality takes; its commercial exploitation by adults; the attitudes of participants (both adults and children) in this exploitation; and the implications for the future of our sociey if precocious sexual activity among children becomes the norm. We also will take into consideration the ramifications of illicit drug use, which, by 1979, reached $50 billion annually, $15 billion of which was for cocaine, the caviar of the upper class. Drug use and its altering of consciousness has served to grease the skids for the decline of American morality.

Central to any discussion of sexual development is the concept of the latency period. As conceived of by Freud and his followers, this period lasts from about age five until puberty. Strictly speaking, it is the time between infancy and puberty when Oedipal strivings are temporarily abandoned and overt sexuality becomes repressed so that the forces of sublimation and superego formation can take precedence in the interest of civilizing the libidinal energies. When sexuality bursts forth again at puberty, it is imbued with a capability for giving and accepting adult love. One might call latency a period of grace, a breathing space between the two waves of instinctual dominance: the savagery of infantile Oedipal conflict and the turmoil of adolescence—which in turn has been made bearable because the libido has become tempered during latency.

Latency is the time when boys despise girls and vice versa, a time when children form close bonds with members of their own sex, acquire a sense of shame, and develop intellectual curiosity and a passionate interest in sports and hobbies. Often thought of as the time of life in which man most truly possesses himself, a blissful "safe place," an earthly paradise, it is a peculiarly American dream which evokes the most poignant nostalgia later on in life, as expressed, for example, in the classic novels of Mark Twain and Booth Tarkington.

But the latency period not only spared the child premature internal conflict over his or her own sexual impulses, it also provided protection from sexual demands from without. The belief that children were ignorant of and immune to sexual feelings has acted as a powerful deterrent against approaches by adults. We examine what happens when this taboo is no longer enforced; that is, we explore what is being done to children by adults—in particular, how children are being drafted into the commercial sex industry and used in pornography and prostitution.

The social changes since World War II have brought with them dramatic changes in attitudes toward children. While experts in the fields of child development and psychiatry were aware of the loosening of family ties and of the greater freedom being granted children to make important decisions about their lives, many regarded these as progress. The direction of "liberating" the children even found itself caught in politics, with some states contemplating, as Sweden is now, a children's "bill of rights." In Sweden children over six years old can "divorce" their parents and live in a choice of foster homes. Denmark has abolished all age of consent laws, now making it legal for an adult and a "consenting child" to have sex. For this author it is absurd to consider that a child of five, six, or seven can give reasoned consent.

New Jersey almost lowered the age of consent for sexual relations from age sixteen to age thirteen. The bill had already passed the legislature, was signed by the governor, and, in fact, was due to go into effect October, 1979, as part of the new criminal code, when its existence became public knowledge. A police lieutenant in Paramus, New Jersey, made note of the new criminal code and the lower age during a department briefing session. Once he publicized the situation, the resulting public outcry brought about immediate changes. The New Jersey legislature restored the age of consent to sixteen. Of course, there are a variety of ages of consent, ranging from thirteen through seventeen, in many states. The trend, however, where changes are written into the law, is to lower the age requirement.

Sadly, what appeared to so many people to be liberation has ended up as legalized sexual exploitation of children on a scale never before seen in the United States. While there have always been individuals and institutions that degraded children, historically those children were from lower socioeconomic classes; for example, black slaves and, even earlier, Indians. It was so widely accepted that "anything went" with socially subordinate groups that even respectable public figures of the day thought nothing of using slaves sexually. Thomas Jefferson once wrote to George Washington that two fourteen-year-old girls would be available for sexual relations if he came to visit.

The changes we see now in the United States as we enter the 1980's are part of an ostensibly more egalitarian view. Everyone should do "it." In fact, one song made popular in 1979 beats out the words in an insistent rhythm, "Do it, do it, do it till you're satisfied!"

Children, preteens, and teens, who buy the most tapes and records, heed the messages in such songs, as well as those in movies and television shows, and become the most firm believers in the popular culture of the day, no matter what day it may be. Today so many children are "doing it," whether satisfied or not, that the only group in the United States with an increasing birth rate is nine- to sixteen-year-old children. In fact, in 1978 the Department of Health, Education, and Welfare reported that 9,000 babies were born to girls eleven years old or younger. This number is only for live births and does not include abortions, miscarriages, and unreported births or pregnancies. We might also note here that the rate of pregnancies increased 13.1 percent among black and Hispanic girls, 50 percent among white girls.

Just how far society has moved in its views on morality may be seen in the schools. Colleges have in one generation gone from providing separate, chaperoned housing to establishing co-ed dorms. Their health services dispense contraceptives and make referrals to abortion clinics. Many colleges, with the exception of some religious schools, have proclaimed that they do not act *in loco parentis* anymore. In other words, drug use and sex behavior are not their concern.

High schools, junior high schools, and even elementary schools are more heavily involved in the childhood sexual revolution. In fact, the lower the age and grade, the more sexual ferment and change one sees. There seems to be a continual scream of headlines about rapes in school, sex clubs, and very extensive drug use beginning in grades five and six. Confirming national statistics, every child interviewed for this study by grade seven had either used nonprescribed medication, was about to, or had a good friend who was using such drugs.

On April 25, 1979, the House Select Committee on Population reported that,

(a) One out of every five American children aged thirteen or fourteen had had sexual intercourse.
(b) Fewer than one third of these sexually experienced children used contraception regularly.

(c) More than one half of all illegitimate births in the United States involved teenage mothers.

(d) Pregnancy was the single most common cause of dropping out of school for girls.

The committee chairman, Representative James Scheuer (D.) of New York, observed that these facts underline the woeful inadequacy of the government's response to the needs of American children. The committee concluded that funding for contraceptive research and family-planning clinics must be increased. However, a larger problem that the committee could not address itself to is the schizophrenic American attitude toward sex, especially sex involving children. While everyone agrees that a problem exists, government agencies and private foundations find their hands tied by legal impediments, such as the prohibition of services for minors without parental notification or consent.

In general, we see governmental inadequacy in this area at all levels—federal, state, and city. For example, while every knowledgeable citizen bemoans "kiddie porn," the federal government encounters serious problems in condemning it. There is a widespread fear that prohibiting a ten-year-old from appearing in a pornographic film might violate that child's First Amendment rights.

While New York is the only city to have a "runaway squad," it becomes an empty gesture when the facts are known. For in a city of almost eight million people, with a police force at full strength of 28,000 officers, there are only six police officers assigned to the "runaway squad"—one sergeant and five patrolmen. This coverage provides New York, a mecca for runaways, with approximately one quarter of one police officer covering any of the five boroughs during the three shifts that police officers work.

Across the country, Los Angeles, the other major U.S. runaway center and also the center of kiddie-porn production, has the only juvenile vice bureau in the country. This squad also consists of one sergeant and four patrolmen. In fact, it was only at the insistence of Sergeant Lloyd Martin, head of the squad, that it was formed at all in 1977. Even though Martin had amassed statistics to demonstrate the extent of the runaway problem, Los Angeles began its juvenile vice bureau only when it received a federal grant from the L.E.A.A. (Law Enforcement and Assistance Administration) in 1976.

This negligence by city governments assumes serious dimensions when one takes into account that New York City and Los Angeles are the two major magnets for the one million runaways reported annually by the Department of Health, Education, and Welfare. (Our research leads us to estimate the number of runaways at closer to 1,300,000 children.)

There are occasional attempts by individuals and organizations to take action and "save children from the obvious degradation they are sinking into." One dramatic example of this was flashed across the country when two vice-squad policemen flew to New York City from Minneapolis, Minnesota, in 1977. They proclaimed their determination to wipe out the infamous "Minnesota–New York Pipeline." They claimed that each year the "pipeline" transported 400 girls as young as thirteen from the twin cities of St. Paul and Minneapolis (which, in turn, attracted girls from neighboring midwestern states such as Wisconsin and Kansas) to New York. Girls from these farm areas are much in demand in the porno/prostitution field. Principally of Scandinavian origin, the girls' wholesome, blond, and blue-eyed good looks bring the highest prices.

The senior officer in the team, Lieutenant Al Pahlmquist, in addition to being a seasoned vice cop also runs a rehabilitation center for ex-prostitutes called Midwest Challenge. The team's prowling of the streets of Manhattan, especially of the Minnesota Strip, a section of Eighth Avenue between Fortieth and Fifty-fourth Streets, was in vain. The officers went home a week later without having rescued a single girl. However, blaming their failure on conflicts with the New York Police Department as well as on excess publicity, they vowed to return. They did so three months later, accompanied by a group of young ex-prostitutes who had been shunted through the Minnesota–New York Pipeline, and who were working with Lieutenant Pahlmquist to rehabilitate other young prostitutes. This time the group brought vans and printed cards that guaranteed free transportation to Minnesota, with no requirement to stay there. Girls could be flown there, or they could come along in a van. The immediate take-off option was offered to counter the threat of the pimps' intervention to forcibly keep the girls locked into prostitution. However, sadly, again not a single young girl returned to Minnesota. Very obviously, the needs and views of youngsters were not met with this appeal. Perhaps it sounded too much like the parents' appeals they had heard so often.

As we notice in the chapter on runaways and pornography, the vast number of children, perhaps 500,000, who are involved in the pornography and prostitution business indicates that there is a complete break with traditional Judeo-Christian standards. Most adults, as the 1970's drew to an end, seemed upset and confused by the fact that pimps and cult leaders seemed to reach so easily children who were alienated from their parents. Are the traditional values of middle America so at odds with the needs and aspirations of most American children as to be irrelevant? If this is so, then the family is in even more serious trouble than most experts feel, and this bodes even more ominously for the capacity of today's children to grow into healthy adults.

Has liberation become libertine? Has the vaunted liberation of children turned them into sacrificial lambs on the altar of the sexual revolution? At the close of the seventies, the pressure for "change" in all areas seems irresistible. To Americans, who are constantly bombarded with advertisements for "all new" and "improved" products, any change is equated with progress and seems desirable. Yet five major social revolutions in the latter part of the twentieth century have upset and changed values. The resulting "new morality" has had devastating effects on children.

The sexual revolution has affected all of American society, but most dramatically it has affected American women. The concept of marriage as an institution solely or primarily for the procreation of children has been seriously challenged. This challenge is a blow to a centuries-old morality which dictated that sex and marriage were for procreation, not pleasure. If nothing else, the sexual revolution stated that it is acceptable to expect sexual fulfillment. This was the logical outgrowth of Freud's revolutionary school of psychoanalysis, which put great emphasis on pleasure and dared explore such controversial areas as childhood, and even infant, sexuality. Freud shocked the world when he wrote that children receive sexual gratification of some kind from earliest infancy, starting with nursing.

Next came the contraceptive revolution. For the first time in history, effective means to have sexual intercourse without the consequences became available. Thus, we backed up the psychological change of the sexual revolution with the medical means effectively to eliminate unwanted pregnancy. There were, and are still, however, laws on the books in many states that forbid the sale of contraceptives to minors, and in some states the prohibition extends even to adults without a doctor's prescription. But in most states these laws have been changed, and we now see contraceptives displayed at drugstore counters, distributed in storefront clinics, and even bootlegged in junior high schools. Since prescriptions are needed for birth control pills, young children who cannot purchase them legally procure them on the black market in school, much as they procure other drugs. Our research shows that the availability of birth control pills to preteenage and teenage youngsters is widespread.

There are still a great many individuals who believe that permitting the sale of contraceptives encourages promiscuity among children. Children and adult advocates of planned parenthood dispute this, arguing that by not making contraceptives available, society may stop children from having "responsible sex," but it will not prevent them from having sex itself. The safety and certainty of contraception in avoiding the unwanted consequences of sexual activity have certainly influenced young people and helped many to relax their anxiety about the dangers of sex. Women, as childbearers, have been the most directly affected by the contraceptive revolution as well as by the sexual revolution.

It is no wonder then that the old double standard which was dying during the early 1970's was declared dead in 1979 by Dr. John DeLamater, Professor of Sociology at the University of

Wisconsin. He had just completed a six-year study on sexual attitudes and behavior of young men and women. His results showed that the overwhelming majority of his respondents felt that "it is okay for men to have sex and that it's also acceptable for women." In fact, 94 percent of the men and 87 percent of the women agreed that making love before marriage was all right for both sexes. The findings are cross-cultural, irrespective of religion or socioeconomic background. They are certainly different from the Kinsey results of 1953, which showed for one thing that only 35 percent of college females had ever masturbated. Among blue-collar women the percentage was considerably lower.

The next revolutions were the feminist and civil rights revolutions, which left women and young girls integrally involved in society, and with women's issues becoming increasingly viewed as part of the civil rights struggle. The last social revolution still ongoing in the United States at the end of the 1970's and continuing into the 1980's is the "gay" liberation revolution. In an atmosphere which challenges such a broad range of existing sexual and moral beliefs, there are few basic "truths" that children can hang on to. Young children particularly are most easily influenced by what is *au courant* and are eager to be "with it." Since the current dictum is that everybody does his or her thing (a popular 1979 song dictates "doing it" till you are satisfied), many children believe these fads to be truths to live by.

The only children in all the research who appeared immune to the cultural pressures involving sex and morality were those with strong religious beliefs and/or who also felt loved by their parents. Parents' income, race, socioeconomic background were all of no significance in affecting children's choices of moral codes.

While sociologists working in the field of human rights acknowledge that there have been strides in establishing beachheads to protect children, even from their own families, many experts are now concerned about the future. By 1979 all states had passed child abuse laws to protect children from physical abuse in the home. However, protection from sexual abuse is not legislated and, in fact, has only become a topic to be discussed by psychologists, psychiatrists, and sociologists in the last three years. Children's "rights" in America have progressed to a dangerous state. In freeing children from their parents and moving them earlier into the mainstream of society, which may be "liberating," we have set them up for exploitation. Where there is less parental control there is also less protection. We see that children who run away, as explored in the chapter on runaways, are forever receiving new labels. Thus, we now speak not only of runaway children, but also of throwaway and walkaway children, children whose homes became nonexistent, or whose families expelled them.

There is among sociologists a school of history called the "Eternal Constant." This school holds that there have always been certain modes of behavior in any culture. The ancient Greeks and Romans, for example, certainly exhibited certain behaviors, and events have recurred since time immemorial, so there really is no cause for alarm. We reject this argument vigorously, as it does not take into account the casualties—the youngsters who grow up survivors of a revolution they were drafted into, knew nothing about, and did not ask to be a part of.

There is no question that a diverse number of self-interest groups have quickly leaped in to fill the gap between parent and child.

In the past a great many parents deferred teaching their children about sex, rationalizing that the child was not yet ready. With the loss of the latency period, however, an accelerated development, which telescopes from infancy through early adolescence to almost a lifetime of experiences, has foisted these experiences on the shoulders of unwitting youngsters—ready or not. Gone are the halcyon days when little boys had time to join boys' clubs, build clubhouses, and play ball. Some, of course, still do but the numbers decline. The same goes for little girls, who once played with dolls and hoped some day their knights in shining armor would come along, marry them, and live happily ever after with them.

So far, society has all but ignored these changes in American childhood. There is a tremendous frustration among those who research the field, as well as among those in the criminal justice system, about the seeming inability of the courts and the police to cope with pimps' brutality. Between 1974 and 1977, the government finally acted on a small scale in New York City and put several pimps in jail, not on charges of sexual exploitation or brutality, but for income-tax evasion. One begins to suspect, as Dr. Judianne Densen-Gerber and others in the field have suggested, that our society does indeed hate its children.

We see the casualties of the sexual revolution all about us. High schools which at one time expelled pregnant girls no longer do so because they would be depriving so many youngsters of an education, which would even further jeopardize their futures. Schools in the United States began admitting pregnant girls, but around 1962 insisting that they attend special classes in buildings isolated from the mainstream of junior high and high school students. Then the number of pregnant girls became so large that it was no longer economically feasible or politically wise to separate them. So, for the most part, they are now mainstreamed, with only a few school systems still isolating pregnant girls. Their presence may make parents and teachers uncomfortable, but it probably has a lesser impact on already savvy teenagers.

The feminist revolution, the contraceptive revolution, and the sexual revolution have freed female children from the restraints of the culture and its Judeo-Christian morality. It is interesting to note that while there is only a slightly larger number of boys who are sexually active, though they do become sexually active younger, the number of sexually active girls has increased tremendously since 1960. The gay revolution has probably also had more of an impact on young women and girls in junior high and high school than it has had on boys. There are many reports across the country of young women in high schools and colleges having lesbian affairs because it is the politically correct thing to do. In fact, so slavishly do children follow what they consider to be the "right" thing to do, that during the latter half of the 1970's, when it appeared that heterosexuality might be in vogue again, many young women who were political lesbians formed relationships with young men. However, they would insist on including their homosexual partner so as not to denigrate their love for women.

We find that, in general, many children are unable to relate to each other on a one-to-one basis. American youngsters, particularly those aged eleven to fifteen, tend to go to parties in packs, to "turn on" in packs, and to make love in packs. The old need for privacy and exclusivity lessened considerably during the 1970's. Only in the latter part of 1979 did we begin to sense a slight resurgence of interest in coupling and in exclusivity.

However, children, in packs or alone, when they are on the run from society, find that the morality of the street becomes the dominant code. In the chapter on runaways, we will see just how extensive the network is that hustles children away from their parents to various big cities and how influential the moral code engendered by that network is.

It is an interesting and saddening observation to note the direction taken by contemporary sex-oriented photo displays. Starting in World War II, G.I.'s were regaled with a variety of pinup photographs of famous actresses. For the most part, these were "cheesecake" shots which showed a great deal of leg but not much more. Then we moved during the early to mid-1950's to complete nudity. Once nudity was accepted by society, the next step was to show simulated male-female intercourse in soft-core stills and films. Next came hard-core pornography where, instead of simulated lovemaking, there was actual heterosexual interaction, often of a variety of perverse types. The next big push was in gay pornography, which depicted men and women in various kinds of homosexual interaction. This was followed during the early sixties to midsixties by portrayals of bestiality, which involved the use of animals in sex. Then came kiddie porn, which featured children as young as six, seven, and eight. Kiddie porn seems to have blossomed into a multibillion-dollar business in its own right.

In fact, kiddie porn is the fastest-growing income producer for the pornography business in general.

In order to be able to get some appreciation of where we are headed in the eighties, we conducted a survey among college youngsters who a decade ago were children of ten and eleven. The findings show that some of the effects of early sexual exposure indeed remain and traumatize children.

This book pinpoints where the sexual revolution has brought us. It also points out ways in which we can surmount the damage to children and help to raise successfully a generation of sexually educated and moral children who can become adults with dignity and status, capable of forming satisfying relationships and building families.

Chapter 2

A DECADE OF CHANGE
1969–1979

Young people have always followed the dictates of a culture which is parallel to, but completely separate from, that of their elders. Within the youth culture, the most powerful force is peer pressure—peer pressure to conform not only to certain styles of dress and modes of speech, but also to a group morality. The basic underlying question of this chapter is just what social forces create that group morality? It is my belief that today, more than ever before, the overriding influence on the child culture is the adult culture. Adult mores are being foisted onto children who, in effect, are being denied their childhood.

The primary vehicle for transmitting adult values to children today is television. We know that children spend an average of forty-nine hours a week watching television. We also know that they spend more time watching television than they spend doing anything else except sleeping. In their study, *Sex on Television*, Silverman, Sprafkin, and Rubinstein* say:

> We have no idea what kinds of confusions are provoked, what kinds of attitudes are fostered, and what types of behaviors are valued and/or mimicked, and what kinds of lifestyles are vicariously accepted or ridiculed because of the televised sex children can currently sample.

The effectiveness of observational learning—learning by watching television and films—has been documented by Maccoby and

* Asterisks throughout indicate reference in Bibliography.

Wilson, and Bandura and Walters. They show that children readily imitate adults on the screen, especially the adults they most admire. Horton and Santagrossi propose that the problem is compounded by the fact that children spend most of their viewing time watching shows produced for adults.

The youth culture of the seventies, as influenced by the commercial adult world of television, films, and songs, is one in which changes dictated by peers are affecting younger and younger children. The accelerated changes may be seen in such areas as drug use, sexual practices, curfew, smoking, drinking, and allowance. So rapidly have mores changed that the youngsters who matured during the seventies—the "Now Generation" —are set far apart from their parents and even from older siblings.

The research presented in this chapter documents the social changes which have taken place in the lives of the children of the seventies. This chapter also compares male-female interaction of a decade ago. Two facts epitomize those changes. The first is that according to a 1979 report by the House Select Committee on Population, one out of every five children in the United States has had sexual intercourse by age thirteen or age fourteen. The second is that more than half of all the 1978 illegitimate births in the United States involved teenagers.

The research was conducted by the author, who has worked as a consultant to schools and clinics since 1965. The population studied consisted of 2,795 females ranging in age from eight to seventeen and, for comparison, 240 college women aged twenty to twenty-one. I focused on women because I believe they are the carriers of moral standards. Even in these sexually liberated times, it is more likely to be the woman who sets the limits for sexual behavior within a relationship.

The young women responded to a fifteen-item questionnaire, which was pretested and refined by a jury of fifty-five youngsters enrolled in an experimental psychology class at a private school in New York City. Respondents attended private and public schools in urban and suburban areas of New York, New Jersey, California, Connecticut, Minnesota, and Pennsylvania.

For the purposes of this study, they were divided into three groups: sexually inactive, sexually average, and sexually active.

• The *sexually inactive* girls attend religious schools, where no pregnancies have been reported in the past ten years and where drug use is uncommon. This group consisted of 640 girls aged eight to seventeen.

• The *average* group is just that—a typical cross-section of middle-class girls in private and public schools. This group consisted of 1,971 girls, also aged eight to seventeen.

• The *sexually active* group is composed of 184 girls who have children, are pregnant, or have had abortions. These girls ranged in age from eleven to seventeen.

Before interviewing began, the jury of peers helped translate what various items on the questionnaire would mean to young people. In some cases this resulted in modifications of questions. For example, part of our jury felt that we should ask, "Do you smoke marijuana?" because of its widespread use. However, school administrators vetoed the question in that form. So it was worded more vaguely: "Do you smoke?" Our jury assured us, and experience proved them right, that children in this age group would understand the question to include marijuana.

The rest of the questions are based on middle-class American attitudes toward dating and marriage.

The first and second questions, about grade and age, are separate items. So many of these children have taken time off from school that their ages and grades no longer correspond. In addition, there are always a few gifted youngsters who have skipped grades and are younger than their classmates. We found that it is better not to assume an average age in an elementary school class; rather, it is more accurate to consider a flexible range of ages for any given grade.

First Date at What Age?

A child's first date is a milestone in her life. The age at which the child is permitted to date also tells us something about her parents' views. While later social practices require less and less parental approval, the first date—which is conducted from the parents' home—still requires parental consent. The child is beginning formalized male-female social contact, which increasingly will take her out of her parents' home, both physically and symbolically. Parents' enthusiasm about dating in general and about particular social partners creates a new tension between child and parents. At this juncture children learn whom their parents consider to be appropriate social partners. They also may learn their parents' expectations indirectly from reminiscences: "When I was your age I only dated ————," or "I never stayed out past midnight until I was ————."

The word, "date," incidentally, became almost passé during the 1970's. It was replaced with "hanging out." Many children objected to the concept of dating as a relic from their parents' generation and not appropriate for their life-style.

For some children the process of separation from their parents is a relatively easy one, but they are the minority. They are children who have a healthy relationship with their parents, feel themselves to be loved, and may even feel closer to their parents though living apart. In addition, these youngsters can move closer to or away from their parents in a flexible way based on circumstances and needs. Children, though they may find it hard to acknowledge, do need their parents, perhaps even more when beginning dating activity. Sadly, the ones who are more threatened by dating and separating are precisely the ones who have had the least positive parental contact. The question that children must find answers to at this stage of their lives is who they are in relation to others in the outside world. This is vital because out of the dating process come the expectations and needs to be met in marriage. Dating the other sex develops intimacy, dependency, and trust. In general, youngsters from homes where the parents love each other in a healthy way will have the least difficulty finding healthy relationships. Since a child's first view of the other sex is the parent of that sex, if the relationship between mother and father is poor, it will affect the child negatively. He or she will have to struggle to develop trust relationships with the other sex, even though the need for such relationships is even stronger for this child than for other children. It is striking also how children's relationships with the other sex mimic their parents'. Some children, of course, will overreact and, by going to the opposite extreme, seek to relate to members of the opposite sex in a different way. This rejection does not often work, nor does it provide the freedom from the parent-child bind that the child seeks. It shows the youngster still being overinvolved with the parents instead of establishing his or her independence in positive ways.

Parents of the same sex as the youngster generally serve as role models for the children. Although the youngster will change with time, and with the influence of new role models and peer pressure, the initial presentation is a reflection of the parent mixed with how the child thinks she or he should look and behave.

The results of this survey-questionnaire showed the first date is significant in both groups, i.e., the eight- to seventeen-year-olds and the college group. In general, children from parochial schools and those who have strict religious upbringing tended to date later and to have less early sexual experience. The tables are all in the Appendix.

It becomes clear, too, that the group of children below seventeen years of age compared with the college group have had very different early dating patterns. Those below thirteen, in the sexually inactive group, showed that 26.6 percent had already had solo dates, followed in succession by the moderately active group with 34.5 percent, and the sexually active group with 39.5 percent, while the dramatic difference is reflected in the college group, of whom only 10.6 percent had dated by this age. In addition, though each of the younger groups had some solo dating activity before age ten, none of the college group had dated alone by age ten.

There are certainly similarities among the younger children in dating early. While there are differences that are significant between them, especially between the extremes—i.e., the sexually inactive and the sexually active—it is still a difference of 13 percent. The generation gap is seen, however, in the spread of 29 percentage points between the college group's early solo dating and that of the sexually active group.

Dating in groups is considered a learning activity. But early dating as couples probably is a needless hazard and source of tension for children. It is our opinion that children—particularly those under ten—should not be subjected to the stresses of having to make the significant choices related to sexual activity which solo dating promotes at this early age.

First Unchaperoned Party

The question posed here was, "At what age were you at your first unchaperoned social party?" Respondents could check "Not Yet" or give an age.

Parental supervision is a necessity to keep standards of a particular group viable and functioning. Youngsters have poor impulse control and often will rush into things that they regret later. Parties are places where abandon is more the rule than at other times in a child's life. Depending on the era, a party is an occasion to indulge in drinking or taking drugs or some other forbidden behavior. Everyone expects to step out of character at parties. The expectation of emotional release at parties is such a prevailing one with this generation of children that "partying" is a vital activity in their lives. The word, "party," itself goes from being a noun to a verb, as in "Do you want to 'party' tonight?" One doesn't need an invitation or a crowd to be able to "party." Two or three participants or perhaps a close friend will do. Partying is spontaneous, on the spot, casual, uncrowded, and frequent. Upper-class children reported partying at least several times a week, which is much more frequently than lower-middle-class children. The time between school dismissal and dinner seemed a favorite for brief parties. Evening parties, which would mean encountering a parental presence in the home, were not favored except for weekends, when parents might be out. For many, especially those private-school youngsters who have shorter school hours and more money, a regular routine for a majority was to go straight from school at perhaps 2:10 or 2:25 to a peer's vacant house to get stoned till approximately 4:30 or 5:45, when they would have to report home. A party simply requires several joints, perhaps some wine—or, occasionally, hard liquor—and a few good friends. Interestingly, many children who do not use drugs at all complained that they did not get invited to parties because they were regarded as deadheads.

The real difference that is the decade gap (since technically we are comparing a decade of difference) shows up again in comparing early unchaperoned parties. A look at partying by age twelve shows again, as reflected below, that while there are differences between the groups compared on the basis of sexual activity, these are not significant between the average group and the sexually active group. Compared with the college group, however, there is a spread of 24 percent by age twelve, and this is a tremendous difference.

If we look at the ages of twelve and below, we see the following statistics. For our preteenage population, the numbers show that 26 percent of the sexually inactive group, 33 percent of the moderately active group, and 38 percent of the sexually active children report going unchaperoned to parties. Again one can see the disparity between these groups and the twenty-year-old group, only 14 percent of which report going to an unchaperoned party between ages ten and twelve, with none having gone to parties before age ten. In the inactive group, 25 percent said they have not yet been to a party alone.

Youngsters learn much about parental attitudes from parents' actions. There is a difference between respect based on trust and the *laissez-faire* attitude shown by parents of many children in this study. Having no chaperone at parties for very young children sends a message that anything goes. In the past, children would take pride in being trusted by their parents to "do the right thing" and to be left on their own *occasionally* at parties. Today it is different.

Of the many youngsters interviewed, though, those who felt

close to their parents took pride in their involvement with them and expressed pity for the friend who hardly ever saw his or her parents, who themselves were out partying or traveling. While these children had unlimited funds, maids, and empty houses, they were also the most forlorn. There is an initial *braggadocio* attitude of "I can do anything I want," but this fizzles out quickly. These children generally try to latch on to some other friends' parents, a teacher, or other sympathetic adult for guidance. Those who don't may look to the streets for some kind of guidance and companionship.

Thus, we can see that going to an unchaperoned party does represent a significant step in the social life of children who are perhaps a bit young at age ten, twelve, or fourteen to run their own parties. About twice as many children in the eight- to seventeen-year-old group as in the twenty-plus age group indicated participating in party activity by age twelve.

Age Started Smoking?

The question, "Do you smoke?" as used by children today generally means, "Do you smoke marijuana?" If cigarettes are meant, then that has to be specified. While parents may have memories of fearing being caught with cigarettes, today's youngsters are experts at handling marijuana by the time they reach junior or senior high school.

Heavy users—"pot heads" or "heads"—by children's standards seem to be peers who get stoned almost daily. Children who are only weekend users or who partake only two or three times per week are average for this group. Some youngsters become mini-pushers to earn the money for their own marijuana and pills. They will buy a pound of marijuana, cut it up into smaller quantities, and sell it to their friends. Many reported having all the paraphernalia needed, including scales, rolling papers, and other items "stashed" in their homes. Some children reported that parents would be upset if they knew the extent of their usage, while others claimed that their parents knew and either tacitly or overtly approved. Twelve percent reported that their parents themselves used pot in the youngster's presence. In all cases parents who were themselves pot users were more lenient and accepting of the child's use of pot and pills. If the parents themselves also took other nonprescribed medication, then they were in the position of offering their children hallucinogenic substances on a fairly regular basis.

Strangely, we had no difficulty in obtaining information about drug use from the youngsters we questioned. In fact, many would refer friends who volunteered to be interviewed. Our major obstacles were school administrators, who seemed to fear public knowledge about drug use as well as sexual activity among students, and some parents. (The parents, ironically, often looked to the schools to guide their children and to understand this "new generation.") Obviously, discovering drugs is a serious thing, but unless drug use is blatant, most schools would rather not know about it. No such resistance was encountered in religious schools, where few children used drugs or were promiscuous. Schools, public and private, which had reputations for heavy drug-dealing were the most reluctant to cooperate. With this in mind, we further modified our question, "Do you smoke?" to "At what age did you start smoking?"

One can see the socially dictated need for smoking in all the young groups. There is a staggering difference, however, between them. Contrary to the teen argument that smoking pot is healthier than cigarettes, much of the literature, including a study by the author entitled "The New Morality on the College Campus," showed that those youngsters who used marijuana *also* smoked cigarettes nearly twice as much as youngsters who did not smoke marijuana. It is more correct to state that it is not either/or but rather both or none.

The figures below show the prevalence of smoking and its relation to the various groups studied. While no one in the sexually inactive group had smoked before age ten, and a minuscule 2 percent of the average sexual group had done so, a full 18.7 percent of the sexually active group had smoked. In the over-twenty group, none had smoked before age ten. By combining ages eight through twelve, we come up with a majority—51.1 percent in the sexually active group—while the others trail with 16 percent for the moderate group and 11 percent for sexually inactive. By age sixteen most of those who would smoke have already begun. By seventeen there is little change in smoking habits. Note that the sexually active group had only 24 percent nonsmokers, while the sexually inactive group had 59 percent nonsmokers.

Remember that smoking is not a solitary activity for youngsters. Many report that they need the "high" to feel sexually aroused and to perform better. We might conclude that 76 percent of the sexually active children live in a drug culture. Smoking is just the tip of the iceberg in terms of sexual activity and altered mental states.

"What Is Your Saturday Night Curfew?"

We selected the Saturday night curfew since it represents for most youngsters the night they do the most socializing and stay out the latest. The song "Everybody Loves Saturday Night," sung by Harry Belafonte, tells us about Saturday night's significance for children. It represents their initiation into adult-like social activities. One can, or at least one used to, measure increasing maturity in correlation with ever later curfews. However, with today's changing social life, curfews are not valid measurements. Many youngsters don't come home at all. Many hang out for a long period at other children's homes or in parks. They may sleep in vans with friends and travel long distances on weekends while stoned. The absolute deadline seems to be a thing of the past.

Yet families of some children still demand observance of a curfew, with "grounding" being the punishment for breaking the rule. In some families a curfew must be earned, while in others it is a right. Curfews are usually negotiated so that they satisfy the parental need to control and the child's desire to conform with peers' curfews. Many a child, despite complaining about parents waiting up for him or her, expressed gratitude that they at least cared. They felt sorry for friends who had no curfew. These "throwaway kids" are the most neglected group. It is significant to note that there is a group in each category who had no curfew.

Curfews have been disturbed by the sheer amount of travel many children go in for now. For example, attending a rock concert may necessitate late-night, long-distance travel. To some extent girls still have a slightly earlier curfew than boys, but the latitude granted to boys is fast vanishing. Many girls, even in the eight- to ten-year-old group, insist on equal terms and conditions.

Saturday night curfews must be compared between the three child groupings. The results here are dramatic in showing a steady, dramatic diminution in curfew as one moves from the sexually inactive group, with 16 percent having to be home by 11:00 P.M., to 9.6 percent for the average group and to only 3 percent for sexually active children. Home by 1:00 A.M. is only slightly different, as follows: sexually inactive, 34 percent; moderate group, 20.2 percent; and sexually active, only 8 percent.

Although 86 percent of the twenty-plus age group claim they have no curfew, most of them are college students who do not live at home.

Of the younger children, the finding that so many of them stay out late on city streets says a great deal about parental supervision or lack of it. Some youngsters reported that they had to stay out late to come down from a high before going home. Most children, however, did not worry about this and claimed that their parents either did not know or did not care if they were stoned. Most, no matter how young, took great pride in stating that they were able to "handle" their highs. They bragged that they easily could pass any parental scrutiny and had in fact been doing so for a long time.

"Do Your Parents Wait Up?"

What good are curfews if they aren't enforced? Although families have a great many ways of keeping tabs on children, waiting up for them is probably the most effective even if it is also somewhat controlling. Many children, despite grumbling to their peers about curfews, will often with a sense of pride tell them that their parents really care enough to wait up for them.

Generally speaking, a truly involved parent is one who communicates with a child in a positive way. Preaching, maintaining a distance, and not setting an example are poor ways to raise children. Children at all ages need to know that their parents really care. Being available is evidence that this is true. Being available does not mean, however, to cover up for basic neglect, swooping into children's lives periodically in an intrusive way. It means, rather, a physical presence combined with a commitment to keeping open parent-child channels of communication.

Table 5

"Do your parents wait up for you?"

Ages	Yes
10–12	100 %
13	86.8%
14	61.4%
15	44.4%
16	43.4%
17	37.5%
20+	8 %

Table 5A

"Do your parents wait up for you?"

By Group	Sexually Inactive	Sexually Average	Sexually Active	20+
Yes	45.3%	41%	17.6%	20.4%
No	54.7%	59%	82.4%	79.6%

What can be seen very clearly here is a steady decline from the 100 percent reported "yes" for children in the ten- to twelve-year-old group to only 37.5 percent in the seventeen-year-old group. However, one also must note the abrupt drop-off at age fourteen. This is a decrease of over 25 percent from the thirteen-year-old group. Continuing downward, figures for all the succeeding ages are relatively proportionate. The precipitous drop at age fourteen implies a change in parental supervision. Is it merely coincidence that the average age for runaways has become fourteen? Or that figures for pregnancy and venereal disease begin to climb at fourteen? Note the high percentage of parents who do not wait up for children in the sexually active group.

The Ideal Age for Me to Marry Is

Most very young children express the wish to be married someday. Often, too, they have in mind a particular person they would like to marry. Once the children have gotten past the stage where they say they want to marry Mommy or Daddy, they begin considering others who are more appropriate.

We have found that as children go through preadolescence and into adolescence, they become more cynical about marriage. It seems less and less important. Corresponding with this, we found that younger children wished to be married early, older children later. In addition, there are many youngsters who increasingly express a desire to never marry or have children. By the time these young people reach their early and mid-teens, increasing numbers of them are voicing interest in having a baby even if they do not marry. This certainly is revolutionary for the middle-class child, especially for middle-class girls. It is a rejection of the traditional wife role their mothers assumed. That young people express this rejection openly to adult interviewers shows how strongly they feel about it.

Many reasons for disillusionment with marriage have been proposed. One is that so many children live in divided families. Almost every child interviewed, even if he or she came from an intact family, had at least one friend whose parents were divorced. An idealism about having children, about building a family, is missing. Perhaps the disparity between the idyllic state they fantasize about and the strained and imperfect situation they see around them confuses young people. Since marriage and family have been the cornerstones of Western society, we should take a close look at this issue and at the children's responses to the question about ideal age at which to marry.

At first glance one finds that the children in the sexually active group favor marriage at a very young age. Also for the first time, we find the other two child groups postponing marriage. For many young children, there seem to be two major age ranges for marriage: These are twenty to twenty-three, and as they themselves move from age thirteen to sixteen, they go from preferring twenty to twenty-three to twenty-four to twenty-seven as ideal marriage ages. In general, as children move into and through their teens, there is a further rise in the ideal marriage age.

It must be pointed out that for the sexually active child, the thought of marriage is not a fantasy. Many of these children are now or have been pregnant and are involved in long-term relationships with men. Some of them practically live with boyfriends while still nominally living at home; some others are about to marry because they are pregnant.

A look at the 9.6 percent figure shows the urgency for early marriage among sexually active sixteen- and seventeen-year-olds. That figure is more than four times higher than that for sexually inactive children of the same age. Yet, in indicating the more realistic age of twenty to twenty-three for marriage, the inactive and moderately sexually active groups predominate. That the sexually active group indicates a desire for early marriage explains the very early marriages and, perhaps, the frequent breakups and divorces that follow. Correspondingly, the moderately sexually active and sexually inactive children marry later because, for one reason, they do not *have to* marry early. In general, the younger the couple and the less education, the higher the incidence of divorce.

A logical follow-up question is how important is marriage

to children? Do children from all groups view marriage as the same thing? To give us the answers to this question, we posed the following query: "In my opinion marriage is very important _____; important _____; not important _____." To see if the sexes respond differently, we included male subjects' responses and compared them with those from our female population. Surprisingly, we found no significant differences between their responses. Male and female youngsters both said that marriage was important to them. Whatever societal influences are acting upon young people are making them expect more equality in marriage and other areas of socialization. This would seem to reflect, in part, that parents may be treating children more equally as well. Feminists' encouragement of little boys' dolls and little girls' trucks and cars appears to be having some effect on the middle-class child.

The results listed for the importance of marriage are interesting in delineating several distinct groups. There is a group of approximately 35 percent for whom marriage stays "Very Important" without any significant change as they progress from age ten to twenty. The remaining 65 percent of the population show variability. Gradually, year by year from ten to twenty, they reflect a growing trend which slowly but surely diminishes the importance of marriage. While we start out with 0 percent regarding marriage as "Not Important" at age ten to twelve, it climbs to a high of 37.5 percent by age twenty. There is however a corresponding drop in the "Important" column figures from 68.4 percent, which is the all-time peak at ages ten to twelve, to a drop below 50 percent by age thirteen. This figure stays below 50 percent until age twenty, when it drops further to a low of 25 percent. For a child to say that marriage is not important while still living in the parents' home is quite significant. In the "Not Important" column there is also a progression downward. By age seventeen 20 percent, or one fifth of all respondents, have changed their views and hopes and see marriage as not important. By age twenty this leaps to 37.5 percent, well over one third of all respondents.

Does this mean that these children are turned off to marriage?

It seems more likely that they very quickly begin to perceive its relative place in their lives, based on their own needs rather than on their parents' projections for them.

Politics

For many young people, involvement in politics is a way to find out how the world really works and to acquire some power in it. Idealistic youths who still believe that they can change the world and make it a better place represent a dynamic, activist force in America. It is, after all, youthful volunteers who fill out almost all election campaigns. They are drawn to certain political figures, such as the Kennedys, who champion causes and defend the underdog. Children can readily identify with minority and powerless groups in our society. Since these youngsters do not have to work for a living, they have free time to devote to campaign work. Many schools give students time off or course credit for doing political community service. Educators and others have found that youngsters mature through their contact with adults and benefit from the positive identification with a cause or person.

No group felt that politics was more important than the sexually inactive group did. If we add together the "Very Important" and "Important" percentages, we get a total of 94 percent. Though there are those who feel that these youngsters sublimate and spend their energies in other than directly sexual areas and that that is why they become so involved, politics seems a healthy outlet. The inactive group's score is closest to that of the twenty-year-old group, who are college students, and we know that college students are highly politicized.

However, an evaluation of the "Not Important" column shows that a cynical "turned off to the system" view grows fast. Younger children feel politics are "Not Important" by only 12 percent, and this progresses slowly through age twenty, where 25.5 percent are being turned off. There is a slight decline at age seventeen, when many look forward to voting for the first time. There should be provisions to reach out to youngsters to sustain their idealism and avoid the turn-off we see here.

Politics, of course, brings us to the topic of values. The question we posed is, are values changing too rapidly, rapidly, slowly, or not at all? One must bear in mind that children, by virtue of their age, have a limited historical frame of reference, and the primary values they know are the ones they were raised with. From hearing parents and teachers talk about their experiences, children acquire a second-hand frame of reference. Yet, as all politicians know, today's youngsters are tomorrow's voters. So how do they feel about values—are they stable or are they changing too rapidly?

The column "Too Rapidly" demonstrates dramatically that there are qualitative as well as quantitative differences between the three children's groups. There is a significant progression from the sexually inactive group that values are changing "Too Rapidly" of 19 percent to 30 percent for the average group, to 57.1 percent for the sexually active group. The college-age group remains at 14 percent "Too Rapidly," indicating that this group is much closer to the sexually inactive group. While the sexually inactive youngsters are anchored securely to their parents' values, youngsters in the sexually active group generally have broken away from traditional societal values and are being swept along by contemporary currents. The question itself, "I feel that values are changing . . . ," was suggested originally by our pilot group of students as being indicative of what they themselves perceived as wider, and perhaps deeper, differences that are a part of sexual values. Having no strong ties to parents or to viable ideals, the children in the sexually active group are the most swayed by cultural pressures. Songs, slogans, the "now" thing is what they believe to be the "real" thing. These youngsters even more than others experience a crisis of ego identity, since so little of their belief system is grounded in history or in a realistic projection of the future. In addition, these youngsters are also isolated from their families and from the support system a family offers. Values are important for stability—even more so for children than for adults. Everything is changing for children, from their bodies and their families to the world. A close-knit family with stable values can lessen the anxiety associated with this tumult.

Dating

What kind of people do young children find attractive and wish to date? We have already seen that even very young children expressed strong personal preferences about the other sex. Looks, size, personality merge into a concept of sexual attractiveness. Boys traditionally note overt sexual features and value these more than do girls, who often say that personality—character and a sense of humor—count more.

To find out just how youngsters choose partners, we posed the question, "People I date have to be ————." Responses were so varied that we had to group them into eight categories: religion, sex, money, intelligence, looks, sense of humor, other, "personality." In all of my years as a psychological researcher, I have not seen so many idiosyncratic preferences by children. For example, many children insisted that their dates have a good sense of humor. In terms of clinical adolescent psychology, considering the depression and suicide rate of adolescents, we can see the need for a funny partner to help relieve depression and despair.

Table 10
"People I date have to be ————."

Trait	Sexually Inactive	Sexually Average	Sexually Active	20+
Religion	6%	2.5%	0%	0 %
Sex	0%	3 %	9%	8 %
Money	0%	0 %	14%	1.4%
Intelligence	17%	13.8%	7%	12.9%
Looks	14%	25 %	21%	6.8%
Sense of humor	2%	2.3%	0%	2.7%
Other	52%	41.3%	28%	60 %
"Personality"	9%	12.1%	21%	8.2%

Apart from the obvious scatter of preferences, we can see that "other" is the most popular category for all groups. This attests to the very personalized traits that each child desires, though they may change their minds from month to month, or even from day to day, about what it is they really like. At the moment that they "feel" something, it is "a must"; they believe in it strongly enough to make it into an article of faith.

A very important observation must be made in the sexually active column. Flashing danger signals should alert us to the unique danger facing this group. The emphasis on money and sex stands out starkly. As we note in the chapter on Project Alert, potential prostitutes show an early and very strong desire for money, and for people who have it or can get it for them. Now if we compare the "Money" responses—the sexually active group's 14 percent with the inactive and average groups' 0 percent each, and even with the twenty-plus-year-olds, who showed just over 1 percent interest in money—we realize that some idealism has been replaced by the need for immediate material gratification.

In the category labeled "Sex," if we look across from left to right, we see that the sexually inactive group lists it as 0 percent, the average group at only 3 percent, and the sexually active group at 9 percent, which is the highest of all, nosing out even the twenty-year-old group, though they are considerably older the average group at only 3 percent, and the sexually active group's rating of intelligence its own narrow needs; only 7 percent of these youngsters, which is the lowest figure in any of these groups, showed some appreciation for intelligence. It is far too intangible an attribute for them to relate to. This, of course, sets them up for getting involved in activities which offer a fast buck. These children, who become the runaways and the prostitutes, have a built-in vulnerability.

It is quite obvious that there has been a tremendous change during the past decade. One cannot simply lump all children into one category, though there are dramatic differences between their life experiences and the values of children raised just a decade ago. In addition to the quantitative differences, there appear to be qualitative differences in the relatedness to the family structure as the central position of their lives and as the prime source of information, attitudes, practices, and values. Equally as important are the different lives and life-styles of children in the ten to seventeen age group, based on sexual activity. The children in the sexually inactive group come close to those of a generation ago in attitudes and experiences.

Children date earlier, they spend more money, abide by curfews less often. The increasingly loosened ties to parents, and the laxity of parental supervision as well as a possible disinterest by those adults in being parenting figures, is also seen clearly. The lack of generational boundaries and a nonidentification with parent-generation values are evident. However, this is a two-edged sword, as we note that the ranks of those parents who wait up for children thin out dramatically after age thirteen. There seems to be a *laissez-faire* approach to child-rearing by parents in this category. It is possible to speculate as well that the rise of venereal disease, the social ills of runaways, and pregnancy are perhaps more than coincidentally related to the dramatic falloff of parental interest and supervision after age thirteen.

Of interest to parents is the fact that by noting values and areas of development studied in this chapter, there are ways of anticipating future directions of rebellion. Thus, perhaps running away can be avoided, and children who may get into difficulty by being swayed by the peer and pop culture can also be reached ahead of time. Crisis prevention is always more effective and desirable than crisis solution. Although this chapter did not deal with drugs, the other two parts of this unholy trinity for children—sex and smoking—are still ways that children show their need to break out of what are perceived as childhood restrictions and to act out rebelliously. For girls the risks are higher than for boys, though there has been a more equal interest in sex, smoking, and "independence." As one thirteen-year-old girl said, "Well, he said he loved me, and we make decisions together, but I'm still the one pregnant."

Things not only have changed but continue on in a state of

flux. For children who have stable values and are attached to their religion, and whose family ties are intact, there is less revolutionary and more evolutionary change at a more tolerable pace. For these children the winds of change do not blow so harshly, while for children who are eagerly chasing after the "now" thing, the world is topsy-turvy.

Chapter 3

PREGNANT MINORS— MAJOR PROBLEMS

"I'm glad I had the baby," Susie said. "She's such a beautiful child, really smart and alert. I really love her a lot. But the responsibility—when I think of it, a child is a lifelong responsibility. I feel that I don't know who I am yet, and I didn't think about how long it is that I am going to have her.

"And sometimes I get annoyed at her. I get impatient and frustrated when she's crying and crying and crying, and I feel that I want to hit her. I get so scared, I think, 'My God, could you actually beat up your own kid?' I've never done it, but I could see myself. I'm not ready to look at my whole life ahead knowing that I have to take care of this person, because I still have to look after myself, and it's much too difficult with the baby, too."

Susie was twelve years old when she became pregnant two years ago. She refused an abortion and is now, at fourteen, the mother of a ten-month-old baby girl. Susan does not fit other characteristics of the pre-seventies stereotype of the unwed mother. She is beautiful, bright, and artistic. She comes not from a ghetto, but from a very well-to-do family. She has gone to the best private schools; her father is a successful industrialist in the Northeast; she has grown up in a home where the children see more of the domestic help than they do their parents. There are millions like Susie in America today. Planned Parenthood says that the incidence of childbirth in the early teens has reached epidemic proportions. Of the sixty million women who became mothers in 1975, almost thirteen million "became parents before they became adults," according to a report issued by the First Interhemispheric Conference on Adolescent Fertility.* The rate of childbearing among teenagers in the United States at this time is one of the highest in the world.*

One half of all teenagers have intercourse before they finish high school, and three out of ten girls who have intercourse become pregnant.* One in five of all live births in the United States—over 600,000 every year—is to an unmarried teenager.* While the birth rate in general has declined drastically over the past several years, it has increased among girls under fourteen.* Nine out of ten of these child mothers keep their babies, refusing—usually in the face of intense opposition—to give them up for adoption.*

For the past twenty years, Charlotte Andress has been the director of New York City's Inwood House, a home for unwed mothers which was founded in 1830 by a group of ministers. During that time she has seen some startling changes: "When I first came here, ninety-five percent of the girls who delivered their babies placed them for adoption. Last year, only one girl out of two hundred gave her baby up for adoption.

"The most dramatic change in attitude came about after July, 1970, when abortion became legal in New York State. Girls from the middle and upper classes were getting pregnant just as rapidly and as often as before, but they no longer came to us for resident services. There seemed to be no more need for them to hide, and an almost instantaneous change in the mores made it acceptable for a girl from a middle-class family who got pregnant and was not going to abort to stay home; her parents accepted the pregnancy much more easily.

"That was a predictable enough result of legalizing abortion, but what surprised us was to see how often, even if the girl decided not to have the abortion, she could discuss the whole thing quite openly with her family and live at home throughout pregnancy. When the baby was born, the family would welcome the new grandchild and help take care of it.

"Sometimes those who want to keep their babies will set

themselves up in an apartment with the financial help they get from their families and live on their own, but these aren't the very youngest girls, of course.

"Our clients used to be women in their twenties and thirties, but now the vast majority are teenagers under eighteen. Last year we had a pregnant ten-year-old, and we've had many between eleven and fourteen. A number of our thirteen- and fourteen-year-olds already had had an abortion and were now carrying a second pregnancy they refused to abort.

"I'm still startled by how young some of these kids are; it's hard to believe they're physically able to get pregnant. Some of the girls tell me they've never menstruated, and yet they not only conceive, they carry the baby to term."

Dr. Adele Hofmann, Director of the Adolescent Care Unit of New York University–Bellevue Medical Center, describes the physical changes which have taken place among young women:

"First of all, there's an increase in fertility; over the past seventy-five years, the average age for the onset of menstruation has dropped from fourteen and a half to twelve and a half. We think this is related to better nutrition, which makes girls ovulate sooner. Many of these kids have just one period before they're pregnant; they don't know what's happened to them.

"The second factor is what we call an increase in fecundity. These girls not only get pregnant at a younger age, they can also carry the baby to term. Fewer babies are lost now during pregnancy than used to be, again because of better nutrition and better prenatal care."

But even though it is now possible for increasingly younger girls to bear children, both mother and baby run grave risks. A child's body may be capable of conception, but it is not yet ready for the stress of pregnancy and childbirth. Babies born to girls fifteen and under are much more likely to be premature and to weigh less at birth than those born to women twenty and over. Low birth weight is an ominous prognostic sign; it is an important factor in infant mortality, and it is associated with birth defects, neurological problems that may mean permanent mental retardation, and many childhood illnesses. Babies born to young teenagers are two to three times more likely to die in their first year.*

As for the mother, risk of pregnancy-related death is sixty percent higher for girls under fifteen.* They are more likely to suffer from toxemia and anemia, and the babies' demands during pregnancy compete with the mothers' nutritional needs for their own growth, making them more susceptible to illness later on.

The reasons for the rise in teenage pregnancy are multiple and complex. The subject has just begun to be studied in depth and conclusions so far are tentative, but some hard data are emerging. What is obvious is that the lower age of puberty is meeting a rising rate in sexual activity among very young adolescents who do not use birth control.

In comparing the Kinsey Report of a generation ago with a 1976 study by John Kantner and Melvin Zelnik of Johns Hopkins University in Baltimore, the greatest change noted has been in the number of sexually active girls.*

Dr. Hofmann agrees:

"As far as boys go, it's about the same, but many more girls are having sex earlier. About eighty percent of non-college-bound boys are sexually active, a little less among the college-bound. In Kinsey's day about twenty percent of girls were sexually active—a figure that has been escalating since the turn of the century. We're now seeing over half the girls in this country sexually active in their teens; the figure is beginning to approximate that of the boys. I feel that this is an expression of the growing equality between the sexes: Girls are beginning to do what boys have always done."

The reasons behind this activity, however, are unclear. Is the physical sex drive manifesting itself earlier, or are girls succumbing to pressures from their environment? Most authorities agree that the more closely knit and more affectionate her family, the less likely a girl is to be sexually active at a very young age—regardless of economic class. It is no longer true—if it ever was—that it is mainly children from the ghetto who "get into trouble"; the deprivation that results in sexual acting out is not economic in origin but emotional. Nevertheless, even girls from highly supportive families often find peer-group pressure overwhelming.

The issue of sex education in public schools has become urgent in the past few years as studies increasingly show that children can be highly active sexually, even promiscuous, and at the same time remain sublimely ignorant of the most rudimentary facts of life. Kantner and Zelnik found that only two out of five of the girls they polled knew that the middle of the menstrual cycle was the time of greatest risk of pregnancy. Anything from Coke to Saran Wrap—but usually *not* including the Pill, the IUD, or the diaphragm—is considered adequate contraception. One girl who became pregnant at fourteen said, "I started having my periods at thirteen and a half, and I was kind of skinny, so I really didn't think I could get pregnant. I would just do what some of the other kids had suggested, like after having intercourse I'd stand up quickly, and I'd go to the bathroom right away afterward, and then take a cold shower."

The increase in fertility among the very young means that any gap between the onset of menstruation and the use of effective contraception is hazardous; it is no longer true that young adolescents are protected against pregnancy by a period of infertility when they first begin to menstruate. Nevertheless, Planned Parenthood has found that by far the majority of teenagers had been sexually active for at least a year before they first used any contraception at all.

They are, however, aware of the depths and dangers of their ignorance. In an adolescent opinion poll conducted by the First National Conference for Teenagers on Sex and Human Sexuality, in 1978, 95 percent felt that schools should offer courses in human sexuality; that instruction on birth control should be included in school health programs; and that information on subjects such as masturbation, homosexuality, and venereal disease should be made freely available. The breakdown by age showed this consensus was virtually unanimous in later adolescence— 98 percent of the nineteen-year-olds felt that sex education should be offered as a credit course. But even among eleven-year-olds, 79 percent were in favor of sex-education classes, and 86 percent wanted to be given information on birth control.*

The need for such instruction reached the point of emergency in 1977, according to Dr. Margaret Gregory in the New Jersey State Department of Health. She called for mandatory sex-education classes in the public schools, beginning in the fifth grade, after it was discovered that 12,500 New Jersey school-girls—some only ten years old—had delivered babies in 1975, and that 2,600 had had abortions.* "Frankly," Dr. Gregory said in a public statement, "I would regret having to force sex education in districts where there is local resistance, but I regret even more the destruction unwanted, unplanned pregnancies wreak on the lives of the child mothers, the fathers, and the babies."

Despite this alarm, most communities still find the notion of sex education in public schools distasteful; only six states and the District of Columbia require it. The conservative position is that sex education will not reduce the number of illegitimate births—since these are steadily increasing in spite of more widely available contraception—and that instruction will be construed as advocacy.

In a national survey of teachers in 1976, three quarters of the teachers polled considered human reproduction and sexuality to be "controversial" subjects, and more than nine out of ten thought birth control methods or abortion were "very controversial." * "Controversial" in this context usually means that the opponents are a vocal, influential, and feared minority. A number of public-opinion surveys have consistently shown that the majority of American parents—eight out of ten—favor both sex education in the schools and making contraceptives available to unmarried teenagers.*

Planned Parenthood believes that most adolescents would avoid pregnancy and childbirth if they could, and that the reason for the dramatic increase in teenage pregnancy is that until very recently, laws, policies, and practices have denied adolescents access to effective services to prevent or terminate unwanted pregnancies. Although some recent changes in the laws give teenagers the right to contraception and abortion at their own request, many doctors and health services still refuse to comply with such requests without written permission from parents.

But most people who have worked closely with pregnant teenagers feel that in any case making contraception widely available is only part of the answer and that the problem goes much deeper. All adolescents harbor strongly ambivalent feelings about their own sexuality, feelings which are often not fully resolved for many years—if ever. Children from ten to fifteen are still not ready to cope with the realities of sex; they are not equipped even to acknowledge them, let alone deal with the turbulent complex of sensations and emotions and mysterious physical changes that accompanies a developing sexuality. Children this young are still unsure of their physical command of themselves in the world; they scarcely feel settled into their bodies before they lose control of them again. The muddle of folklore, wishful thinking, and denial which characterizes their beliefs about contraception and pregnancy poignantly reflects an internal chaos.

The explanation girls most commonly offer for their failure to practice birth control is that they are too young to conceive. They think of themselves as children still, even though they have begun to menstruate. Their bodies look unformed and infantile, they know themselves to be entirely dependent, and they therefore deny the possibility of pregnancy, even though consciously they recognize that all the physical conditions for it have been met.

The persistence of myths such as that having intercourse standing up will prevent pregnancy, that the first few months after the onset of menstruation are "safe," that you can't get pregnant if you have intercourse infrequently and irregularly (as most teenagers do), and that getting up quickly, running around, and showering immediately afterward are safeguards against conception derives from a simple lack of information, but it is also related to a need for these children to deny both the fact and the meaning of their own sexual activity. Although, for reasons we will explore later, most young teenagers who do become pregnant insist on carrying their babies to term and keeping them afterward, it is equally true that most teenage pregnancies are inadvertent. They occur because children this young are often unable to confront with any degree of clarity the fact that they are having sex—sex that has consequences—at all.

Sometimes a sexually experienced child who rejects contraceptives is simply afraid that her parents will discover them, but further investigation usually reveals an ambivalence on the part of the child herself. Birth control means planning ahead; a girl who has armed herself with a contraceptive is saying that she intends to have intercourse at some future time, and a surprising number of very sexually active teenagers are unwilling to admit such a degree of premeditation even to themselves. Sex to them is still so freighted with guilt that it has to be spontaneous, a yielding to impulse; they need to feel swept away by the passion of the moment, which the calculations of contraception would spoil. They do not, in short, really want to be fully aware of or fully responsible for what they are doing—all the more so since the excitement is not pure pleasure. Some girls also exhibit infantile persecutory anxieties in the pervasive fear of being poisoned. This fear appears in the reluctance to use contraceptives, especially the Pill, which alarms many girls. "I'm not putting any foreign substance into my body!" says one fourteen-year-old, who is a constant and indiscriminate consumer of "recreational" drugs.

Dr. Peggy McHugh, Director of the Pediatric Gynecological Clinic at Columbia-Presbyterian Hospital in New York City, is a firm believer in the Pill for teenagers, although she recognizes the difficulties:

"Thirteen-year-olds can't use a diaphragm because they won't touch themselves. In order to be fitted, they have to feel inside with their fingers, and they refuse to do that.

"There can be medical problems with the Pill because giving it to a young girl will stop her growth, but a girl who's already menstruating will not grow much more anyway. If she starts menstruating at nine or ten, she's going to be short in any case;

there is very little growth left in a girl once she starts menstruating. And, frankly, I'd rather see her give up a quarter of an inch of height than be pregnant at eleven. In my experience very few kids have any trouble with the Pill *per se*, but the fantasies related to it cause a great many problems. If you go out on the street and ask kids about the Pill, you hear all about the people who had strokes and who died or went blind. They read every single thing in the [New York] *Daily News*, and they know all the pathology, but of course they never quote the number of people using the Pill safely."

Many doctors feel that taking the Pill every day is not suitable for adolescents, who tend to have sex irregularly and seldom. Kantner and Zelnik's 1976 study found that two out of five of the teenagers interviewed had not had intercourse during the previous month. The ideal method of birth control for teenagers has yet to be found, but research is now under way on a pill which need only be taken after intercourse.*

A girl who finds herself pregnant and refuses abortion doesn't necessarily do so because she wants the baby. Fear of abortion—stemming mainly from guilt—can be intense among adolescents. Judy, the president of her eighth grade class, who did choose abortion when she was thirteen, found that the experience left a lasting mark:

"The clinic looked like a death factory. That may not sound very liberated, but it was all I could think of, with the efficient nurses walking around and everybody trying to look so calm and cool—and it was all only a cover so people wouldn't panic and show their real feelings.

"When my turn came, I went in thinking, 'Oh, well, it will only take a few minutes, and they say it doesn't hurt.' I was going to have suction, so there wouldn't even have to be any cutting. It was all going to be very easy and I would be out of there fast, just as good as before. But while I was lying on the table and they were busy adjusting all these things and the machine started going with that high-pitched whine of the suction, suddenly it hit me that they were ripping my baby out of me. I started to sob, but the doctor didn't care or even notice, so I just held myself back the best I could until it was over. Sure enough, it didn't take long and it wasn't all that uncomfortable, physically.

"Still, for the next several hours while I rested, and even though Ron, my boyfriend, stayed with me, I couldn't stop crying. I managed not to get hysterical, though, and when I left I thought it was all over. But the next few nights I woke up screaming in my sleep from these awful dreams about killing babies. When you think about it, it wasn't just an egg and a sperm, it was a fetus, a living human being. It was my baby.

"I think kids ought to be more serious about sex and not take so many chances. Everybody always tells you that you can just go and get an abortion whenever you need to, and I have to admit that if I ever did find myself pregnant again I'd probably go through it again, but I could never take it casually now the way I did before. I knew it was the right thing to do, and Ron is still friends with me, but it's not the same anymore. I can't just laugh and enjoy sex the way I used to, and think of it as a fun thing.

"I had the abortion over a year ago, but I still cry and get the shakes when I think of that dreary day when I went to the clinic. Ron and I have a fairly good relationship, but I don't feel we're in love anymore. I still have those crazy nightmares. I'd think twice, maybe even three times, now before I'd have intercourse with anyone."

Susie, who had her baby, is one of many who did so simply because abortion seemed a worse alternative:

"When I went for the pregnancy test and they told me it was positive, I just sat there. 'What?' I said. 'You're pregnant,' she told me again, and I couldn't believe it. I started crying. I didn't know what to do. 'You can get an abortion,' she said.

"I didn't know what else to do, but it seemed to me I couldn't do it just like that. I told her I'd have to think about it, and went home and called Gary. He got real uptight. He didn't want to talk to me about it on the phone; he said he'd see me the next day in school. We sat outside after lunch, and he said, 'I'll give you the money to get an abortion.' Suddenly, I decided not to do it.

Suddenly, it just hit me, he was so sure I was going to get an abortion, and that made me stop right there and say, 'No, wait a minute. Maybe I'll have the baby.'

"I did some research on my own and read up on abortion. I found out that when the baby is still just a fetus, it moves and everything. I saw a movie about it. Once I learned that, how the baby is alive even before it's born, I decided there was no way I was going to have an abortion. It would be like murder. I decided to go through with it and have the baby."

The cases of Susie and Judy typify the attitude of teenage girls toward abortion, whether they choose it in the end or not. Such feelings stem partly from guilt, but they also owe a great deal to the fact that, as we shall see later, a child of twelve or thirteen is still close enough to infancy herself to identify strongly with the baby in the womb, even if the womb is her own. She is much less likely than an older adolescent to see the baby, initially at least, as a threat to her future. Her first impulse is to protect the unborn, less from a mature maternal instinct than from identification with the baby as a still undeveloped, still vulnerable self. Many adults, especially parents, failing to understand the feelings behind the resistance, label it as a spoiled, stubborn lack of realism; but abortion can be an extremely serious trauma for these children—sometimes more serious than carrying the baby to term. Kathy, fourteen, a pretty cheerleader whose mother is president of their town school board in California, is one of these children. She communicated something of this anguish:

"It was like I wasn't grown up yet, and my whole life was a dream, a big bad dream. I just had to get an abortion. It was like a devil inside my body, and I had to get it out. I was too afraid to have it. What would my friends think? What would my parents think? I didn't want them to think that I was a whore or something. I couldn't keep that baby, it would be too much to live with.

"Even now, I have this big secret inside, and I don't know how I can live with it. I think about it a lot, and while I'm glad I had the abortion I still feel awfully guilty. Sometimes I think about it and how it would have been if it had grown up and I had kept it. I mean, I really had to have that abortion. I panicked. I felt all kinds of things going on inside of me. But I knew the baby would be so mad at me, and I felt so guilty."

Sixty percent of pregnant girls under fourteen have abortions; 40 percent have the baby, says Dr. McHugh. In the group aged fourteen to sixteen, the percentages are reversed.* How many of the girls who deliver are reacting against abortion and how many want the baby—may even have gotten pregnant deliberately—is impossible to guess, but many of the teenage girls who give birth keep their babies.*

Black and Hispanic inner-city children are still more likely to be sexually active while very young, are more likely to become pregnant, and are more likely to keep their babies than white children of the middle class.* The rate of increase for all of these conditions, however, is much more rapid among the latter. Most observers agree that sexual activity has a different significance and purpose for the two different economic groups.

"For all of these girls, having a baby means instant adulthood," says Dr. Hofmann. "But you must remember that inner-city kids have no options in their lives; they can only become mothers anyway. There's little point in aspiring to anything else. Many of these kids are locked into chronic depression. It's painful to be an adolescent. At that age you begin to see the limits to hope, but if you have a baby your status changes immediately to that of a grown-up. The baby liberates you from your adolescence. You get out of school, and people notice you and pay attention to you.

"The white middle-class kid has more alternatives and therefore gets much more pressure from her parents and peers not to keep the baby. Poorer children have a lot less permission for ambivalence than middle-class children do. With middle-class kids, their mothers are letting them know, 'You can get that abortion.' These parents are able to organize and help the child. My observation of inner-city kids is that their parents have problems handling abortion."

Dr. Elizabeth McAnarney, of Strong Memorial Hospital in Rochester, New York, has found that "the kids who are having babies are the ones who are not very successful in other areas of life. The baby then becomes a way of being powerful. It's this girl's way of proving that she can be something and become a somebody."

Among children of the ghetto, having a baby is more likely to be a response to a grim reality. High unemployment, poor chances for lasting marriage, desperate economic conditions, lack of incentives to stay in school all conspire to make pregnancy seem the most attractive possibility open to them. On top of all that, many of these children come from fundamentalist religious backgrounds, says Dr. McAnarney. "That means that even though their religion bans sexuality, abortion is not an alternative for them. If a kid becomes pregnant, she is stuck with the baby."

Among the affluent the situation is more complicated, say some experts. "In the middle- and upper-middle-income classes," Dr. McAnarney says, "the children who are keeping their babies are the ones who are much more sick socially. It's the least capable girls who are opting to keep their babies and try to raise them. For one thing, the younger they are, the more likely they are to keep the baby, being totally unrealistic about what it will do to their lives and about the care a child needs.

"I think the fate of these babies and their mothers is going to become a very big problem for our society in the near future. When the mothers are so young, they don't know anything about caring for a baby, and there's so little going on in the way of interaction between the mother and the baby, it's quite frightening to see. It's a very poor indication for the next generation."

From the beginning these child mothers are living in such a tangle of delusion and denial that not until the baby is born do they understand what has happened—sometimes not even then. Their adamant refusal to abort seldom accompanies a full realization that a baby is actually growing inside their own bodies; their grasp of this fact can often be amazingly abstract.

For one thing, the younger the child, the longer it often takes her to realize that she is pregnant—sometimes not until the fifth or sixth month, maybe not even until immediately before she delivers. One reason for this is the irregularity of menstrual periods at the onset of puberty, so that even a girl who is fully aware of the possibility of pregnancy easily can fail to recognize the significance of missed periods. But what is more likely to be at work when the pregnancy is discovered very late is a defensive denial, grounded in fear and fantasy.

"It's very hard to help these younger girls," says Dr. McAnarney. ". . . it's difficult to plan for them, and they really cannot manage to see what is happening to them. Very often they don't even realize that there's a baby in there until the baby actually appears. Even though they know they're big and can see that their bellies are growing, they seem to feel that it's just that they've gotten fat. They don't understand that there's another human being inside of them."

"Our experience with the eleven-, twelve-, and thirteen-year-olds," Dr. Hofmann says, "is that they aren't really capable of appreciating that they're pregnant. They think it's no different from having a tumor; these are pre-formal thought adolescents. When they keep their babies, it's because they can't even appreciate what's going on, so they can't mobilize any action or make any decisions about it."

There is some evidence that pregnancy among very young girls should be considered less as social pathology than as simply one manifestation of a more general difficulty in coping with the physical disturbances of puberty. Another common condition among young teenage girls is *anorexia nervosa*, a pathological refusal to eat, which is believed to be related to an unconscious rejection of their own maturing bodies. The links between teenage pregnancy and anorexia have yet to be studied, but clearly they are related as opposites, both being disturbances of the body image having to do with the need or the refusal to ingest, and both following a pattern of denial: The anorexic denies that she is starving—she feels fat right up to the moment of death—and the pregnant girl denies that a baby is growing inside her body.

In her clinical practice at Columbia-Presbyterian Hospital, Dr. McHugh sees some wild distortions of the body image as related to sex:

"It starts with the idea that you can't use any protection because then it can't be spontaneous, and if it's not spontaneous it's not right. So you can't carry a diaphragm, you can't put foam in —and, of course, IUD's are absolutely out. They fall out, they stick inside, you can't have babies afterward if you've ever used them. Kids think that if you plan to have sex, something bad will happen to you.

"Then they believe that if he comes inside you when you're having sex, it [semen] will come out of your mouth. The fantasies are incredible about where it goes, what happens to it, what it is that comes out, what it means, what it's made of. It gets all mixed up with the idea of blood.

"And they think that after having sex you mustn't move around for fear of something happening down there. They're afraid all their insides will fall out because they've opened up during intercourse. On the other hand, they believe that the way to keep from getting pregnant is to jump around right afterward. They're totally confused. Most of the time they know it, but they're afraid of looking foolish and they don't know how to ask for help."

Once the fact of pregnancy has been established, the girls who insist on having and keeping their babies continue in confusion and fantasy. It is generally agreed that a child mother is sending out some sort of distress signal to her own mother, but psychologists are divided as to how to interpret it. Some see the child's unconscious purpose in having the baby as a sexual challenge to her mother, a form of Oedipal rivalry with her. Others believe it to be an expression of a need that precedes the Oedipal phase: the struggle to develop out of the infantile state of total identification with the mother and to establish oneself as an individual with a separate existence.

Dr. Irving Markowitz, Medical Director of Family Services at a New Jersey clinic, believes that teenagers who keep their babies are doing so as a way of gaining status: "They can be mothers themselves, in competition with their own mothers. That accounts for the tenacity with which they hang on, their unwillingness to give up the baby."

Another factor in these pregnancies may be the girl's awareness of her mother's unhappiness that her own childbearing years are coming to an end; the grandchild is then an attempt at restitution and consolation. Very often the grandmother does welcome the baby, accepting the gift as it was intended. Nevertheless, the families of these child mothers are usually deeply disturbed. Most characteristically, there is a long-standing emotional impoverishment owing to the psychic or physical absence of one or both parents, leaving a child whose early experience is dominated by feelings of loneliness, helplessness, and anger. Having a baby then becomes a way of starting over, hoping to make it come out happily this time.

"It's an affirmation of their gender roles and their identity, which they are having a lot of trouble with," says Dr. Hofmann. "In the younger age groups, below fourteen, the baby becomes a younger sibling; it's the 'baby doll' syndrome."

The younger mothers who have refused to give their babies up for adoption usually drop out of school and stay home with their families, relying on their own mothers' experience and skill in child-rearing to help them over the first difficult months with their babies. This is considered the most hopeful, if not the only feasible, resolution for all concerned. But even the family's acceptance of the girl and her baby into a warm and welcoming environment can menace the baby's chances for healthy growth.

Drs. Joanne Fineman and Marguerite Smith, of the Department of Child Psychology and Child Development at Boston University Medical Center, have studied a number of these babies, their mothers, and the mothers' families over a five-year period. The girls were between fourteen and seventeen, were living at home, and had no continuing contact with their babies' fathers.

As the babies approached the ages of two, three, and four, those who had been born to mothers under seventeen tended to exhibit a particular syndrome of disturbed growth:

"We saw, in a majority of the observations of the infants of adolescent mothers, that focused eye contact on the part of the baby toward the mother was intermittent and unstable. The babies tended to gaze indiscriminately at other human faces or at inanimate objects in the environment. It was consistently difficult to get the babies to focus and to maintain a fixed gaze. Their visual behavior seemed remarkably similar to the babies diagnosed as failing to thrive, even though they were not malnourished or starved-looking."

Drs. Fineman and Smith related this behavior to a general inability to form loving attachments:

"It became very clear that their psychopathology centered around the incapacity to attach and remain attached to care-giving figures, and that modification of primitive aggression had been poor or incomplete. . . . We found that most often we settled on the diagnosis of 'developmental deviation' to describe the failure of consistent loving object attachment and the wildly aggressive attacks directed toward adults or peers who had to frustrate or limit them, or who were approaching them with nurturing and loving behavior. All of these children . . . failed to achieve age-appropriate internal controls over their destructive impulses and were fragile in their capacities to love consistently and to accept loving approaches from their care-givers. The term 'care-givers' is significant; more often than not, the biological mother—the adolescent—loses in her struggle to be both mother and developing girl and, through some external intervention . . . the baby is placed in a foster home, usually before the age of two years. . . ."

The trouble begins during pregnancy with the formation of a competitive triangle consisting of mother, baby, and grandmother:

"Most of the adolescent mothers, during the pregnancy and after the birth of the baby, regressed to a more ambivalent tie to the grandmother. . . . [When mother and baby come home from the hospital] the baby becomes the center of controversy and the focus of rivalrous confrontation. The baby's mother alternates between her wish to be nurtured as she sees her mother nurturing the baby and her need to possess her infant; this is the stage at which we have seen most regression and revival of hostility between mother and grandmother.

"Gradually, such primitive ambivalence pushes the mother

and daughter further apart, and the solution becomes a separation. The baby is likely to be placed in foster care, and each member of the triad has lost a crucial love object."

This, then, is the sad scenario: The younger the pregnant girl, the less likely she is to accept abortion, the more likely she will insist on keeping the baby once it is born, and the greater the likelihood that the baby will be the loser in its mother's struggle to be both mother and developing girl. The baby will, within a year or two of its birth, be sent to live among strangers in a foster home.

Miss Andress of Inwood House, like most other experienced observers of child mothers, is familiar with this phenomenon:

"What we see here is that in a tragic way the younger and less prepared the girl is for life, the more strongly she is convinced that she needs the baby and will be perfectly adequate at taking care of it—before it's born. The trouble begins when it's a few months old.

"We have one difficult case now, a girl who had a baby with us four years ago. She is now living with her baby in a foster home, is a freshman at Brooklyn College, and has ambitions to become a lawyer. The foster mother has noticed that she doesn't take very good care of her baby. He's only four now, and from the time he was eighteen months old she neglected him. She wouldn't change or feed him or even play with him. The foster mother had to do it all.

"We've been talking to this girl and have finally been able to convince her to surrender the baby for adoption. Now she's going her own way with her plans to become a lawyer and talks of her baby as a 'surrendered child.'

"In the worst cases, there is not just neglect, but active violence done to the babies. Some of these girls were abused children themselves, which we now know means that most probably they will become abusing mothers. Often when you try to correct them and tell them, 'Don't hit that baby,' they get very angry and yell at you, 'You can't tell me anything. This baby's mine, I can do whatever I want.' This is absolutely horrifying, of course, and we have sometimes gone to court to take the baby away from an abusing mother until she's convinced us she can take care of her child properly."

Compared with the recent intense focus by public and private health and welfare agencies on the predicament of child mothers, very little attention has been paid to the fathers, owing to the double standard which allows them to escape both scrutiny and censure and to the fact that few of them have physical reason to seek help. Statistics here, therefore, are scarce, but there is general agreement that at least as many boys try to act responsibly when their girl friends become pregnant as try to escape, dropping the girl and vanishing from the scene.

Kevin, sixteen, was confused when he and his girl friend, Lisa, learned that she was pregnant: "It's . . . it all happened so quickly. Like the week after she thought that she was, like the week after her period didn't come, she went and got tested and the test said that she wasn't pregnant. Then they said, well, come back in a week or so and you'll find out whether you are or not because it might be too early to show up. That's when it showed up and like a week later she had the abortion. And it didn't seem as if she really had had an abortion. It was like, there was no long waiting to really think about it. I still, it still hasn't really hit me yet that my girl friend really had an abortion. It's hitting me now."

Lisa's mother refused to let Kevin see the girl right after her abortion. He tells how he felt: ". . . like she felt as if Lisa shouldn't see me that day, and I thought that was so totally wrong, who better to be with than the person that . . . and also I took part in it, you know? I mean like it's partly mine, so I wanted to be with her, too, and it was like so weird. . . ."

There is even some evidence that an increasing number of boys choose to become fathers, rejecting abortion for their girl friends even more strenuously in some cases than the girls themselves. Usually, however, these boys are deeply torn; the same ones who most vehemently oppose abortion are often those who disappear after the baby arrives.

As a rule, the forces acting upon a teenage girl that propel her toward pregnancy are not at work in adolescent boys, or not to the same degree. The affirmation of gender identity, which is perhaps the single most important psychological struggle for boys and girls of this age, can be achieved by girls through motherhood; but the gender identity of boys, which may be temporarily confirmed by the fact of fatherhood, will once more be threatened by the urgent needs of a growing baby.

Dr. John Ross, of the Department of Psychiatry at Albert Einstein College of Medicine in New York City, says in a recent study of paternal identity that by the late teens a boy has developed a sufficiently solid sexual identity to give him a ". . . foretaste of genital love and psychosocial independence and responsibility. But as far as parental identity is concerned, adolescence typically constitutes a 'moratorium' when an unwanted and irresponsible paternity is to be avoided."

Miss Andress sees this avoidance as universal:

"We find that many of the boyfriends are the same age as the girls, with rarely a difference of more than five years. Sometimes the boy is even a couple of years younger, either in school himself or a dropout, but almost never is he in any sort of economic situation where he can support a baby. Young as he is, though, he may already have impregnated as many as three or even more girls, and he has no interest at all in this particular girl who is pregnant and in our institution."

Among the child mothers we interviewed, one, Nadine, has so far succeeded reasonably well both in caring for her baby and in keeping her own life going:

"I was fourteen when I had my baby, Tad. He's now two. He's certainly changed my life. I wouldn't give him up for the world, but to tell you the truth, if I had it to do over again, I think I would have tried harder not to get pregnant.

"My boyfriend was maybe the ninth boy I'd ever gone steady with, but he was the first that I slept with. A lot of my friends had been sleeping with boys since about the age of twelve, and I know one girl who started when she was eleven, so I was a little slow—I was thirteen before I slept with Larry.

"My father is a dentist, he's a highly respected professional man, and I always felt a sense of security with both my parents. I don't mean that they never have arguments, but they usually get along pretty well. So I was looking forward to marriage; I thought life could be beautiful.

"But I was very silly and careless about my sex life. I started having my periods when I was thirteen and a half, but I was very skinny and I never thought I could get pregnant. I was almost in my sixth month before we found out, because I didn't put any weight on right away; and when I started showing, everybody just thought I was filling out at last. At first, I'd even get compliments, especially when my breasts started to get big. My family took this as a sign of maturity, and of course my boyfriend just loved it.

"It wasn't until around the end of the fifth month that it occurred to me that although my periods had always been irregular, I'd never gone that long without having any at all. So Larry and I went to a testing lab, and the report came back positive.

"I was scared out of my mind. It was very late, near the end of the second trimester. I remember they said that, because to me a trimester meant having three semesters a year in school instead of two. Larry really went through some changes. He was going to marry me; we would elope. Then he decided I should have an abortion. When it turned out to be too late for that, he got very cool and quickly put a lot of distance between us. We're friends again now, but for a long time we were anything but.

"By this time my mother had to tell my father, and it was very bad. He got very, very upset. He thought I'd let him down and acted as if I'd done this terrible thing on purpose to hurt him. We had a secret family conference where we discussed the various options, but my father had already made up his mind.

"He pressed me very heavily to give the baby up for adoption. I thought about it, but the longer I thought, the worse it seemed. I really felt that if I was going to carry the baby through the whole pregnancy and give birth and all, I should at least have a chance to see if I could be a good mother to it afterward. I felt that if after six months or a year I wasn't doing a good job with it, then I could give it away without any doubts or qualms.

"By this time I was in the ninth grade—I'd gotten pregnant over the summer—and toward the end, the last three months, my belly began to stick out and all the kids at school knew. I couldn't sleep very well because I couldn't roll over, I couldn't climb stairs without a lot of puffing, or get into any of my clothes. On top of everything, my father would hardly speak to me—he acted sullen and annoyed all the time. My parents had decided that if I was going to have it, I should at least be 'responsible' and agree to give it away, but I fought them like a tiger.

"After I had the baby, I tried living with him at home, but right away there was trouble, starting with his name. My father wouldn't let me name him after anyone in the family, and of course I wasn't going to name the baby after *his* father, whom I wasn't speaking to. So I had to give him a neutral name, but I think it's beautiful.

"The baby was very cute right from the start. It's true he was a little small when he was born, I guess because I'd been smoking, and the first six months when I didn't know he was coming, I didn't take care of myself. He was a little slow in sitting up and doing the other things babies do, but he seems to be catching up nicely. Right now he is really my main reason for living.

"But my father kept saying absurd things, like he couldn't get any sleep because of the baby's crying. The baby was so good he hardly cried at all, and never at night. Really, I think my father was embarrassed about our neighbors and relatives all knowing that I'd gotten myself pregnant, and here was this constant reminder of it right in the house.

"Anyway, when the six months were up and my parents started nagging me again to give the baby away, I refused. I stayed home for a little longer, but the tension just became too great. I couldn't stand all the noise and arguments anymore, and I decided to move out. I was lucky to find two girls, a little older, who were looking for a third to share their apartment.

"I work part time, and I even went back to school. The schools are wonderful. They arrange special classes for girls like me so we can take care of our babies, too. I have hopes of going to college, although my grades aren't quite up to the nineties and ninety-fives I used to get before I dropped out. I still want to be somebody special, but the world is going to have to accept me with this baby. I'm not ashamed of him. I expect him to be a very proud, upstanding man someday, and I feel I'm giving him a good start and being a very good mother to him.

"I *don't* feel like a martyr, and I *don't* think I'm throwing my life away, as my parents keep telling me. I think now I have a reason to live and a reason to work hard.

"My parents do help me out a little financially, but it's clear that I'm going to have to make it mostly on my own, that I won't be able to lean on them anymore. One of the first things that made me aware I was no longer a helpless kid, and that I was now going to have to think, act, and earn like an adult, was realizing that when my baby woke up and cried, he was crying for *me* and not my mother. It really makes me feel good to know that I can make him happier than anyone else can, and that I'm the one he wants and no one else. There are certain things I miss, like when the other kids at school are getting ready to go to dances, or even when I see younger kids playing outside, I sometimes feel that my childhood has just passed me by too quickly. But then just holding my son in my arms makes me forget all that.

"I've stopped nursing him—he's being weaned now, but that was a wonderful experience. Nursing him not only made me feel closer to him, it convinced me that there's nothing more important in the world for my body to do than serve another human being. I know now that I will definitely never give up my baby. If any of the boys I date don't like it, that's tough. So far none of them have complained, because they understand that my baby comes first; I figure that any boy who loves me will love my baby, too, and accept us both.

"Right now he still has my family name, and we'll keep it that way until I get married. Then we'll have my husband, whoever he is, adopt him and give him his name. I used to think I wouldn't get married until I was twenty-five or even thirty, but I realize now that I can't wait that long if my baby is going to have the experience of a father in his life. So far, I don't think he misses it. As long as I'm there, he's happy. I can't tell what the future will be, but whatever happens, I'm going to face it with my baby."

Despite her intelligence, strength of will, and courage, all of which are high, the odds against Nadine and her baby are higher still. Ninety percent of the girls who give birth at fifteen or younger never finish high school; pregnancy is by far the most common reason for dropping out of school. Ninety-one percent have neither full- nor part-time employment, and most eventually go on welfare.* Nadine, as a daughter of prosperous parents, has escaped the scars of poverty, but she still must cope with the difficult demands of both her baby's infancy and her own adolescence, which has only just begun.

Nadine's mother, Mrs. Howard, takes the long view of her daughter's situation. Clearly, however, she has yet to completely accept it:

"Certainly we still love Nadine, and she is still my child, although it's a little awkward now to call her 'my baby,' even though I feel that I still should, at her age. But she's a mother herself now. I love our little grandson, too, I think he's precious, but I really can't say that I feel a wholehearted joy when I hold him or play with him. For a few minutes I can forget myself and totally love this little boy, but then there's always a stab of pain when I look at him and remember how he came to be.

"We've always thought of ourselves as a very enlightened, liberal family. Certainly my husband and I always thought we could accept almost anything. But no matter what theoretical constructs you have about how you expect to react to certain situations, you can't know for sure until they actually happen, and this shook us to our foundations. It's safe to say it even shook the foundations of our marriage.

"When we found out that Nadine was pregnant, we went through some pretty traumatic moments. Her father became especially bitter; he changed dramatically, in fact. Well, you know that's why I'm talking to you here in Nadine's apartment and not in our own home, where she should be. He felt that not only was he being embarrassed, but that in some way this whole episode was intended deliberately to hurt him.

"I know I went through some serious soul-searching, asking myself over and over where we went wrong, what kind of misleading messages we might have given her. Of course, we soon realized that we didn't have total control over her moral standards or ideas, that maybe she was influenced by her friends, too. But we couldn't be satisfied with that.

"We had always been a very close, loving, warm family. If you had told me just a couple of years ago that this would happen, I would have said you were crazy. Of course, I also would have said that if it *did* happen, well, that's simply one more symptom of our sick society, and that's just the way things are these days. I would have been rather glib about it.

"The acid test came when she told us she was pregnant. It was a little too late to have one of the safe, easy abortions using suction, and it was a decision between either a serious procedure that late in the pregnancy or having the baby and giving it up for adoption. We really wanted her to give it up. We felt that she had made a mistake, but that it was a mistake she could learn from, and that from now she would be a little older and much wiser.

"But it was Nadine's choice to keep the baby. I still can't understand why she wanted to give up being taken care of, being a loved child, for the uncertainties and pressures of instant motherhood. I know one or two of her friends must have had abortions. I talk to some of the other mothers, and they tell me they worry all the time about abortions, VD, and running away.

"Actually, none of the girls we know have been runaways. They're all excellent students, and all well loved and cared for. They've always had everything they ever wanted. All they've had to do was snap their fingers, and we've given them everything. I really can't see what we did wrong. I guess I simply have to acknowledge that this is the way things are happening now. My child is a product of the times. I'd like to believe that we could influence her ultimately as to what life should be and the kind of life she wants to have, but it's really up to her.

"My husband had all kinds of glorious plans for her. He hoped that she would become a dentist, too, and join him in his practice, even take it over some day. She still talks about going to graduate school—or maybe it's law school or something else by now, but, frankly, I have my doubts. She's having enough trouble finishing high school, in spite of all her motivation and crusading claims that she's going to build a life for herself, and that this is not going to be a stumbling block but a stepping stone. I *hope* so, but deep down I doubt it. Maybe I'm pessimistic because I've seen what happens to unbridled idealism, but I believe that many parents are totally at a loss with today's morality.

"It's not that I didn't discuss sex with her; I even offered to take her to my gynecologist to be fitted for a diaphragm or get pills. But she kept saying everything was fine, she knew what she was doing and had everything under control. I suspected that she was probably having intercourse. She certainly was very involved with her young man. I guess I should have insisted on some kind of birth control, but even if I got it for her I couldn't force her to use it, could I?

"It's frightening, the way generations repeat themselves. My grandmother from the old country, whom I never met, got married when she was about fifteen. She had a child at sixteen, and another ten children after that. But, you know, when we look back at our roots and remember how they struggled and slaved and had all those children—most of whom died—it really was a hard life. That's why they came to the new country, looking to America for something better. What I mean is, it wasn't easy building up the kind of life we have now. It's a very good life. Yes, we work hard, but we also have education and leisure. All we wanted to do was to pass on the benefits of our life experience to our children. Then, suddenly, like a ghost from the past, your own child repeats the pattern you thought you'd shaken off forever.

"Nadine talks very bravely about taking care of herself and being able to look after herself and the baby financially, but I doubt it. We're helping her out, and of course we will continue helping her because we feel that's the least we can do. Certainly we are very involved. My husband feels funny about the baby's having his name, but what other name is he to have?

"Nadine is quite confident that she can still get married. She thinks the baby will have no effect on her chances, and that no young man will be upset about having to take on a baby, too. Well, maybe that will turn out to be so—I don't know. I think she hasn't thought through what's going to happen when she has other children with her new husband, and this baby starts to ask questions.

"It's so absurd, she's really a little girl at heart. She still reads the teen magazines. I sometimes come over to baby-sit so she can go and play with her friends, or go bowling with the other girls, or just sit and giggle with them about movies and romances and rock stars. I do hope this will turn out not to have hurt her, that she can still build a life. I hope being a mother won't become the whole focus of her life, and that she can still grow into the independent, proud person we always hoped she would be.

"My husband and I were both so upset by this we went to see a psychiatrist for counseling, and he told us to relax. Can you believe it, he said that this is happening everywhere now and the best way for us to handle it was just to accept the reality that our child is a product of the times? He insisted that it was not a tragedy. My husband became very angry. He told him that it was easy for him to say that because it wasn't his child, but how would he feel if it were?

"But we understand that the morality we grew up with and

the expectations we had are not the ones children grow up with these days, and it has created a rift. Our other child still gets along well with Nadine, loves her as much as ever, and loves playing with the baby. I believe that we really are out of step with the times, and that kids now are marching to the beat of a different drummer."

Chapter 4

FAMILY SEX GAMES

Not surprisingly, if we look at the early life of a child who becomes a prostitute, or a mother at twelve, or a performer in pornographic films, or who in any other way is acting out a precocious sexuality, we usually find that the roots of deviance reach deep into the family structure. Very often the deviance appears in patterns of neurotic dependence and role-playing that have been recurring for generations.

What are sexual family games? How do some families get involved in them? How do the players get the roles they do? Why do they persist in playing them?

Most experts in the field of family interaction agree that family sexuality is determined by the relationship between the mother and father. Kaufman and Peck found that "the personality structure of the mother or of the father considered independently would not be sufficient to produce the acting out. The girls reacted to their mothers' unconscious desire to put them in the maternal role. They at the same time received gratification from the fathers as parents who loved them in this pathological way." *

The support the parents give each other, either unconsciously or consciously, in part accounts for the continuation of the game, as we will see in most of the case studies in this chapter. The tacit understanding between parents also accounts for D. Browning and B. Boatman's finding that, in their study group, less than one third of the parents who discovered sexual offenses took any steps to help the child.*

Some experts blame this violation of the normal protective parent-child relationship on the turbulent social changes in contemporary society. For example, Margaret Mead suggested that the feminist movement may have disturbed traditional family stability by "denigrating motherhood and diminishing the importance of fathers." *

Mental health professionals are becoming more aware of the extent to which family games are played. However, identifying the characteristics and the victims is difficult because family sexual interaction is by nature deceptive. Alvin Rosenfeld says, "Though molestation is the chief complaint in some situations, most cases of sexual abuse are presented as common childhood difficulties and are detected only when the clinician has a sufficiently high index of suspicion."* The presentations in this sphere which at first seem to be only common childhood problems are, according to Rosenfeld:

1. Genital difficulties;
2. Common childhood problems;
3. Alterations in behavior; and
4. Acting-out behavior.*

What usually inhibits sexual acting out within families is what L. A. Berman and D. R. Jensen call "modesty training." * In this chapter we will see some abuses of modesty training, some excesses beyond its "normal" range. We also will explore some of the important questions Berman and Jensen raise, such as, how is modesty training carried out? Just what is the normal range of modesty training? How is adult personality affected by modesty training during childhood?

As the nature of modesty training is determined by the parents, so is all family sexual behavior initiated by the parents. E. M. Litin says, "Unusual sexual behavior evolves by the adaptation of the ego to subtle attitudes within the family. Perverse sexual acting out and many unusual heterosexual patterns result from unconscious permission and subtle coercion by adults." * (L. Kolb and A. Johnson noted that similar family dynamics were described by adult homosexuals.*) Parents who play family sexual games use their children for their own ends. S. A. Szurels, who studied delinquent children who were not gang members, said, "Parents unwittingly seduce these children into the expression of the parents' own forbidden impulses, thus affording the parent unconscious vicarious gratification." * The case of Edna and Sabrina in this chapter illustrates one form of this vicarious gratification.

From the start, parents set the rules and the tone of the game. The child, whether from inexperience, isolation, or fear, may accept the game as normal. Litin describes the parent-child dynamics well when he says, "Concomitantly the parent defines a pattern of unusual sexual behavior. This behavior may be genital, or it may be pregenital and perverse. The child regards it as partially condoned and acceptable and therefore carries out the act. It may feel very little guilt and shame." *

The parent conducting a sexual game usually chooses one child to bear the brunt of it, one child to seduce. "Seduction" here means a pathological tempting of the child. It can be in the guise of tenderness, or it can be overt passion. Either way, the adult imposes upon the child an adult form of sexuality completely inappropriate to the child's age and position.

R. D. Laing and A. Esterson's classic study of the schizophrenogenic family constellation, Sanity, Madness and the Family, showed how a child may be chosen—may even, in a sacrificial gesture, choose itself to play out the role of family scapegoat.* The arrangement, painful as it is—and it can lead to loss of sanity —is still, in a pathetically inadequate way, effective in establishing an equilibrium that holds the family together.

What binds the structure is the understanding of all members that certain forces will never be acknowledged for fear that the situation might explode. Instead, these forces are focused on one family member who serves as a symbol for all the inadmissible feelings and impulses of the others.

Laing and Esterson were concerned especially with the early environment of young people who had been hospitalized for schizophrenia. Since we will be concentrating on those who act out sexually, and who therefore are probably not as disintegrated as psychotic children are, we will not be dealing with families in which the conflict is so deeply repressed. The meaning of the family games discussed in this chapter is very thinly veiled; indeed, these games are only a short step away from the overt incest that will be the subject of the next chapter. Still, there is a degree of disguise in that the child is being manipulated in such a way as to conceal the incestuous motive behind what is done to him or her in the game. At some level both parent and child probably are quite conscious of the meaning of their behavior, but they have an unspoken agreement to call it something else.

Bear in mind that there are, of course, components of sexuality in childhood which involve tenderness and affection, appropriate expressions which fuse into the burgeoning sexual drive at puberty to form adult sexuality. From Freud on, many psychologists and psychiatrists have noted that aspects of child-rearing involve elements of sexuality. For example, B. Glueck remarks that some activities associated with nurturance and hygienic care of children may be considered sexual in that they involve "contact with the child's genitalia or produce in the child an emotional response of a sexual nature." *

Healthy childhood experiences include kissing, hugging, washing, wrestling, and other kinds of physical closeness, but with limits, limits that recognize the child's need for a sense of self and preclude overstimulation of the child for prurient adult motives. A child who has had a warm physical relationship with parents will carry those feelings into adulthood, integrating them into a personality repertoire which includes warmth, tenderness, affection, and a healthy pride in self and family. We all know the mental health axiom, "Battered children become battering parents." So, too, children who have not been teased, taunted, and touched inappropriately are able as adults to show love for one another. They have no pain to overcome in forming intimate relationships.

The children you will meet in this chapter have suffered a variety of pathological family interactions. Many of them are

angry at their parents for exploiting them. The parents who exploited these children did so out of different emotional needs, but
all of them have one thing in common: They are unable to sustain intimacy with their children without sexual involvement,
and they have created a family scenario in which each member
plays an assigned role in maintaining the fiction that the discharge
of parental sexual tensions upon at least one of the children is
simply normal family love.

The most common pattern of quasi-incestuous acting out is
the "Children as Harem" game. This is usually played in families
in which all the children are girls, with an age span of not more
than ten years between the oldest and the youngest. The father
typically is a big, blustering bully, dominating the family with
frequent emotional outbursts and temper tantrums which terror-
ize everyone. An enormous amount of time and energy is spent
trying to placate Daddy in a futile attempt to soften his explo-
sive temper. These efforts are never successful. Venting his rage
upon his family is one of the few satisfactions life has to offer
him. Such a man generally suffers deep humiliation and frustration in the world outside the home. Usually he has failed, or feels
he has failed, to become successful in his work, and is often
trapped in an underpaid, menial job.

At home he compensates by playing the domestic tyrant.
Nothing is good enough for him, everyone is always failing him,
especially his wife, who is a constant disappointment in every
way—as mother, wife, housekeeper. The whole family is continually letting him down, and his favorite way of discharging his
accumulated anger at the mess he has made of his life is to
threaten to leave them. The children live in constant fear that he
will desert them; his occasional absences are periods of great
anxiety. Miserable as it is to live with him, they are nevertheless
terrified of abandonment.

Usually in this situation the mother plays the hapless victim.
She passively suffers the storms of physical and verbal abuse,
making no effort to deflect them or even to protect the children
from their father's blasts of rage. On the contrary, she often
turns to them for comfort, as though she were a child herself,

which intensifies their sense of helplessness. By withdrawing from the battle, she effectively plays into the father's need to denigrate her.

In families in which the father does not resort to physical violence, freezing silences are the preferred tactic, with one or both parents communicating with each other only through the children: "Ask your father if he would be good enough to . . ." or "Try to explain to that cow that . . ." The children are thus caught in the no-man's-land between their parents, compelled usually to side with the father as the stronger force, the one who has the most to give if only he can be mollified.

At this point one of the daughters is singled out as the favorite. In some families all the daughters vie with each other for the privilege of pleasing Daddy, but most commonly one is chosen early and is pulled closer than the others. This is apparent first by the absence of shouting and anger when she is around. Soon she discovers that she is much more powerful than her mother, for she can actually make Daddy happy and keep him calm and good-humored. Next, the work of soothing him assumes an openly physical form. His commands become "Sit near me," "Come sit on my lap," "You sit in the front seat with me, they can all go in the back."

The age of the child when this begins to happen can vary. It may not start until early adolescence, but it is usually well under way by the time she is five or six. At that age the erotic intention behind the strokings, spankings, and caresses still can be masked as innocent playfulness with a little girl. The mother is usually subliminally aware of what is going on, but is incapable of protesting against any of Daddy's whims. She instead laughs—perhaps a little too quickly—at these signs of his special favor. She may well find that the temporary peace makes smothering her suspicions worthwhile. In any case her complicity—"It doesn't mean anything, she's just a baby"—paves the way for more serious father-daughter intimacies later on.

If the child should protest—which rarely happens—her complaints must be very loud and urgent before the mother will respond. If the mother is playing a passive-aggressive role herself, her own laments will drown out those of her daughter, who then will be caught between dreading her father's approaches and feeling guilty for her selfishness at being preoccupied with her own discomfort and doubt rather than with her mother's unhappiness.

Lucille

Lucille, seventeen, is the older of two sisters in an upper-middle-class family in Connecticut. Throughout her childhood, her mother was a passive and compliant shadow in the house, totally dominated by the father, who made constant companions of his daughters. All through her elementary and high school years, Lucille's father would take both girls to the baseball and football games he loved. He is a burly bear of a man who tends to be very physical with everyone, but he always seemed to be even more so with his two girls, especially Lucille. He would often tell her, "You are the son I never had," as he gave her what she called "bear hugs that almost broke my back."

He also had a habit, whenever he wanted to talk to her, of bursting into her room without warning in spite of her protests. He seemed to need to speak with her most urgently whenever she was changing her clothes or taking a bath. When this upset her, the family treated it as a joke, making fun of Lucille's "pretensions." "Look at her, she thinks she's a regular young lady," her mother would say, although Lucille was already in high school. Or "Stop making such a fuss, it's only your father. We're all girls together here anyway."

Throughout her adolescence, Lucille never had the privacy she desperately craved. When the family moved into a new apartment with one large and one small bedroom, the parents decided to give the small one to the other daughter and to divide the larger bedroom with a partition, Lucille taking one half and their taking the other. When Lucille, without fully realizing why, fought against this plan, she was quickly overruled. Now she had to contend with the embarrassment of hearing the sounds of sexual intercourse coming from her parents' half of the room, and with her father in even closer proximity than before, no longer bothering to conceal his enjoyment at being able to barge in on her without warning. When she talked on the telephone, he openly listened in on the extension and even intervened in her conversations with her friends.

The crisis came just at the time Lucille thought she had at last broken free. A gifted student, she graduated from high school at fifteen and a half and won a scholarship to an out-of-state university. The previous winter both her father's mother and sister had died in an accident (his father having died several years before). The night before she was to leave, her father took her for a long walk, during which he put his arms around her and said miserably, "Well, I've lost my sister, I've lost my mother, and now I'm going to lose you, too. You're running away from me." Feeling guilty and helpless, she hugged and kissed him, promising that he was not losing her and that she would never desert him. Throughout the term, he called her every night, demanding to be told that she still loved him best and would always belong to him.

Under such pressure she found it impossible to concentrate, did poorly in her courses, and after a couple of months dropped out and returned home. At midyear she made a second attempt to escape from home and enrolled in another college. This time she held out for the whole semester, but her grades were marginal and again she returned home. Her family accepted these failures with remarkable equanimity, considering that she had gotten almost straight A's throughout high school, her father especially not disguising his pleasure at having her back. Her sister and mother, too, were relieved each time Lucille came home to stay—the father was always better-tempered when she was around.

The following year she capitulated and made no attempt to leave home, hanging around the house doing odd jobs, writing poetry, playing her guitar. But she was listless and unable to focus her energies. Now, a year later, she has made a third attempt at yet another college. Whether she finally will succeed in breaking loose is still in doubt.

In such situations, symbolic domination and overt physicality always coexist in a ratio that varies from family to family, depending on its religious and socioeconomic background as well as on the father's needs and how strongly they are repressed.

Joanne

My father would never let me go out at night with my friends until I was fifteen and finally threatened to run away from home. But then when I come back, he makes me tell him everything, every little detail, like where I was, with whom, for how long, what did we say, were there any boys—especially that. Then it's terrible. If there was a boy, he wants to know everything about him, his name, what he looked like, where he came from, how old he was, and everything he said to me.

But it's never enough. After all this tremendous buildup, he asks me with a scary smile, "All right, Joanne, what did he do to you?" Nothing, I swear, nothing. But he never believes me and keeps on questioning me like a detective. At first, I'd be honest and deny doing anything because I really never *do* do anything. But, finally, I got tired of this barrage of questions night after night, and I've found that if I tell him some little thing, like the boy kissed me good night, that makes him happy, it satisfies him, and he says, "Aha, I knew it! I know my girl, don't I? I know you better than anyone else in the whole world."

Then he makes me promise not to do it again, and goes on and on with gory details about what happens to girls who let boys fool around with them—always there's a tragic ending, the girl always dies from an abortion or something, and then he ends it with "Do you see what happens when you leave your father? You must listen to me and stay with me so I can protect you, nobody loves you like I do."

Finally, it's over, after I've apologized, with a big kiss and a long, tight hug, while he keeps asking, "So do you still love your daddy, Babykins?" I always have to answer, "Yes, I do, you know how much," and then he says, "Of course you do, of course you do, you're my baby and always will be, and I love you." Then he insists that I have some dessert, some ice cream or something, and finally he lets me go to bed.

This is an example of a moderate degree of dominance. What will save Joanne is her awareness that her father's interest in her is prurient and voyeuristic, an awareness which enables her in some degree to manipulate him in return for her own protection. If he should intensify his demands or attempt an actual seduction, she will be able to defend herself—or even leave home if it comes to that—without carrying any additional burden of guilt. Lucille, on the other hand, in whom this awareness was suppressed, responded to her father with guilt, depression, and a paralysis of the will.

In the eroticization of the parent-child relationship, the first step is invasion of privacy. Banning locked doors, opening letters and eavesdropping on phone conversations, obsessively examining a daughter's dresses and underclothes, caressing and stroking her body under the guise of ordinary parental affection or of keeping it "pure" from the touch of strangers, are steps along a continuum whose end point is incest.

But although the child's entanglement in the parent's complex of needs may stop short of this ultimate violation, he or she can still suffer from severe and permanent emotional damage that can include a pervasive general anxiety about sex which may persist throughout life; an equally pervasive emotional instability which with any additional stress may lead to a breakdown; and a greater susceptibility to using drugs and more difficulty breaking the habit once it becomes established than the average adolescent drug user has.* The normal sexual crises of adolescence will also be greatly exacerbated, with schoolwork coming to a virtual standstill and grades dropping alarmingly.* Inevitably, as the child becomes more independent, he or she is likely to withdraw abruptly and completely from the suffocatingly heavy emotions of the family atmosphere and seek a substitute family elsewhere.

Intimate Stroking Games

But the child may be unable to pull away if the father is less inhibited than in the previous examples, in which case the sexuality may become overt and brutal, almost a violation of the child's body by force—in all but the most technical sense incest, stopping short of penetration. It is most often and most aggressively pursued by fathers rather than by mothers, amounting as it does almost to rape, and because it is often a husband's response to his wife's withholding herself for some strategic reason of her own. Usually, however, when matters have gone this far, the child is locked into compliance by the mother's attitude which says, often in so many words, "Look, he's the provider. What do you want me to do, break up the family? Then we'll all starve. He's not hurting you, he loves you. He may not be perfect, but he does support us and take care of us." Or, worse, any appeal to the mother is met by a counteraccusation either that the daughter is slandering her father or that it is she who is seducing him. In these cases there is a double denial that can raise the level of unreality which pervades the household to alarming heights.

This type of game generally gets under way in early puberty when the child is from ten to thirteen years old. What the father claims to be doing is concerning himself with his still-innocent daughter's chastity, protecting her from boys with evil intentions, or even from herself. This begins with admonitions to stay away from "bad" boys. He tries to keep her close to the house, unless she is actually in school or going out with him and her mother, but soon moves from such general warnings to specific and graphic anatomical descriptions of *precisely* what it is she is not to allow them to do to her.

But soon the father becomes impatient with the inadequacy of his words, especially when his daughter is developing so quickly into a woman right before his eyes. At that age every day seems to bring new changes, painful reminders that she soon will be moving out of his control. Now the questioning becomes more prolonged and intense as his anxiety rises. Depending on the pattern of alliances prevailing within the family, the mother may join the father in this verbal assault, or she may side with the daughter and try to stop the inquisition by reminding him that he, too, was once young and eager to learn about life, and that the daughter is now entitled to her time for experimenting. If the mother puts her foot down firmly enough, she may succeed for a while, but usually it is only a brief respite.

Sometimes, indeed, the mother's intervention, if it takes the form of "It's her turn now," only seems to provoke the father. The restraints, however feeble, that previously prevented him from open physical interference with the child have been loosened (indeed, the mother's own motives in choosing such a defense of her daughter also must be considered suspect), and now he begins ritualistic inspections of the girl's body, especially the pelvic area, to see if she is keeping herself "clean." He quickly progresses from surface scrutiny of buttocks and pelvis to separating the labia for prolonged internal "examinations." If, owing to infection or premenstrual secretion, there is any sort of vaginal discharge, she will be hard put to convince her examiner that it is not semen, since such discovery strengthens his case for even more extensive and frequent checkups.

Helen

My father and mother separated when I was two. He was in the Navy, and I didn't meet him until I was five, and all I remember then is going to visit a ship and looking at all the sailors. When I was nine, he came home and stayed until I was twelve, then left again, came back when I was fourteen, and left again for good. I left home myself at sixteen.

He was of German and Welsh descent, a short man

with a Napoleon complex, very religious and very violent. If you didn't answer him with "Yes, sir" or "No, sir," or if you looked at him crosswise, he would simply slap you across the face forward and backward—he called it his "backhander." When he was angry at me, he would grab me by the kneecap and squeeze that funny bone part that really hurts. He would grab my thumb and twist it, and he liked to slap. When I was little, he loved to pull my pants down and lay me across his knees and spank me. No matter how hard I screamed, he'd keep whacking away on my backside for five or ten minutes, leaving real welts. In fact, he loved it when I screamed.

And he'd beat me for the craziest reasons. For instance, if I'd had a fight with a neighborhood kid and the kid had beaten me up, when I came home my father would take me back to the kid and order me to beat the kid up, then he'd drag me back home and beat me up himself. Or if I didn't shine his shoes properly—he had me waiting on him all the time—he'd turn me across his knee and smack me.

My mother was okay until I was nine, when he came back home, but after that she never seemed to care enough to intervene or try to protect me. She just retired to her bed, reading and drinking and taking very little interest in the house. The only time she showed any concern at all about my growing up was when I was ten and she said to me, very casually, "Some day you're going to have a period, and you're going to bleed," and that was about it. It was ten o'clock at night and I was ironing—I even remember the time. And, you know, I didn't even get my period until I was fifteen.

But I think my mother and father had a brother-sister relationship. I don't think they were sleeping together anymore by the time I was ten or so, but my father became very suspicious of me and any of the boys I knew. I used to be so humiliated when I'd come home from a date. If I had too many creases in my dress, he'd insist I'd been doing something wrong. In those days, you know, young teenage boys had these jalopies, these falling-apart cars, and ten of us kids used to pile in to save gas. But if I came back with my dress wrinkled, which was hard to avoid with us all jammed in on top of each other, he'd make me turn around to see if there were any stains on my skirt—he used to stare silently at it for a long time. Then he'd make me take off the skirt so he could look at my pants. Right before my period, I used to get a kind of white discharge, and my father insisted it was due to fucking.

I could never stay out beyond 9:30 at night, even when I was almost sixteen, and even if I came home before the curfew he'd still check me. And for every five minutes I was late, he'd make me stay in the house with him for a week. If I was twenty minutes late, if the car broke down or something, I couldn't go out for a month—he literally kept me indoors. I wasn't allowed to have any friends in the house, either. Anybody who came to see me had to stand outside and talk to me through the screen door. They couldn't even come into the yard to play with me.

A significant element in this story is the mother's indifference to her child, to the point of eventually removing herself from the scene altogether, which left the father in complete control.

In the next stage, there is no longer any pretense that the stroking and fondling is anything but sexual in its intent and effect. It is all being done to keep the girl safe from contamination from the outside: "I want to keep it in the family and not have her become a whore," one father explained. Even with this degree of consciousness, however, the sexual play often remains indefinitely at the level of manual manipulation without crossing over into intercourse, fellatio, or cunnilingus. The father is then able to tell himself that he is acting out of a sense of duty, that his aim is only to preserve his daughter's "reputation" and not his own erotic gratification.

Sarah

My father started asking me questions about myself when I was eleven. At first, I thought it was just that he cared about me, even though they made me uncomfortable—questions like, did I know I wasn't too young to get pregnant? and did I make sure that the boys I knew respected me? I didn't know exactly what he meant, but I assured him that the boys all respected me and that I had a lot of respect for myself.

I started to get scared when I was about twelve and a half. I came home late one night, and he insisted on coming into my room to talk to me. I was used to that; my goodness, we had so many of those talks. I was fed up with them, but I couldn't say no to my father. He was a very violent man with a bad temper, and I didn't want to get him angry with me. But this time he insisted he wanted to examine me. First, he checked my breasts to make sure there were no teeth marks or hickies, then he started to fondle them, which scared me. I said, "Dad, what are you doing?" But all he said was, "How does it feel?" I told him it felt nice because I didn't want to offend him; it didn't, though, and I wanted him to stop. But he just smiled and said, "See, I'm doing it just for you, and you like it."

This went on for a while, until pretty soon he started demanding to examine my crotch. I didn't know what to do. If my mother ever found out, I think she'd kill me or kill herself, and my father might end up killing all of us. But every night when I come in, I can count on it like clockwork, ten minutes later he'll come walking into my bedroom, close the door quietly—we have a big house, though, and my mother would never hear—watch me undress, and then start to play with me. Sometimes I've even had to fake orgasm.

Many times I've thought about suicide, and several times when I was taking pills—downers—I would drink a lot of alcohol with them thinking that that might take me out of my misery. But what really scares me now is that these last few times my father has insisted not only on touching me and putting his finger into my vagina, but now he's telling me he's going to have relations with me. So far I've held him off, but I won't be able to keep him off forever. I'm going to have to do something, but I don't know what. I keep thinking if only I'd never been born or if I were dead it would solve all my problems.

Sarah has been made to feel not only helpless but guilty. The absence—psychological if not literal—of the mother makes this almost inevitable. The child feels that she is somehow responsible both for her mother's having faded away to a ghostlike presence in the house and for her father's unhappiness, and that if she refuses to make it up to him by consenting to replace her mother, she is only compounding her guilt.

Liann

It started the week before my ninth birthday, with my stepfather, Jerry, lying on the couch. He began playing with himself, fondling his penis right in front of me. My mother was out of the house emptying the garbage or something, and it was, "Come here, honey, and sit on my lap," as though I wasn't supposed to know what he was doing.

Just a few weeks after that he started taking an interest in my hygiene—did I take my shower right? was I getting myself clean? This went on until I was about eleven. He supervised my shower, he bathed and sponged me and wiped me dry. I just assumed this was what people, grown-ups, do. And he continued to get me to sit on his lap, hugging me, kissing me, stroking me, and giving me extra money. And not just extra allowance; I could get almost anything I wanted.

Then he started worrying about did I get enough exercise. He had me doing all these crazy exercises—like the bicycle, where you lie on your shoulders with your rear end and your feet in the air—while he watched very closely. He made me do this without any clothes on, too, but I finally refused. He didn't like that one bit. He kept coming up with more ideas for exercises I could do, trying to bribe me, how nice he would be to me if I was just a little bit nice to him, but it was so creepy I couldn't stand it.

Between the fear of retribution and the temptation of bribery, the child is effectively trapped. Children who are subjected to sexual intimidation by their parents or stepparents seldom escape serious psychological injury. A high percentage of runaways are fleeing from these kinds of pressures in their homes.

Come-into-My-Bed Game

When we think of incestuous games, we consider the most dangerous and damaging—and most common—ones to be those between father and daughter. Mother-son games are not taken so seriously. There are several reasons for this: Male children are customarily thought of as having more autonomy from the beginning than female children, and therefore as being less susceptible to harmful influences from adult women. It is much more likely that a pubescent daughter may be impregnated by her father than a mother molested by her son. In America at least, a mother is not considered a sexual being. This is especially evident when children are discussing the incredible fact that their own parents obviously must have had intercourse at least once per child. Many a little boy receives his first black eye defending his mother's virtue. As the old joke has it, "Papa maybe, but Mama never."

But for the very reason that she is the original love object of all her children, it is easy for a mother to go on to bind a young son close to her in an erotic liaison which appears to be "normal" mother love. And the easiest and most natural way for it to evolve is from an exaggerated concern over hygiene, the mother seizing every opportunity for stripping the boy, checking his bodily orifices for cleanliness, and then soaking him in a tub as she long and lovingly strokes and kneads him under cover of washing him. As he gets older, these baths take on additional significance as rituals of purification, rinsing away the effects of imagined unclean sexual thoughts and acts. This tends to become a compulsion, which is simultaneously furiously denied.

Father usually sense what is going on but don't know what to do about it, although they feel very sure that it has been going on for too long. As a rule, one son only is singled out for this special attention, and the father intervenes sporadically and ineffectively if at all, and then only when the child is approximately between the ages of nine and thirteen—before that it could be innocent, and afterward it's too late. But such intervention is usually blocked by the mother's angry counteraccusations of prurient thinking.

The boy himself is caught in a classic bind. On one hand, in his relations with his mother he totally, on a conscious level, represses the sexual component, but at the same time, he becomes increasingly secretive as he approaches puberty. Their special relationship is cemented by the mother's habit of secretly slipping him extra allowance, or permitting him special privileges denied the other children, on condition that such favoritism is concealed from the father: "Don't tell Daddy, he'd be angry with me if he knew," or "Your father won't understand, so there's no need to say anything to him about this," which of course alienates him still further from his father, making it impossible to confide in him about anything. Such tactics on the part of the mother can permanently corrode any potential trust between father and son.

If the mother is single or separated from her husband and living alone with her son—which happens frequently now that one out of every two marriages ends in divorce*—the balance of forces in the power struggle shifts somewhat. Certain manipulative strategies are now pointless, since the father is no longer there to witness them; on the other hand, the mother's need to hold the son close to her in the absence of other satisfactions, sexual or social, can become intensified.

Scotty

From the time I was four years old, I would climb into bed during the day with my mother, and I'd lie next to her and play with her hands and stuff. My father died when I was five, so my mother and I were quite close, even though I had an older brother. But he didn't seem to spend much time in the house, so I pretty much had my mother to myself.

I would lie with her in bed, play with her hands, stroke her face and her back, and she never stopped me. At the time I didn't know about the rest of her body, but I loved playing with that part of it, her hands and her face. I used to go crazy, I loved it so much. I can still remember that special feeling of closeness, and her particular smell. She had such a nice, clean smell about her; in fact, everything about her bed and pillow was very nice. I really liked the contact with my mother. I don't know if that's what's driving me crazy now and making it so hard for me to communicate with girls, but it sure felt good then.

My mother was always very attentive to my needs, sometimes even making my brother jealous. I remember when I was as old as thirteen and fourteen, I'd be outside on the street playing stickball with my friends and all, and she'd call me, "I want you to come home now, Scotty, it's time for your bath." But sometimes my mother wasn't home. She had to work to support me and my brother. Then I went to my aunt's house, my mother's younger sister. She lived on the next block, and she would bathe me. They used to take turns; when my mother was working, it would be my aunt, but on the weekends when my mother came home earlier, she'd be the one. Sometimes they'd argue about who was going to get to bathe me,

apparently they both vied for this big privilege, which I
didn't even realize at the time was such an honor.

Somehow my brother, Jack, managed to stay out of all
this; in fact, when I was still little he ran off and enlisted
in the Navy when he was barely seventeen. After he left,
my aunt came to live with us, and I got all my baths at
home. I used to lie back in the tub and love it; they would
soak me and wash me and dry me very thoroughly and,
I guess, very lovingly. It was such a nice, passive feeling;
gosh, I guess those were the days.

When I got to be twelve or thirteen, I started feeling
funny about it, kind of strange, that maybe there was
something wrong about this and perhaps it shouldn't be
going on, but I didn't say anything. I guess I should have
known something was happening because I started masturbating when I was ten or eleven, and I remember clearly
getting erections in the water while my mother and aunt
were bathing me, and yet it didn't bother them. They never
said anything; they totally ignored it.

But bathing wasn't all. I remember seeing my mother
walk around the house nude, and she had beautiful breasts,
big, beautiful breasts with red, red nipples that stood out
straight. I always had an ideal picture of my mother as
almost like a goddess type of woman, especially when I
was away at camp. I was about nine then, and she'd write
to me. It was weird, I felt very uncomfortable being away
from her. But the business when I was home of her walking
around without clothes and making only a pretense of
closing her door, or—what used to drive me even crazier—
she'd walk around in see-through nightgowns.

She did this till I was about fifteen or sixteen, and I
finally had to move out of the house. I guess I thought
I was going to have intercourse with her, unconsciously,
because I got up out of bed; I thought that was what she
wanted me to do. She wasn't dating anybody, and it had
been such a long time since my father died. I suppose she
needed some man. I'd be half-asleep when I got out of

bed, and I really didn't know what I was doing, but I knew she was out of bed. I'd follow her, and we'd make some excuse to talk or go into the kitchen, and she'd make hot chocolate or milk and cookies, and then I'd go back to bed.

But what used to drive me really berserk was when she'd come in to kiss me good night. I didn't realize then that all mothers who do that don't kiss their sons on the lips. And my aunt would come in right after my mother, and she'd kiss me good night on the lips too, only she would linger just a little bit longer and press her bosoms against me. It absolutely used to drive me crazy.

When I was between ten and twelve, I used to masturbate three and even four times a day, but even then I just almost never seemed to get any sense of relief. There were times when I would go into the living room. It had French doors which you could see through, and I would sit there masturbating and hoping that either my mother or my aunt would notice me. The shade on the door was pulled up, but nobody ever said anything. I'm sure they must have seen me, but nothing was said. This room connected with the kitchen, and everybody would be in there while I was in the living room beating my brains out masturbating, and I wouldn't pull down the shades—sometimes by accident and sometimes deliberately. Maybe I forgot, but unconsciously I guess I realized that I wanted them to notice what I was doing, and then I felt guilty, but nobody ever said a word.

The strangest thing that really freaked me out was that I would be lying in bed trying to go to sleep, with all these crazy sexual thoughts tumbling around in my head and feeling kind of disgusted about it. And even up until this year, my aunt would come into my bedroom, sit down on the side of my bed, and lean over and kiss me good night. She had no pretense, she would come right in, sit down, and lean over me and stroke my hair. You have to understand that my aunt was not married and had no kids, so I felt I was her kid as well as my mother's, and that she somehow needed to have some kind of affection with a kid.

Then she would kiss me on the mouth—sometimes her mouth would be open—and stroke my face and call me "bubbala." At first, I thought, "Oh, the poor thing just needs somebody to hold," and even though it was funny it actually felt weird. But I just used to take it, but then it started to get to me, and I realized she was doing it not so much because I was her bubbala, but because she was in some way getting her rocks off. I always felt very weird. I mean, at the time maybe it didn't feel that bad, but afterward it always left me feeling very weird. I mean, to this day I still feel weird.

Scotty's brother, Jack, evidently always refused to succumb to these seductive maneuvers. Even before he left home permanently to join the Navy, he stayed away as long and as often as he could, from the time he was very young. This meant that the full weight of the two women's frustrated sexuality—and their intensely jealous competitiveness—fell upon Scotty alone.

It is common, as such cases demonstrate, for one child to be singled out as the locus where all these forces converge, the other children escaping them altogether. There are many studies on why a particular child is chosen for this role. One theory, which experts such as Dr. I. Bieber hold, is that physical beauty may be the determining factor. The best-looking child, or the one whose appearance most appeals to a particular parent, may be most at risk.*

Often it is the youngest child who becomes the victim. Precisely why is unclear, but one possible explanation is that whereas the strivings of the eldest child are directed outward, away from the family and toward the world, the aim of the younger child is to emulate or surpass his or her older sibling. If the family is a disturbed one, the child is more responsive to the emotional ferment around him or her. It also is probable that the parents were happier and more hopeful when the first child was born. The youngest child is likely to have arrived toward the end of the mother's childbearing years, always a period of crisis; if she does not succeed in resolving it, she may cling to this last reminder of her waning sexual powers. In Scotty's case the death of his father and the departure of his brother effectively sealed him into the emotional pressure cooker that his home had become.

The next case is an exception to the pattern just described. Here the mother managed for a time to hold all three of her sons equally close, maneuvering them into competing for her favors. All three have suffered from the disturbances in development that crippled Lucille and Scotty. Since no one of them had to bear the full weight of the mother's incestuous impulses and because of their competitiveness, they were able to eventually move away from her emotionally.

Walter is from the Midwest, born and raised in Ohio. He is the middle of three brothers. The father was a traveling salesman, and the family was consequently somewhat rootless, which prevented Walter from forming friendships outside his family.

Walter

When my mother would put us boys to sleep at night, she'd kiss each of us good night in turn. But there was a funny thing; we would all compete to be the first boy to get kissed because he would be the favorite that night. The other two boys would make a big fuss about not wanting her to kiss them anymore because now her lips were not clean. But she would give us all a really long kiss anyway, right on the lips, with a big hug to go with it. It felt great.

I didn't realize then how much trouble and strangeness went into us going to sleep. My father was away in the Army for a long time, and my mother stayed home alone with us boys. And whenever he was away—before he was drafted, he was on the road a lot of the time on sales trips

—she would alternate. What I'm trying to say is, she would have a different boy sleep in her bed with her each night. She would come in, give two of us our good-night kisses, and choose the other to spend the night with her. This was a very exciting thing. I remember how I used to look forward to it. I mean I was really turned on by the whole atmosphere, the smell of her bedroom, her nightgown, and getting to snuggle up next to her with her arms around me, and this went on from as early as I can remember up till I was about twelve, when my father got out of the Army and came home.

And somehow we knew not to tell my father any of this; occasionally she would remind us, but we really didn't need reminding. It's funny, even though kids talk so much and we used to get into a lot of fights—and a kid will use anything he can think of against another kid in a fight— none of us ever dropped a hint to our father about what we were doing with our mother.

To this day I still don't feel close to my father. I see him as a terrible person. He had an awful temper whenever he was home. He'd yell and scream and sometimes even hit my mother. He never hit us, but we were always afraid that he would. We never fought back when he hit her, either, I guess because somehow we felt that maybe she deserved it because of the secret stuff with us.

Anyway, it just got us all scared. We were terrified living in that home. Life was no picnic. I can remember once when I was very little, lying in bed with my mother, holding her, and feeling myself get an erection. I was humiliated. I didn't know what to do about it. I wasn't even ten years old, but she didn't seem to mind at all; she just hugged me and kept me with her that night the same as always. The whole thing was strange. It feels freaky even talking about it now, but I'm glad to get it out.

When the child is old enough to become uncomfortably conscious of his mother's erotic clinging, he can sometimes mobilize enough ego strength to take deliberate evasive action, such as sleeping as often as possible at a friend's house. When the mother of one thirteen-year-old who used this strategy protested, he agreed to stay home but insisted on returning his friend's hospitality and having him stay over in turn. The mother tried to supervise the visitor's hygiene as well as her son's, but her attempts were frustrated when the son insisted she bathe the two of them together. Perhaps even she was apprehensive about exposing the extent of her involvement with her son to a strange child. In any case, with a confused mumble of excuses, she withdrew. The intimate bathing of her son also stopped after that, and she never again attempted to manipulate him seductively in any other way.

A child who—unlike Scotty and Walter—has a peer group outside the home from whom he can draw strength and to whom he can appeal has a much easier time extricating himself from a smothering mother. However, one of the most insidious effects of such a binding relationship is precisely to destroy the child's capacity to form such friendships.

Cute Cuddly Game

It is easy for adults to deceive themselves about the erotic quality of their interest when the child is small. A baby is considered anybody's toy; the notion that even an infant has a right to have the integrity of its body respected is alien to us.

Therefore, the games one parent plays with the baby usually are met with indulgence, if not encouragement, by the other. These games also tend to become fixed at the infantile level; it is that phase alone which is attractive to this type of parent. (Note that the daughters we discussed earlier became objects of erotic interest to their fathers only at puberty; they had not been molested as infants.)

Karen

Almost the first thing I can remember is my father hugging me and then putting his hands down the back of my pants and squeezing my bottom. It seems to me now that even then I sensed that I shouldn't say anything about it to my mother, but I never objected when he did it and my mother never said anything, although she must have seen him. And it felt good—to be honest, it really felt good.

And then I remember once when I was about seven or eight, we had company for dinner, and I was hugging my father for some reason, and he put his hand down the back of my pants and felt my ass, and at that moment I felt embarrassed. Obviously, I knew this was not something for other people to see, and I said to him, "Why don't you do that when nobody else is around?"—which when I think of it now is really kind of seductive. Anyway, he never did it again after that. I guess I had made it so blatant he just had to stop.

The focus of erotic interest in a baby is almost always the buttocks, an interest which naturally lends itself to being disguised as affectionate playfulness, since, although we now know that sexual identity may declare itself as young as six months, babies appear to be both sexless and genderless under the age of about two.*

The inability of some parents to let go of their children when the time comes for them to go away to camp, to go to school, to work, to marry, may have its roots in infancy, when the baby, at a time when its dependence is total, is bound too closely to its mother or father by a sexual manipulation that tries to pass for innocent cuddling. But the child is never deceived; indeed, it is just the gulf between what the child knows is happening and what it can speak about that causes the damage.

Avery

I'm embarrassed to admit it but when I was between ten and fifteen years old, I used to baby-sit for my young niece, who was then about three or four, and I seem to have developed what I guess has to be called a fetish. She was the most adorable little kid with the cutest ass, and I would use any excuse to change her when she got dirty so I could feel her ass and play with her. I used to call this "going under," and sometimes I'd reward her afterward with a cookie or a piece of candy or even a few coins, but always warning her not to tell her parents.

To tell the truth, I think the kid liked it, too. I had a special way of doing it. If she was wearing pants, I would slip my hand down her pants, or if she had a short skirt on, I would slip my hand up her skirt over her panties and then down over her buttocks. I never touched her anywhere else, I never played with her vagina, but somehow I always found her ass irresistible. I would get the most horrendous erections and be unable to control my breathing. It was terribly embarrassing, but I couldn't stop myself.

What's interesting is that I baby-sat for this kid for about four or five years, and she never once said anything to her parents. And after that, in school, I would play with the other kids, and when I got friendly with another little girl, and occasionally even with another little boy who had a cute little ass, I would ask them if I could go under. At first, they would look at me in a puzzled way, but when I explained what it was, most of them let me do it. I never let myself keep my hand there too long, though.

Not only parents but other relatives, family friends, or even, as in this case, older children may exploit young children in this way; in 80 percent of all cases of child molestation, the offender is someone the child knows.

Sherry

My mother and father did not get along very well, and she would often come and sleep in my bed with me. She became a real health nut where I was concerned. I had all kinds of stomach problems when I was a little kid, and she was always examining me. Until I was twelve she would take my temperature every day with a rectal thermometer, and for several years before I got my period, when I was ten and a half, she would do internal examinations on me, looking into my vagina. She seemed to be obsessed with my body, and was always patting or stroking or touching me in some way.

It began to get very creepy, and I would welcome any chance to get out of the house, like visiting friends or going away to camp. I had a hell of a time convincing her to let me go to camp. She hated the idea of me being away for so long. She kept saying I'd get sick of it, that I couldn't make it without her. But the truth is, I now realize, she needed me a lot more than I needed her.

When I was eleven, I got colitis and from then on, forget it. She was at me constantly, with reasons why she had to feel my stomach and pat my ass and check my temperature. Finally, when I was thirteen, I refused to let her touch me unless she used an oral thermometer. At least in this one area, although it seems like a small thing, I wanted to have some sense of dignity.

It is quite common and probably normal for parents occasionally to have sexual feelings for their children. The younger they are, the more most children need, and provoke, loving physical contact, which at moments may become eroticized for the parents. It is dangerous only if, as with Sherry's mother, it leads to something more serious, such as an obsessive need by the parent for such contact.

Ellen

When I was little, my father used to squeeze me so hard I'd say I couldn't breathe, and he'd laugh and say he was going to squeeze all the air out of me. It wasn't just my dad, either; my brother got in on the act, too. He would wrestle with me, pin me to the ground, lie on top of me, and squeeze, pressing his whole body against me. I'd developed early and had sizable breasts from the age of ten, so this hurt quite a lot, but I couldn't figure out any way to stop it.

They set me up as the cute baby so that even when I cried, I was just being adorable. If I went into a rage and screamed for my mother, she'd just stupidly reply, "You're all having such a good time!" And one day my brother was squeezing me so hard I broke wind, and I was so humiliated I began kicking and scratching until finally he eased off, although at first it seemed to excite him even more.

After that I got violent all the time, until one day when I was thirteen, while we were involved in one of these idiotic wrestling matches, my sanitary napkin fell off. Then I really got hysterical and kicked my brother as hard as I could in the crotch. That ended the game for good.

When unmistakable signs of maturity command the attention of parents or older siblings, it usually is enough to put an end to such games, unless the pathology is severe.

Single Parents' Game

Our 50 percent divorce rate has meant an enormous increase in single-parent families, and the increasing vogue for split custody means that many children divide their time equally between each single parent.* This is undoubtedly preferable to the anxieties of living with both parents in a home torn by anger and resentment, but it can bring its own set of problems. A lonely mother or father who has not yet found new friends and lovers may cling too tightly to a child who may be the only link with a happier time. Or the child may be used as a surrogate for the other parent, and loved or hated or manipulated accordingly.

Maria

My parents separated when I was seven, and when I first saw my father after a few months had gone by, I was surprised at how much he had changed. He took me home with him to his new place and told me, "We're going to share this pad when you come here weekends."

It was a small one-bedroom apartment, which meant I shared the bedroom—and the bed—with my dad. The bed was a studio couch that opened up to become a double bed. Sometimes there was another lady there, usually not the same one twice, and then I would go to sleep in the studio bed, but wake up in the morning on the couch in the living room. It took me a while to put together that that meant his date was sleeping over. The bedroom door would be locked, with orders not to come in.

I was jealous; what right did these strangers have to sleep with him? My mother was the only one who belonged there, and it seemed to me that if she wasn't there, then I should be.

My father was very affectionate, and after we went to bed at night and in the mornings, we'd play together for hours, rolling in the bedclothes with me climbing all over him, and we'd be hugging and laughing. I slept with him, except when he had a date, until just a year ago, when I became fourteen. He was good-looking, too; I thought he was the most handsome father in the world.

My mother was more discreet. She rarely brought her dates home with her, and no one ever slept over that I knew about until she and my stepfather became engaged. And somehow I knew—maybe he told me, but I don't think so—not to tell her that my father sometimes slept in bed with me. Occasionally she would ask me who he was seeing, just as he would ask about her. It made me feel very important, but I was uncomfortable about it, too, so I would usually just say I didn't remember, and if they really wanted to know, why didn't they call each other up? I used to have fantasies that they would get back together again and live happily ever after.

I felt that somehow it was my job to keep my dad happy so he wouldn't need these other women—like standing in for my mother until they got themselves straightened out and could live together again with me. For a while I made a game of it. I would call him up at the office, and he would be very cute on the phone, and sometimes when we'd go out to the movies or to a restaurant, he would call me his "date."

He'd even take me along on his real dates sometimes. He'd try to put me in the back seat of the car, but I wouldn't stay there. Even when I was little I felt I should be sitting next to him, and I made enough of a fuss so he'd let me sit in front between him and his date. Boy, did they hate that! My mother loved it when I'd come home and tell her about it. But when I got my period and had to have napkins and stuff, he got very uptight. Maybe my becoming a woman biologically was too much for him to handle.

It is not easy for a single parent alone with a child to maintain the parental role firmly; mothers and fathers need to see themselves and their actions reflected in each other. As Maria's story shows, it is harder for separated parents to resist the temptation to make the child a confidant, a spy, or a conduit for conveying covert messages between the households. Many children adapt all too quickly to this role, playing one parent off against the other, which further encourages the blurring of boundaries.

Annie

My mother must have thought I was plain stupid. When I was ten or eleven and woke up in the middle of the night, I would find her door locked. Obviously, someone was in there with her. Once she forgot to lock the door, and I opened it and saw a man sleeping with her.

My dad had died a few years earlier, and my mother was becoming a swinger, the merry widow. She had lost a lot of weight, and had had her face and even her breasts lifted. She kept showing them off to me. "Don't I look good?" she'd want to know. But she always went through this little charade every time a man stayed over, of having him out of her bedroom before I got up, mussing up the couch so that it looked as if he'd slept there, and then, when I came out of my room, she'd say to him, "Good morning, I hope you slept comfortably." But the funny thing was that after she took the trouble of putting on this act, she'd still make it obvious that he'd slept with her by leaving some of his clothes on her bed.

And at the same time, in a funny way, she kept urging me to "discover sex." I think she felt she was discovering sex herself. She was always putting pressure on me to go to dances. She sent me to this creepy dancing school and seemed disappointed that I hadn't managed to get laid by the time I was twelve. She told me sex was a healthy and beautiful thing, and I shouldn't be afraid of it. It became almost an obsession with her that I should start seriously dating.

It was funny—the other kids used to be so surprised when we'd talk about our parents; they all wished they had mothers like mine. Some of them even used to come to her with questions about sex. Her answer inevitably was, "Go and find out for yourself. Sex is great, and experimenting with it is even better." She used to clip articles from the newspapers for me saying that even girls of eleven and twelve can use a diaphragm, and she'd tell me I should let her know as soon as I was ready and we'd go to the doctor to get me fitted.

The fact is, she pressed me so hard to start having sex that I turned off to the whole idea. Especially since wherever we went, she'd strike up a conversation with some man and usually end up picking him up. If we were waiting in line for airplane tickets or to see a movie, there'd always be some guy. I used to get very annoyed, but she always turned it around, saying that the guy approached *her*. Did she think I was stupid or something that I couldn't see or hear what she was doing?

So here I am at fourteen, still a virgin, and if I have my way, I'm going to stay one until I'm at least twenty-one. I've sworn a really solemn vow that if I ever do have sex before twenty-one, I'll make sure my mother never finds out, and probably not even after twenty-one. I really think she'd get off on it more than I ever could.

Separation or divorce creates a sudden vacuum in the life of the parent, who is abruptly deprived of the whole domestic structure of his or her life—a loss which is almost always followed by severe depression. If the parent has a child living with him or her full or part time, inevitably the child will be pulled into the empty center, first as solace and comfort, later perhaps as love object. Many parents have reported drifting unaware during the days immediately following the separation, when shock and depression were at their worst, into such a relationship with their child, and then, after a few months when the depression had begun to lift, finding it difficult to resume normal parent-child relations. The child, too, often finds the intensity of the parent's need exhilarating and may develop a heady sense of power upon realizing how dependent an adult has become on him or her. To some children this power is so intoxicating that they scheme to keep their parents hostile and apart, in case they should be thinking of reconciling.

Once the parent has extricated himself or herself from such an entanglement with the child, guilt may induce the parent to ignore or forget that the relationship ever carried such a powerful sexual charge, and to deny that the child is suffering or resentful of its ending. When that happens, the child will often threaten to run away or commit suicide, and sometimes carries out the threat. What lies behind all this, from the child's point of view, is often the simple fear that just as the parents have abandoned each other, so the child, too, will be discarded when the parent falls out of love with him or her. It is essential to make the children of divorce understand that whatever the parents may do to each other, neither parent will ever divorce the child, but will always be there to love and care for the child.

Son, You'll Never Find a Girl Like Me

Among the seductive mothers we discussed earlier, an important subgroup are the narcissistic mothers. With these women the involvement with the son is more superficial, although its effect on him may be profound and harmful. The superficiality tends to be characteristic of all the relationships formed by these women. For the other seductive mothers, their male children are true objects of desire; the narcissistic mother has enlisted her son in the service of her own self-image. Her relationship with him is characterized by flirtatiousness and vanity, not by evidence of a deeper sexual need.

Larry

I thought I would burst from the pressure inside me; even masturbating twice a day didn't relieve it. Even now, when I close my eyes, I can visualize my mother so clearly it's as if she's still standing there in her nightgown, with her nipples standing out on her breasts and her long black hair hanging down behind. And that perfume that used to drive me crazy—I can still smell it.

I think I began masturbating when I was about five. I didn't know exactly what I was doing. All I knew was that it made me feel a little better, and I would be frantically pulling, jerking, and rubbing anything I could reach. But that was nothing compared to what I felt when she'd pull me over to her and press me against her, with my head sinking in between her breasts—she didn't wear a bra. I'd get paralyzed with excitement.

My biggest fear was that my father would catch me like that and kill me—I never realized that my mother never did it when he was at home. They didn't have a particularly good relationship. My father was in the retail business, which meant he had long hours at the store. He used to make me work there, too, and he treated me very mean, shouting and slapping me at the drop of a hat.

It was very different at home. My mother was a strikingly beautiful woman; I think she had won some beauty contests when she was a girl. Anyway, she was certainly prettier than any other mother I'd ever seen. She'd been having an affair for a number of years—I mean, I know now it was an affair. At the time I just saw him around a lot. He seemed to be a nice man; at least he was always nice to me, nicer than my father. But she used me to cover for her. She would say she was taking me to the movies or the park, when really she'd be going off with him.

She was very sensuous; she'd spend hours in the bathtub doing her beauty treatments, and she'd always forget to take her towel with her, so I'd have to bring it in to her, which I didn't mind at all. My younger sister used to get mad and complain that I shouldn't be going into the bathroom when my mother was there, but I just told her to mind her own business.

I always felt my mother had a very special relationship with me. My father felt it, too, I think, and let out on me all the hostility he never would dare show to her. He never actually laid a hand on her that I can remember; she was really almost the goddess on the pedestal. But with me it got to the point where I was constantly feeling very horny and making advances to little girls when I was only nine or ten. I had sex for the first time at the age of eleven with an older woman—a thirteen-year-old girl. I had the feeling my mother would have loved to hear about that, but I didn't tell her. Every so often she would ask me if there weren't any little girls falling in love with her "young heartbreaker."

When I was fifteen, I did fall madly in love with Sally,

a girl in my class, and decided that we had to get married, no matter what. We ran away to Maryland and got ourselves married with fake birth certificates. But then, after we came home, we were afraid to tell anybody. Finally, my mother found out and had the marriage annulled a few months later. She was so furious that I had gotten married that she wouldn't speak to me, as if I'd betrayed her. And whenever she looked at me after that, I felt very strange because now she knew that I wasn't a virgin any longer.

But after a while she began warming up to her old tricks again and started parading around again in her nightgown, the same display that used to drive me crazy. Luckily for me, I decided then to go away to school and went to live with relatives. I think that's what saved my sanity.

One boy from Kansas told me that his high school girl friend wouldn't speak to him after she saw him with his mother at the movies. When he demanded to know why, she said he was going out with another woman. He insisted that the woman was his mother, but the girl flatly refused to believe it: "Not the way you two were hugging and kissing and carrying on, that wasn't any mother you were with."

These mothers are given to exhibitionistic posturing in public with their sons. They especially love to be taken for an amorous couple and to give the son money in advance for restaurants and theaters so he can pay for them both, as if they were out on a date together.

Aging is a terror to these women, both because so much of their identity is built on their physical beauty and because they are afraid of losing their sons.

The seductive mother is dangerous just because she is able to arouse the most intense feelings in her child at a time when he is not at all prepared to deal with them realistically. The sons of these mothers look back on their childhoods—when they gain enough detachment to do so—as a time when they were under the continual threat of being overwhelmed by guilt, fear, and desire in equal proportions. Struggling to cope with this onslaught of unmanageable emotions used up all their energy.

Let's-Turn-On-Together Game

For as long as family life has existed in anything like its present form, so have the various versions of preincestuous manipulation of children. What seems new to our time, however, are the parents who urge their children toward early and casual sexual experimentation. This is a way for the parents to identify with what is young and new, to cling to their own youth, and to deny their aging through vicarious sexual renewal.

Unlike those discussed previously, these parents do not feel any desire for or dependence upon their sons and daughters as love objects. What they are seeking is identification with the freshness of sexual discovery as it comes only with the first experiences of adolescence. These parents can be described as perpetrating a subtle larceny upon their children, trying to appropriate a time of life which properly belongs only to the child, and refusing the role of parent. This annihilation of generational boundaries creates great tension and confusion, setting parent and child in competition with each other and leaving the child without supportive adult authority. It also means that the child is constantly having to establish rules and norms for himself or herself—an intolerable burden for a young boy or girl to bear at a time of such rapid growth and change.

Mothers are more likely than fathers to yield to this temptation because they have always been more involved in the affairs of the children and because the onset of age is on the whole more acutely painful for them than it is for men.

Sabrina

You never really know exactly where you learn about sex, you just pick it up, but I learned about it mostly from my mother. She really seemed interested in explaining all the things I didn't know about it—more than I wanted to know, really. She taught me not only about boys and girls, but about bisexuality and lesbianism.

That was a couple of years ago; I guess I was between eight and ten. Once, one of the girls in the fifth grade said something about a thing called a "blow job," which I didn't understand. When I asked my mother about it, she went into such detail, I found it really disgusting. Uggh! It really was weird. It seemed kind of gross to me at the time, but now that I'm getting older nothing bothers me anymore. If they want to do it, let them do it. It's just not my bag.

There were some things I heard from my friends before my mother had a chance to tell me about them, but she always seemed so disappointed when that happened, I wouldn't tell her I already knew them. But even if I did, she always went into such tremendous detail that at first it would upset me, and then it got to be kind of boring. Certain things I don't think you should hear from your mother anyway, it doesn't feel right. It always comes out wrong, as if she doesn't understand kids at all. Anyway, I somehow felt that because of all this I wasn't like the rest of the kids, I wasn't prissy like them. I liked to walk around in just a T-shirt and panties.

And I always want to be very, very pretty. I always fix myself up, but it seems to be even more important to my mother for me to be pretty and look good and look physically mature. I just want to do it for myself, not for anybody else, but my mother always wants me to look pretty so everybody else will see how good-looking I am.

And I like to get stoned, and one of my fantasies when I'm stoned is that I will meet Kris Kristofferson. I wouldn't go to bed and have sex with him now, but if I was older, like maybe sixteen or seventeen, I'd go to bed with him right away. But my mother thinks it would be great if I could meet him and go all the way with him right now.

I couldn't do it. I'd feel guilty about going to bed with somebody that much older than me.

I have a grandmother, and she got real mad at my mother when she told her some of the things that had been going on. I mean, it's really kind of gross. I know my mother has boyfriends and they stay over at night, but of course they make such a big fuss about locking the door before they have sex. But once I was very upset about something and they must have forgotten that time to lock the door, because I knocked and they said, "Go away," but I had already started to open the door, and I said to my mother, "I have something to tell you." They said, "All right," so I walked in and I got so mad. There they were right in the middle of having intercourse. He was on top of her, and they stopped and looked at me.

I got so flustered, I just stormed out of the house. Imagine telling me it's okay to come walking into the room, and they didn't even stop for more than just a second. I went running over to my grandmother's house, and she really yelled at my mother for letting me come in and see them that way. But my mother wasn't embarrassed at all. She was proud of it and said, "Well, I'm a liberated woman and I do have relations, and there's nothing wrong with it, and I think Sabrina should know about all these things."

I don't think she understands me at all. It's really awful, when I go to any of the rock concerts, my mother always wants to come along, even though she doesn't know anything about the music or who the groups are or anything. When I smoke pot with my friends, my mother insists on joining us—in fact, she'll bring her boyfriends along. One of them has a van, and they'll be making out in the van on the way there and back from the concert. Usually I don't have any boyfriends at all, and it makes me feel very creepy.

But she doesn't seem to think there's anything wrong, far from it. She's always lecturing me and all my friends about not only how great sex is, but how good she is at it, and doesn't she have a terrific body for a fifty-year-old woman, and she doesn't even look thirty. I can't cope with her. Luckily, I do have my grandmother and my friends to explain things in a way that makes sense.

It is not unusual for the children of such mothers to react to their excesses with primness and conservatism, as though instinctively feeling that someone in the family has to maintain an appearance of self-control. That this should fall to the child rather than the parent seems another heavy and unnecessary burden. But Edna, Sabrina's mother, sees it from a different viewpoint:

Edna

I must say I'm very proud of the way Sabrina has been growing up, and of the fact that she really emulated me most of all. Kids nowadays are always talking, talking, talking, and they'll use expressions like "fuck." And Sabrina knows what that is, and she also knows what "suck" is. She knows exactly what "suck" is. But, see, I'm not at all disturbed by that, and I'll tell you why. I grew up with somebody slapping me across the face every time I said "fuck," or asked what "69" was, or if I mentioned the word "suck"; I'd get the hell beaten out of me. So I grew up conditioned to think that all that was rotten and nasty and dirty, and that's why part of my life has been kind of fucked up. Because most of the liberation you hear about when it comes to sex has only happened in the past maybe ten years. So that's why I've gone to the other extreme with Sabrina. I call it "underprotecting" her.

I feel that it's my job to encourage her to fulfill herself in every way. But Sabrina really likes herself and doesn't seem to feel the need to give herself to anybody. She's running around with kids who have had a lot of experience with drugs, and she smokes pot with me, and we've gone to concerts together. We go to the Elton John concert or the Emerson Lake and Palmer, and I'll go with one of my boyfriends and we'll all get stoned out of our minds. I don't know if you smoke or not, but do you know the sensuality when you're stoned out of your mind at a concert? She's surrounded by sensuality just being my daughter. I also let her smoke a little at home, though I don't like her smoking out on the streets. At home I don't mind because I can keep control of it.

She's been resisting my attempts to free her, but one of the reasons she's much freer now—she's in fact liberated—was that this past summer, when she was thirteen, she spent five weeks in the mountains of Tennessee in a little commune. They call it a camp, but it's really a commune, and she walked around all day long without any clothes on. There were twenty kids, boys and girls, all sizes and shapes, and four adults, two males and two females, and everybody was naked most of the time. The day I went up to visit, they had what they called the "sweat tent," where everybody takes off their clothes and goes in. Here were me and Bill, my boyfriend, and Sabrina and the whole camp, at least twenty-five of us, stuffed into an Indian tent having a sweat bath. It was a fantastic experience.

Little by little, our lives have led us back to some very wonderful basics. And this child craves it. She's become a health-food nut; she ate beautifully. She was living a beautiful, free-spirited, happy life there in the camp. Meanwhile, academically she's not accomplishing anything and is doing badly in school.

Edna is honest—or transparent—enough to let us see that her policy of "underprotection" of Sabrina has very little to do with any serious consideration of her child's well-being or even with rebellion against her own upbringing. Edna is terribly anxious to cram as much "sensuality" and as many "fantastic experiences" into her middle age as she can, and she is using Sabrina as her advance guard and ticket to this world of youthful hedonism. But Sabrina is growing up without discipline and a sense of boundaries, and even her mother is compelled to realize that an upbringing totally without values except the pleasure of the moment has consequences: "Meanwhile, academically she's not accomplishing anything and is doing badly in school."

Emotionally troubled children often exhibit the first signs of disturbance in school by a drastic falling off in schoolwork and by trouble with teachers and other children. Sometimes, as in Sabrina's case, this is so conspicuous that it has to be taken as a deliberate signal of distress, a plea for someone in authority—a teacher, guidance counselor, or school psychologist—to notice that something is wrong and to intervene.

The trouble with Edna's philosophy of mindless hedonism is that it ignores something that is very important to her daughter, as it is to most girls of her age: a loving relationship, without which sexual experience is meaningless. Edna's frenetic clutching at anything that can transiently fill the void of her existence is a whole lifetime away from Sabrina's hope for and faith in love and the importance of feeling something for the person she will be sleeping with. Edna's "boyfriends" are not much more than a convenience to her, a cynicism which Sabrina cannot yet possibly understand, let alone share. But Edna never stops trying to force this attitude upon her daughter. She has reported that her conversations with Sabrina often end with the following lecture: "You don't have to marry him. If he seems like a nice boy and has had experience, I'm telling you it could be a very good learning thing for you. Sex is nothing but fun, as long as you don't have to worry about getting pregnant. You're on the Pill, aren't you? Well, then, why not swing? I'm surprised at you, honey—you have such a beautiful, slim body and you're well developed besides, and yet you hardly have any experience. I only wish I'd had your body and a mother telling me it was okay to fool around with boys instead of punishing me."

Edna's claim to be educating her daughter to be a free spirit turns out to be a pathetic lie; it is neither freedom nor fulfillment that Edna is communicating, merely her own desperation.

Sadomasochistic Game

The battered child who has been crippled by his parents can hardly be said to have been participating in a "game," except that sadomasochistic acting out often does have a quality of ritual, a sort of grim playfulness masked as "discipline." It is a horrifying fact that physical abuse from parents has become the number one cause of child death in the United States. Close to three million children have been abused every year for the past five years.* Police and social workers estimate that for every case reported, two or three go unreported.*

Here is a social worker's history of one of these children.

Ernie

Ernie is a ten-year-old boy who has been living with his two younger brothers and an older sister in a home for homeless children. Ernie has been here since the age of four, when his mother ran away and abandoned his father and all the children.

In Ernie's short life, there has been a great deal of physical pain. According to a police report, he was all but drowned in the bathtub by his mother, who held his head under water until she thought he was dead; he was revived only by the swift intervention of the police. When the mother was interviewed, she insisted that Ernie had simply fallen into the bathtub while she was washing some windows and that she had tried to rescue him.

But there was a long record of "accidents" before that. When Ernie was three, she reported that he had slipped and fallen on some glass bottles which broke, and needed thirty-two stitches on his buttocks. When she took him to the doctor, she held him on her lap and restrained him while he screamed and struggled as the doctor was stitching him up. The doctor found her manner remarkable for a mother whose child was in such agony; she seemed to be admiring her own coolness. She told me, "His little bottom looked like two pieces of raw meat. You know, thirty-two stitches is a lot of stitches for a little bottom. But I knew somebody had to hold him down. The nurse wasn't there, so I told the doctor, 'Instead of giving him anesthesia, you know I don't believe in that, it would be better if he felt it and learned to take it like a man, because life is pain, after all,' and I held him on my lap through the whole thing."

Before that, Ernie had had several teeth knocked out when he "fell off the bed." This is not a case of an accident-prone child. In the five and a half years since he has been living in the home, he has not had a single major mishap, nothing more than the minor physical injuries any child accumulates.

While it is usually only one parent who is actively sadistic, the other by not standing up for the child and energetically defending him is in effect giving passive consent to the cruelty of the first.

Jennifer

My father used to grab me around my back from behind and squeeze. When I'd complain he'd laugh, and if I didn't like that, he would put me over his lap, lift up my skirt, pull down my panties, and smack away. I didn't dare cry because if I cried, he would only laugh and go on smacking me longer. I couldn't sit down for several days at a time after he hit me.

Other times, when he really got angry, he would hit me with an iron or his belt. I don't know which was worse, but mostly he seemed to prefer his hand, and even though my backside would hurt so bad, I don't know how his hand could take it either for so long. He would do this for almost anything; I could just be coming back five minutes late, or maybe I didn't say "Yes, ma'am" to my

mother, and the next thing I knew he'd grab me from behind, throw me down, and start whacking away.

Jennifer's story exposes the sexual component in her father's
sadistic behavior. Hitting a child with bare hands seems usually
to be the prerogative of the father, while hitting or burning
the child's hands is a punishment most often inflicted by the
mother. Whether or not she is aware of its meaning, the mother
is enacting a ritualistic chastisement, "punishing the offending
limb," for the real or imagined—or future—sin of masturbation.*

The obsessive nature of the sadistic impulse comes through
very clearly in the following father's attempt at self-justification.

Gregory

I hit her every week on Friday afternoon, right when
I get home from work, so I'll have a good weekend. And
if I don't know what she did, that doesn't matter because
she knows. There have been times when some of my neighbors have complained and even called the police, and a
couple of times they came to get me and I stayed overnight in jail, but I don't care. I think it's a father's job to
teach a child right from wrong, and even if it means I have
to go to jail again, I'm not going to stop.

I feel that discipline is the most important thing a child
can learn in life, and if they don't learn it from their fathers, who's going to teach them? I don't hold with all
these people now that pamper kids and let them do whatever they want. I feel it's very important to make contact
with kids in a way they understand, and anyway a good
smack never hurt anybody. What happened to that good
old idea, "Spare the rod and spoil the child"?

Gregory's claim that present beatings deter future acts is a
common one among violent parents. What does happen is that
a pattern of responding with cruelty to whoever is young and
weak and dependent tends to perpetuate itself from generation

to generation. The brutalized children grow up to do likewise to their own children—it's the only way of being a parent they know.

But many parents do not even offer the excuse of deterrence; they simply regard the child as their personal property to treat as they see fit. Their rights as parents, as they conceive them, do not stop short even of outright torture. And the sexual coloring of the violence inflicted on these children makes it a virtual certainty that they will grow up unable to imagine love without pain, either given or received. This is the genesis of adult sadomasochism, where sexual excitement is always associated with a sense of danger and of being overpowered.

Robbie

I love my mother very much, but I guess I do upset her sometimes. And I think I do deserve the beatings I get some of the time, but not all the time. She just broke up with a boyfriend and has nobody to go out with right now, so she's a little extra tense. Also, we don't have much money, so we can't go to expensive places. We go to the park, and during the summer the men in her office have a softball team, and I used to be their bat boy. I'd give them all the bats they needed, and then we would go to this restaurant that has pinball machines.

I do miss Nick [stepfather who divorced mother two years ago; Robbie has not seen his natural father since he was two]. Nick was nice to me, and he seemed to keep my mother calmed down.

I'll give you an example of something bad that happened. I threw a snowball at this big kid, and he got mad. He ran after me, tackled me—the guy's a big moose—and my glasses smashed on the road. Luckily, the lenses didn't break, but the whole frame was wrecked. If the lenses had broken, my mother would have gone out of her mind. As it was, when I got home I showed the frame to my mother, and she started screaming, "Get out! Get out!" So I ran over to my friend's house for a while. I know enough to get the hell out of there at times like that.

But the scariest is when she gets into certain moods. Oh, boy. First, there's kind of a buildup while she gets madder and madder. Then she grabs me, knocks me around for a while, and eventually knocks me down on the floor. Then while I'm lying on the floor, she has these high-heeled shoes, real pointed shoes with spike heels, and she kicks me while I'm lying there. Sometimes I get kicked in the face, but usually it's everywhere else—it looks too bad afterward when she kicks me in the face. Sooner or later she just gets exhausted from the whole thing, and she'll sit down and fall asleep. When she wakes up, she'll say, "Gee, I'm sorry I did that," but that doesn't stop her from doing it the next time.

She is a good mother, though; I guess I'm not such a good kid. I feel that I get her mad, so she has to scream and yell. I mean, I'm the only one. She has no one else to let it out on.

The hope for Robbie is in his understanding of the unhappiness behind his mother's behavior and his partial realization that he need not feel responsible for it.

None of these family games is unique to our time or our culture. As long as the nuclear family has been the basic unit of social life, the complex of interactions among family members has included pathological patterns of domination and dependence. What may be new is an increasing sense among the parents of these children—that is, middle-class men and women in early middle age—that the only arena of life in which they can enjoy a sense of importance is their own home; that outside the family they are anonymous, insignificant, and expendable. This is one reason why the games described in this chapter are really all exercises in power and submission.

The new religious cults which have attracted so many thousands of young people are essentially neofascistic societies in which dominance and submission are the whole rule of life, not aberrations of one parent. Apparently a generation of teen-agers is growing up without understanding the concept of individual freedom. However, it also may be that the essential feature of these cults, and a primary source of their appeal, is precisely their outright prohibition of premarital sex and their celebration of chastity. To children who have reason to feel persecuted and oppressed by the sexual needs of those in authority, this may come as a blessed relief.

Chapter 5

INCEST

In November, 1979, about 300 social workers, mental health professionals, doctors, lawyers, and nurses gathered in Washington, D.C., for the first national conference on the sexual abuse of children—Sexual Victimization of Children: Trauma, Trial, and Treatment.* Although accustomed to discussing sensitive topics, many conferees were unprepared for the keynote speech given by Professor LeRoy G. Schultz of the School of Social Work, West Virginia University. Professor Schultz, as reported in *The New York Times*, declared that some incest "may be either a positive, healthy experience or at worst, neutral and dull." He maintained that there is no research to support the belief that the trauma of incest often results in neurotic or psychotic behavior.

Not surprisingly, some conferees disagreed.

"I have never knowingly talked to a happy, well-adjusted, unconcerned incest victim," responded Dr. Suzanne M. Sgroi, former chairman of the Sexual Trauma Treatment Program in Hartford, Connecticut. Dr. Sgroi's remarks were applauded by the audience.

The exchange between these two experts is significant for two reasons. One is that until recently, incest was a topic so obscured by taboo, myth, shame, and revulsion as to be virtually ignored. It was less threatening and more convenient to believe that incest was (1) rare and (2) a low-income-family phenomenon. We know what experts have long suspected, that middle-

and upper-income families are not immune to incest; it is just more likely that if they turn to anyone, they will seek help from a private physician who will not report them. Nor is incest rare. For the past thirty years, the official estimate seemed rare, with an assumed incidence of one to two cases per million.* Today, 5,000 new cases of incest are reported nationally each year.* For every one of those reported cases, ten to twenty more go unreported, say experts.* (In a survey of physicians in Seattle, Washington, over two thirds of the doctors admitted that they often do not report such cases to authorities.*) That incest is more widespread than people have believed is the second reason the exchange between Professor Schultz and Dr. Sgroi is important. It is dangerous now, of all times, to trivialize incest and the damage it causes.

Incest—sexual intercourse between persons so closely related that their society forbids marriage—is not a new ill, of course. Ancient peoples associated certain physical phenomena with incest. Galen, the second-century Greek physician, believed that seizures resulted from it. The Bible tells us about Lot and his daughters. Navajo Indians connected incest with witchcraft. Freud related the trauma of incest to hysteria.

The prohibition against incest is probably the most deeply rooted law in human society. There is no known social group which does not practice some form of incest taboo. In different cultures, incest was punished with banishment, castration, forced suicide, and witchcraft rites. Anthropologists and psychologists generally agree that, whatever its origins and functions, the incest taboo is at the root of all morality, protecting the family from destruction by internal conflict and jealousy. The taboo also protects the young from premature sexual stimulation by their first and strongest instinctual love object, the parent of the other sex; it also protects parents from desire for their own children.

In the United States, there was little broad interest in incest until the late 1960's, when reporting of sexual abuse became mandatory under newly enacted child abuse statutes. Between 1974 and 1976, reports of abused and neglected children in

Massachusetts quadrupled.* In 1977, 16,000 cases were reported.* By no means were all of these cases of incest, but the figure of one to two cases per million was beginning to look ridiculous.

About the same time, perhaps as a result of the publicity surrounding the large number of abuse cases being reported, psychiatrists and psychologists treating upper- and middle-income patients made a similarly shocking discovery. Alvin Rosenfeld, in a 1977 paper, reported on the new awareness of the prevalence of incest in the Boston area:

> We were fascinated with the fact that *each* therapist we interviewed was treating several incestuous cases, but had assumed that he was the only one, since incest was thought to be rare. . . . these were not cases of fantasy.

While accurate statistics on the national incidence of incest are still difficult to obtain, city and county agencies which have been set up specifically to deal with incest cases are more accurate sources of figures. Therapists in such programs are armed with information on national occurrence and attitudes. Estimates reported in these programs are of one case per 2,000 households. This is five hundred times greater than earlier estimates. Experts claim that there are ten to twenty unreported cases for each reported one.

The largest incest clinic in the country is the Santa Clara Child Abuse Treatment Program in San Jose, California, under the direction of Dr. Henry Giaretto, who is also its chief therapist. Despite the horror evoked by the very notion of incest, and the deeply rooted shame an incestuous parent feels when confronted with his or her behavior, Dr. Giaretto's case load has been more than doubling every year; in 1978, he saw 600 new cases.*

In Seattle, Washington, the Sexual Assault Clinic of Harbor View Medical Center gets about eighty-five new inquiries a month on behalf of victims of sexual assault, about half of whom are under sixteen, almost all of whom are victims of incest.*

The clinic's director, Lucy Berliner, says, "Considering that we are not one of the major urban areas of the country, I think it's pretty significant that we see that many cases. Dr. Henry Giaretto in Santa Clara County, with a population of only a little over a million, gets the same high numbers, and I just cannot believe that this is because all the incest families are living there or in Seattle. I think it's because of the programs, especially the one in California, which have gotten so much publicity. The community knows about them as a resource, people have a place to come and look for help."

Dr. Giaretto says, "My guess is that there are hundreds of thousands of incidents. I believe that incest is widespread in America."

He agrees with Kinsey and other sex researchers that one girl in four is sexually molested in this country, only 15 percent of the time by a stranger.* Usually she knows her attacker, and the assault frequently occurs in her own home.* Boys are most often the victims of homosexual assault from more distant relatives, such as stepfathers or uncles, and this, too, seems to be on the increase, although statistics are harder to come by.*

Incest is the ultimate betrayal of family trust. When families exploit their children's dependence through the uniquely insidious trap of incest, which sets up unbearable conflicts of loyalties and detaches victims from their own feelings, the consequences are catastrophic. They are distressingly evident in the statistics for deviant adolescents: Among prostitutes, the frequency of sexual molestation in childhood is 92 percent; 67 percent of them experienced some form of incestuous assault.* We have already seen the causal connection between sexual attack in the home and running away—at least 75 percent of the runaways, on the national average, are escaping incestuous abuse.* The same figures apply to cases of adolescent drug addiction: About 70 percent are victims of incest.*

According to Lucy Berliner, "Adolescent incest victims in particular experience suicidal thoughts, and they make fairly frequent gestures in that direction. These twelve-, thirteen-, and fourteen-year-old children feel so bad about what has been done to them that even though they're not responsible they think a lot about killing themselves.

"The more data we gather on kids who are acting out, running away, becoming juvenile prostitutes or drug abusers, the more often we see a history of incest in the background. We're beginning to understand their acting-out behavior as an attempt to cope with an intolerable situation.

"One thing that puzzled us was how a population so deeply involved in incest was so rarely violent. The answer is that for the vast majority of children, the incest begins when they are between five and ten years old, sometimes even younger. Only about ten percent of the cases we see involve incestuous activity which has begun after the onset of puberty."

But perhaps the arguments against incest, like so many other sexual conventions, need to be reexamined; the damage may be the result not so much of the incestuous activity itself, but of the aggression that so often accompanies it. Is there any sort of case to be made for a loving incestuous relationship between a consenting daughter and her father? (Mother-son incest is still exceedingly rare.)

A number of experts were asked to respond to the question, "What, in your experience, would be the consequences of an incestuous relationship between a girl of from ten to thirteen and a very affectionate father who seduced her with great tenderness and consideration?" * Here are their answers.

Dr. Simeon Feigin, Associate Professor of Psychiatry, New York University Medical Center:

"The central problem when a child is involved in an incestuous relationship of any kind with a parent is that the child's basic ability to trust may be permanently destroyed. Knowing that the parent is using the child for his own pleasure, whether sexual or otherwise, is very disturbing to the child and highly disruptive of his development. It's essential for a child to know that his parents' concern for him is altruistic, not selfish—that his happiness or pleasure or freedom from pain comes first.

"When a child is overstimulated, his libidinal energy becomes translated into anxiety, with the result that very often he maintains his sexuality only by becoming detached from his own feelings, like a robot—because the moment he becomes re-attached, the anxiety returns and he can't deal with it.

"In later life he becomes impotent or fearful, and the effects of having been sexually stimulated too early remain a serious problem for the rest of his life. The child cannot master the anxiety. He is too young and the experience is overwhelmingly frightening. When a child is stimulated without sufficient ego development to cope with it, severe anxiety attacks follow.

"Finally, this child would become fixated on the parent and unable to become attached to anyone else. The underlying conflict in a girl who was seduced by her father would probably manifest itself in psychosomatic symptoms or vague feelings of depression, and a sense of unreality—for she herself must know that the experience is unusual, to say the least, and really one of abuse, not love. Her conflict would take the form of 'This is so pleasurable, he loves me—but he is abusing me because he is not letting me be free.' That conflict can lead to terrible disturbances, including even psychoses, because the child's own experience and observation would be self-contradictory, with conflicting elements of love, hatred, and selfishness.

"My own feeling is that without professional help the child would not survive the experience with any degree of emotional health, nor could she sustain any future relationship based on intimacy, love or trust."

Lucy Berliner: "The main problem would be that the child simply wouldn't like it. Kids always know there's something unusual and unacceptable about this behavior, especially since they're almost always told to keep it secret. Even the least sophisticated child knows something's wrong when she's told to keep a secret fom her mother. They just don't like being molested—and they always do know and feel it as a molestation.

"In my experience the father never stops to consider the effect of his actions on the child—and he certainly is not doing it for the child's benefit, whatever he may say. It's nothing less than an abuse of the father's power and a violation of his role as parent, and an exploitation of the child, who has nothing to say about it. And these kids do feel exploited; if you talk to them and listen to what they have to say, you find that even if there was no element of coercion in the seduction or overt threat of force, most of them have nightmares. They dream about violence being done to them, and they're afraid their father is going to return and kill them or their mother. I don't know what further evidence you'd need that the incest experience was not as neutral as some people would like to think.

"But these kids become very adept at hiding their feelings, at placating and ingratiating themselves with adults. Sometimes it's difficult to know what they really feel because they've suppressed their emotions for so long. And they tend to respond as they think is expected of them rather than spontaneously, and the consequences of this can be very harmful.

"In three quarters of our patients, the incestuous experience lasted for more than a year, often for as long as four to ten years, and they felt they couldn't tell anyone because they were so afraid of being blamed for it."

Dr. Jules Bemporad, Professor of Child Psychiatry at the Harvard University School of Medicine:

"I think the problem here is not the sex *per se* but the power relationship. It is the whole idea of this father and daughter doing something that they both know to be wrong and having to be quiet about it. Most incestuous fathers tell the daughter that if she says anything to anyone about what they're doing, he'll beat her up or even kill her. But even if there is no threat of violence, pressure is being put on her to do something with her father that she knows is socially forbidden. The very fact that the child is compelled to do something she feels to be wrong and can't tell anybody about is what does most of the harm— it's the whole aura of secrecy and conspiracy."

Dr. Judianne Densen-Gerber, Director of Odyssey Institute in New York City, a halfway house for children in trouble:

"I think it would be very damaging to such a child. Assuming even the best of all possible circumstances—the father is charming, gentle, cajoles the youngster, and does everything with kindness—it would still be bad. First, she would become fixated on him and unable to transfer her affections to anyone else. Secondly, even if she were able to leave him, too much of her libido would be tied up in sex; it would be much more difficult for her to develop into a meaningful kind of person in life outside the bedroom.

"But I also challenge the belief that there is a 'nice' way of having incest. I've never seen it; lots of the girls who come here have had some kind of experience with incest, and most of them have become drug addicts, prostitutes, or attempt suicides—several of them successful. So I must reject this myth about being nice and sweet and tender, and it just happens to be a father and daughter who are making love. It is not love, it is abuse that the father is heaping on this child. The child is not able afterward to look at herself with respect or think of her father with any trust or respect.

"The sad fact is that what this man is doing is overpowering this child when she has no other option—it's certainly not a relationship of equals. The child didn't ask for it, and the father, who ought to know better, is actually exploiting her, using her in a way that certainly is at variance with behavior that our society condones."

Whatever else it may be, incest is an exercise in dominance; its psychodynamics always include elements of a need for the assertion of power over a dependent and relatively weaker person. Nor does the power have to be solely physical. As we see in this chapter and in the chapter on Family Sex Games, the power need is also for symbolic control over the victim. The need is for total dominance and control over the life of the individual.

As reported in *A Sexual Profile of Men in Power*, the authors state:

> For many, direct physical gratification is not enough; some of the men need to extend their domination over the woman beyond the bedroom, controlling and directing every aspect of her life. . . . Indeed, the actual physical

penetration of the woman sometimes becomes of secondary importance compared with the pleasure of invading her daily existence. . . . It is the need to take possession of another's consciousness.*

Dr. Bemporad believes that "men are increasingly intimidated by mature women. This confirms my power theory—from being overwhelmed by women, they find relief by overwhelming little girls."

But there are obviously other and deeper reasons for the kind of family power relationships Dr. Giaretto has become accustomed to seeing in the cases referred to him in California:

"At first, I was interested in seeing whether the approaches I followed with other clients—with the so-called 'average' neurotic middle-class Americans with whom I was using humanistic psychology—might be applicable to these families. It was a challenge, but I soon forgot that in the struggle of dealing with my own horror. That's the only word for what you feel when you see and hear cases of a father forcing a son to copulate with his mother while the father watches.

"I've had a father here who would strap his daughters up and do a weekly examination on them with gynecological instruments. I've had parents not only poking around, but actually having intercourse with the youngster in front of the other children. And then we've had whole families pressed into scenarios, holding their own group sex orgies at home."

One consequence of an early incestuous relationship—as of any premature sexual activity—is a serious interference with normal development by eliminating or drastically shortening the latency period, that breathing space which channels the libido into intellectual development and the formation of friendships.

In the case histories that follow, the effect of such interference takes various forms. In the first, Elyse's case, her choice of career—in her early teens she became a professional model, actress, and singer—was probably determined by a precocious self-conscious seductiveness evoked by an incestuous relationship with her father beginning when she was very small.

Elyse

Elyse is the younger of two children, with a sister five years older. The family lived together until the exposure of the incest. Elyse began therapy because of recurring depression. She describes her father in the following terms:

"My father is a brute; he's an absolute animal. He not only used to beat up my older sister, he used to slam my mother around pretty good, too. He's a great big man, about six foot three, and very broad; he seemed like a giant to me.

"When I was very little, about five, my father began coming into my bed at night and having intercourse with me. If I was nice to him—which meant giving in to what he wanted to do without resisting him—he would be nice to me. He used to buy me all kinds of gifts, but at the same time he would humiliate and insult my sister.

"I remember the pain of the penetration when I was small, and I also remember him swearing me to silence, whispering that he would kill me if I told anyone. So for seven whole years, until I was twelve, I never told anyone. There were even times when my father would insist on having sex with me twice in one night; to this day I don't know how my mother didn't know what was happening, since he sure wasn't with her, but apparently all the time he kept coming into my room and spending the night with me she never even missed him.

"It hurt a lot, and sometimes he would put me on top of him and enter me with him on the bottom and me on top. That felt funny. But he generally preferred to enter me from above and then lie down with all his weight on top of me while he thrust into me. My pain didn't seem to put him off in the least; in fact, if I made any sounds it seemed if anything to excite him.

"My father was a very successful salesman and could probably sweet-talk anybody into anything, but he never seemed to care much about any of us. He never showed any interest in anything else I did, like school, and if I told him I had gotten a good mark or a part in a play, he might say 'That's good,' or occasionally even buy me something special as a reward, but except for my physical relationship with him, he didn't seem to care very much about anything else that I did in life except please him.

"Sometimes—and I used to dread this even more than sleeping with him at home—he would take me along on his sales trips. This was supposed to be a big treat, but I would be scared because then there wasn't even my mother in the next room to call out to if things got too bad.

"And yet, as I look back on it, it's strange, there were times I now realize when I was being seductive, I have to admit. He used to buy me all kinds of cute dresses and skirts and even little slips, and I remember to this day how I used to enjoy dancing around and modeling some of these things for him. I don't know if I was aware at six or seven that that was the way to arouse men and that my dancing around like that might turn him on, but I was certainly looking for approval. I think I was trying to get some kind of response from him outside of the bedroom. I never succeeded.

"My father always used to tell my mother that he cared a lot about raising us girls right and was very concerned with our welfare, but the only area he showed any serious interest in was our physical growth.

"I understand now why he used to beat my sister up so badly —she was refusing him. She was a very beautiful girl who had been a successful child model, and she apparently was constantly turning him down. But, in spite of the hassles and the beatings, she never told my mother. I never did, either—and it wasn't just the fear that my father might kill me. I felt ashamed and humiliated, and I was afraid that my mother would be angry with me, apart from what she might feel about my father.

"But he was always telling me how lucky I was and how nice he was being to me and doing it all for me. He even said it would make it easier some day when I got married because when some other man shoved a penis in me, it wouldn't hurt. My own feeling at the time was that I never wanted to get married at all—it hurt so much I could never imagine anybody having sex voluntarily. There was almost never any what you might call stroking or foreplay; all that happened was he would get turned on by roughly touching me, feeling my crotch and my bottom. Then he'd just plunk me down, get on top of me, and plunge into me.

"When my breasts started to grow, I didn't know what was happening. I knew that my girl friends were developing breasts, but I was so isolated from other girls—because I couldn't talk about what was going on at home—that I only had heard vaguely about things like periods, and the information really made no impact on me. But shortly after I got my first period, I developed a vaginal infection. Then my mother finally found out everything after all those years, and proceeded to call the police and kick my father out of the house. They ended up getting divorced, and I never saw my father again."

Elyse's case illustrates father-daughter incest in its classic form. First, the relationship is one of brute force asserting itself over helpless dependence. The father made no pretense whatsoever of having any concern for his child except as an instrument—not only of sexual pleasure but also of self-assertion and self-confirmation. (Even where the imposition of force is as raw as it is here, however, one can still see a vestige of guilt expressed in the feeble rationalization that, after all, the child was being spared the pain of defloration later!) Not all incestuous fathers are as brutal as Elyse's, but the need to define oneself through a sadistic exercise of power is almost always present to some degree in father-daughter incest.

The second classic element is the mother who has withdrawn from the family and essentially abandoned her husband and children. Only a woman who was frozen in a posture of denial could have succeeded in refusing to "know" what was going on between her husband and daughter for seven years—and those years among the most critical in the child's development.

The third significant feature is Elyse's "seductive" behavior, which began, as she remembers it, sometime after her father's first assaults. An important trigger in father-daughter incest is the covert agreement among family members that the daughter replace the mother, who has opted out. This not only relieves the father's sexual frustration, it releases him permanently from any fears he may have about his sexual adequacy—how could he be judged by a child of five?

This family collusion, by assigning the daughter a role which subjects her to abnormal sexual stimulation throughout her childhood, means that her Oedipal fantasies never have a chance to become resolved through identification with the mother, and latency is bypassed. Some of the effects of this are poignantly illustrated by Elyse's "seductiveness," which she recalls with so much guilt. It was, as she recognizes, an attempt to attract some affectionate attention from her father. But by this time, she had so little affection from either of her parents, and so much sexual stimulation from her father, that the only way she knew how to ask for attention was by being provocative.

Equally damaging, of course, is the fact that most incestuous activity is associated with pain, fear, and secrecy. The child is terrified by threats of retaliation if she confides in anyone, which, apart from the crippling effects of fear, means a dangerous isolation from the rest of her family and even from the world outside. Few girls who have had incestuous relationships escape serious depression later on—especially when to the trauma of the experience is added guilt for the breakup of the family.

But father-daughter incest is not the only form in which the relationship is one of brutalizing terror. Almost identical elements are present in the following case of brother-sister incest.

Karen

I guess I was about six when my brother, who was seven years older, first approached me. He called me into his room one day, much to my pride and delight. He was a very strong character, always throwing temper tantrums, and he'd never let me in his room. All his playthings looked very interesting to me, but I was never allowed to touch them. But that day he called me into his room, closed the door, and told me he had to do a project for school involving biology and that he wanted to study me. I didn't know what he meant, but I soon found out.

He had me undress, then he pulled his pants down. He was very aroused, his penis looked enormous, and the next thing I knew, without any kind of foreplay, he was on top of me, had forced my legs apart, and with a lot of violent thrusting managed to penetrate me. I was terrified, but I couldn't say a word. I don't remember feeling anything except an intense, stabbing pain. After what seemed like hours, he must have finished and ejaculated; anyway, he withdrew. Then he told me to go and wash up, and quickly walked away from me after warning me not to tell anyone about it. I was absolutely stunned. I didn't know which hurt more, the fear or the physical pain.

This scene was repeated several times a week for the next three years until I was nine. He occasionally tried various other positions besides the straightforward one on top of me, but when he attempted anal intercourse, it was so incredibly painful that I absolutely refused and threatened to start screaming. Most of the experience is like a dream. Although it was fantastically painful, it didn't seem real, not even at the time, and I'm not sure now exactly how it ended, how I managed to bring it to an end when I was nine. All I know is that it finally did end, much to my relief.

All this time my brother was never kind to me. In fact, he seemed more than usually rough and a lot more inconsiderate. He'd go out of his way to humiliate or insult me when I was alone or even in front of friends. He made a point of poking fun at me, questioning everything I did, and accusing me of all kinds of dirty things.

My father was absolutely no support at all. He was an alcoholic and in fact had left us several years earlier. My older brother was really almost the father figure in the family. To this day I've never told my mother about it. Actually, I don't speak to my brother anymore and, frankly, I don't care if I never see him again.

This child, too, endured a long period of alienation from her family. She had three other siblings, but her brother so intimidated her that she never thought of turning to any of them for help.

The next case illustrates perhaps the most damaging consequence of all, alienation from oneself. So many years of mute struggle between the two partners seem improbable, but once the pattern of complicity is established, in whatever bizarre and unlikely form, fear and guilt can maintain the inertia almost indefinitely.

Carrie

I remember being quite happy with my family when I was little, especially in the summers when we would all go away to a resort. My folks would rent a bungalow, and my father came up on weekends. I was a very active kid. I liked swimming and playing ball, and I was also very close to my brother.

It all began one night in summer when I was about six. For some reason my mother had had to go back to the city, leaving us with my father. She had been gone for several days, and my father was out—I think there was some entertainment going on at the nightclub. Anyway, my brother and I were alone. There was only one bedroom in the bungalow, and all four of us used to sleep in the same room. My parents had the large bed, and my brother and I slept in bunk beds, with me on the bottom and him on top. Even though it was August, it was kind of cold and we were afraid of going to sleep alone, so we decided to sleep together on the big bed.

In the middle of the night, I heard my father come in,

but I didn't move. I hoped maybe he'd let me sleep in his bed and he'd take one of the bunks. But he must have taken my brother off the bed, because a few minutes later I suddenly felt him touching me, and there he was licking my legs and vagina and going down on me. I still pretended to be asleep because I didn't know what to say or do. So I just lay still, and after a little while he seemed to have finished.

I couldn't really sleep much that night. I kept waking up, going back to sleep, waking again, and thinking that it must have all just been a bad dream. The next day neither my father nor I said anything about it, and he carried on just as usual except that he seemed to be a little more hostile to me. Most of the time he was fairly nice, but he was never the kind of man that you felt somehow you totally understood.

Well, before my mother came back, it happened again, and again I pretended to be sleeping through it all—except this time besides eating me he also fingered me, which was very painful, since I was all of six years old and still a virgin. But neither of us said a word afterward that time either. Unfortunately, it didn't stop when we came back to Ohio from vacation, even though at home my brother and I each had our own room, and my parents slept together in theirs. He would still sneak into my room at night and do this. And it was not only painful, but sometimes he would get off on me. Now how long can I keep up the pretense that I'm asleep? After a while I started putting locks on my door, but no matter what kind I used somehow he always managed to get the thing open and he'd appear beside my bed and start doing his thing, with not a word between us. Afterward, he'd just walk out.

Often, while he was busy "doing me," I would stir or move around as if to let him know that I was aware of what was happening, but he would simply murmur, "Shhh, shhh, don't say anything, it's okay, shhh, everything will be okay," and he would just go right on with what he was doing until he was good and ready to leave.

I was getting quite frantic, but I felt I couldn't go to my mother. Don't ask me why. Whether I thought that she would be angry with me, or I would get my father into trouble, or both, going to my mother was somehow out of the question. And I couldn't tell my brother about it, either, but I was determined not to let this go on. The truth is, at times it may have felt fairly good if it weren't for the weight of his body on me and the pain of him angrily shoving his finger into me. I felt as if I were being fingered to death. So besides getting more and more elaborate locks, I'd push furniture against the door, and each night I'd go to sleep thinking that tonight at least I'd be left in peace. Wrong. Because somehow, don't ask me how, he found out how to pick every single lock—he'd become an expert burglar—and there he'd be in the room.

It's a frightening thing to know that there's no way you can ever get any privacy. And to realize how vulnerable I was, and also how isolated I'd become in my own home. Once when I was thirteen, I had a fourteen-year-old girl friend, Joan, stay overnight with me. I was feeling very safe when we went to sleep. We both slept in my bed; it was a big bed. My father will never dare to come in now and bother me, I thought. I hadn't even bothered to put the furniture against the door.

But much to my shock and embarrassment, during the night my father picked the locks again. He'd got into the room and there he was, making out with Joan. She woke right up, of course, and started to scream. He tried to calm her down, but she went on screaming and cursing at him until he left the room. Joan jumped out of bed, threw on some clothes, and ran out of the house, and the next thing I knew there was a pounding on the front door, and there was Joan with a bunch of cops.

They took my father in and booked him. Of course, my mother knew nothing whatever about anything and was very upset that my friend would dare make such wild accusations, but she finally decided to believe that Joan was just hysterical. And when the case came to court, it was dismissed for lack of evidence; my father was such a solid citizen and successful businessman, they weren't about to do anything to hurt him, so the case was dismissed.

That obviously was the end of my friendship with Joan, but meanwhile I had been in a terrible dilemma. In a way I still felt a sense of loyalty to my father, but I also realized that if I opened my mouth and spoke, I might finally be free from the terror of his breaking into my room at will and doing whatever he wanted to me. Just at that point, though, my mother made a big issue of how we now all had to stick together, that this was a crisis and it was important to stand up for our father because he was our provider, and all that kind of stuff. So I had some doubts, if I were ever called to the stand—after all, I was there in that bed, too—about what I would really say if it came down to it. But it never did.

I assumed that after this incident my father would leave me alone, but I was wrong. In fact, he continued even more aggressively than before until I was sixteen and a half. After I started getting my periods when I was a little over thirteen, I was very alarmed. I didn't know what it was; I thought I was bleeding because of something he had done to me. For a day or two I was so scared I didn't dare say anything. Then I went to my mother and told her what was happening to my body, and she just looked at me and said, "Oh, congratulations, you've got your period."

This seemed if anything to stir my father up even more, my becoming an adolescent and all that, but the weird thing is that by this time he had been doing it to me for about ten years, but there still was almost never anything said. I would be in bed, he would come in, do his thing, and go out without a word. The rest of the time he was very hostile and nasty to me, and was really cruel to me during the day. He could be very sarcastic and would interrogate me, accusing me of being a lesbian, implying that I was totally perverted, and at the same time attacking me for running around with boys.

Finally, just before my seventeenth birthday, I made up my mind I was going to end it once and for all. Once again I barricaded the door, put three or four locks on it, and, sure enough, early in the morning he somehow gets into the room. This time I started yelling at him, "Get the fuck out of here." I think I surprised him. "Shhh, keep quiet," he muttered. "Get the fuck out of here, you fuck, or I'm going to kill you," I screamed. He kept trying to shush me, but I wouldn't be shushed. I kept screaming and yelling, and I had a little nail file I was all set to stab him with. I was just determined to put an end to it, and finally I drove him out of the room.

A little later I heard a disturbance in my brother's room next door. Apparently my father had gone in there and started to eat him in his sleep. My brother woke up, jumped out of bed, grabbed his baseball bat, and started to go after him. He ran out of the room, ran right out of the house, jumped into his car, and drove off.

The next thing I hear are loud voices from the kitchen. My brother had gone downstairs and said to my mother, "Do you know what that fuck tried to do to me?" and he told her everything, in detail. I felt that pain again, both my own humiliation and fear and also dread that now my father was going to be exposed. My mother called me down and asked, "Did you hear what your brother said?" "Yes," I told her. "Did your father ever do that to you?" "Yes." "Once?" "No," I told her, "many times." Ironic, that after eleven years it should come out in just that way.

They separated after that. There was one attempt at reconciliation, but when my father came back, he again tried to make out with me. This time I was no longer standing for anything. The minute he made a move, I screamed and yelled and threw things at him. He became quite ugly about it.

They finally ended up getting divorced, and from then on I never saw him at all. I wouldn't care if he was alive or dead. The way I feel about him is not as a father. He never showed us any love or affection, never played with us, never took us anywhere or did any of the things that most fathers do. I recognize that biologically he fathered me, but whether he lives or dies, whatever happens to him, really is of no significance to me. I feel that the man is basically an animal, not a human being.

For a long time after he left, I was so traumatized I couldn't let any boy come near me. Then I went through a stage of being a nymphomaniac for a while, but now I realize that I don't trust men at all. I really prefer women, but while I'm primarily gay, I still kind of regard myself as being basically bisexual. I'm living very happily with a lover. She's very nice, and I don't need men for anything.

As in the previous cases, the attacks stop only when the father is exposed—either by chance from the outside, or at the point when the child has mobilized enough ego strength to protest, whatever the cost. The very high cost—the breakup of the family—is precisely why so much is endured for so long without protest. What ends the silence, it should be noted, is *not* the child's discomfort, however extreme that may become. The silence is broken only when she gets old enough to make a conscious decision to act, as Carrie did on that particular night.

In this case a talk with the father, Arthur, gives a rare opportunity to see an incestuous relationship from both sides and to compare the two versions of events:

"I know that you've talked to my daughter, and if it weren't for my years of therapy, I wouldn't be sitting here with you now. But I feel that it's an important thing to discuss, and perhaps it will help to educate other people if you hear my side of the story. You've probably gotten a completely opposite picture of me from my family, but I'm going to tell it to you the way I experienced it. No, I'm not proud of what I have been through or what I did, but there wasn't any other way I could have been.

"It all started a number of years ago. My marriage was already stinko; my wife and I didn't have sex very often, just once in a while when she decided for some reason to do me a favor. But even then it was no good. I felt that I really had no voice and very little power in that marriage.

"The thing with Carrie started when she was quite little, about seven, one summer when we were up at a resort. My wife wasn't there, which happened often, and I spent a lot of time alone with the kids. One night it happened in some strange way that I was stroking my little girl—you know, putting her to sleep—when I suddenly found myself very excited. I was embarrassed and ashamed and even a little scared—and yet, when I stroked her again the next night, the same thing happened. I couldn't understand it. The next several nights I made a determined effort not to let myself get aroused, but it was no good.

"Well, one thing led to another, and gradually the stroking became more intimate. But no matter what I did, I found, strangely, that she was sleeping through it, so I assumed that it must be comforting for her. And it was not only a tremendously stimulating experience for me, but to my surprise I found I was able to achieve gratification this way, too. All along I was very concerned about her, I didn't want to hurt her, but I told myself that I was only making nice on a more physical level than most fathers do—that's all.

"Things went on like this for the next several years, since she seemed both to enjoy it and sleep through it. Even though I had my doubts and kept resolving never to touch her again, I found myself being drawn to her. I couldn't stay away or keep my hands off her. But I always made very sure that I had an orgasm quickly, before I was tempted to do anything more than fondling and poking around her with my hands. Later on I found that I was kissing her, too, as well as touching her all over, and it felt superb. It was a strange combination of the terribly forbidden and the incredibly exciting—both seemed to be operating at the same time.

"I used to have flashes of that same excitement and fear when I was little myself and my mother would take me into bed with her. But then I used to be terrified that my father would come in and find us and kill me. Here I was the father, and this was my own little girl. I don't know exactly what I was so afraid of, but I really was always looking for some way to end it or break it off. I could never find any. I just assumed when Carrie put locks on her door that she had done it accidentally, that she didn't realize that I might want to come into her room that night.

"My wife never said anything, although since we were sharing the same bedroom she couldn't have been asleep all that time. I don't know what she thought, since we never talked about anything much. Sometimes we hardly spoke for days. I tried to justify what I was doing by being nicer in a lot of ways to my little girl during the daylight hours, but now, after hearing what she said in court, I'm convinced that she thinks of me totally negatively. I object to being portrayed as a monster. I do believe I was very disturbed; certainly I didn't have the kind of control that I should have had. If I had it to do over again, I wish that I could have been in therapy when I was much younger so I could have had a more enjoyable relationship on a more normal basis with my daughter. Maybe I would even have been able to confront my wife and demand that we either have a normal adult relationship or get divorced.

"Frankly, knowing what I now know, I would tell parents that one has to be in touch with the feeling of responsibility. I still believe that children have a great deal of sensuality, but that it's up to the adults to set limits on behavior—some things are really unacceptable. Kids have to be protected sometimes even from their own feelings, and certainly it should be the parent who does the protecting.

"I believe that I am completely cured now of the kind of hang-up that tormented me for so many years, and that it is well behind me. It seems almost a lifetime ago, it has that vague surreal quality, but yet I know it happened. At this point I'm sadder but wiser.

"I find that since my therapy I'm able to enjoy and feel good with adult women in a way that I never could before. I find that not only am I doing things in bed with them that are gratifying, but that even the way I relate and talk to them is different. In short, I'm able to live with myself and even like myself —and self-respect is something that is very important to me."

Arthur's story is shot through with self-justification and self-pity, but it also oddly echoes his victim's account. He talks about his lack of willpower, referring to "what I have been through." Arthur says he has resolved his "hang-up" through therapy, but this seems doubtful as long as he still believes that his incestuous attacks on his daughter had little effect: "She seemed both to enjoy it and sleep through it." The ambivalence still runs deep. In comparing the two accounts, however, what stands out most is the extent to which both father and daughter lived in a somnambulistic twilight of unreality because neither of them was able to speak.

In the next case, one of homosexual seduction by a stepfather, the child is also pulled into a complicity that renders him helpless. Here, however, there is no sense, as there was in the case of Carrie, of an unending nightmare, of a childhood lost in the fog of an inadmissible enslavement. Perhaps this is because, in this case, the seducer was a comparative stranger.

Herbert

I was nine years old. My sister and I—we were very close, she was about five years older than I—were living in Rhode Island with my mother and her new husband. She had been married about two years to this man whom I didn't particularly like, but she had explained to us that we needed a man in the house to make it a home. Before she married him, we had been farmed out a lot to relatives throughout the South because my mother was an alcoholic; and after she and my father divorced, she seemed to spend a lot of time just moving around, sometimes with us and sometimes parking us with relatives. Now here we were up north in a strange place with this new husband.

The only real constant in my life was my sister, Joy. We were always together. She was like a little mother to me, and the only one who really cared about me. My mother was a nurse when she was sober enough to work. She had been single for a long time when she met this man, whom I didn't like much, down in Tennessee, and I guess when you're as old as she was—in her late forties—you can't afford to be too fussy. He had a red, flushed face and a big beer-barrel belly, and generally seemed to be a jolly, friendly sort of person, but I guess I sensed something else underneath.

My mother promised Joy and me that from now on there would be no more shuttling from Uncle John to Uncle Harry to Aunt Betty, that we were a family again. She used to work nights in the hospital. She said that the night shift paid better and that her new husband, Larry, would be home during the day, so we would have someone there when we came home from school. Joy and I slept in a little attic upstairs that divided into two small rooms. Mother, who didn't quite trust Larry, had warned Joy to keep a hammer under her pillow in case he came up at night and tried to get fresh with her, but he never did. My mother was on the wrong track.

One night I had a bad cold. My mother was worried that the attic was too drafty, so before she left for work she said to me, "Why don't you sleep down here, where it's warm, with Larry tonight? Would you mind, Larry?" Larry said he didn't mind at all. I soon found out why he was so nice about it. Almost as soon as my mother was out the door, he was all over me, groping me and playing with my penis. I was startled; I didn't know what to do. Partly it felt good, but when he started to stick his finger up my ass, it hurt and I told him so. He calmed me down and promised that everything would be okay, then he slid down and had oral sex with me. I wasn't able to have any orgasm, but there he was eating me. I was shocked and embarrassed.

I didn't say a word to my mother. Even if Larry hadn't warned me not to dare say anything to her, I doubt if I would have, anyway. And, surprisingly, even though I was so close to Joy, I never said a word to her either. Up to then we'd had no secrets from each other. I always told her everything, much more than I ever told my mother. But this was different; I didn't know how to tell her even if I'd wanted to.

This went on with my stepfather for the next year and a half until finally he insisted on penetrating me. When I told him it hurt, he just took out a tube of KY-Jelly, smeared some around my ass, and entered me. It hurt like I never believed anything could, but he seemed to like it, and afterward he tried in his own way to be nice to me. Each time he would give me fifty cents or a dollar, but then he would warn me to keep my mouth shut or else he would really hurt me.

I hated the man. I absolutely hated him. I didn't know anything about homosexuals then. All I knew was how much this hurt, although I had heard somewhere that there were certain men who seemed to like doing things to little boys. I found out that Larry had spent ten years in jail for rape. Occasionally he would talk about what it was like in prison, which was where he had started to have homosexual relations with men.

He was a very menacing figure; he used to warn me, "Don't get me mad, boy." There was absolutely no tenderness between us other than his occasionally giving me extra money, and I was absolutely terrified of the man. He was not only big and heavy—and me weighing all of forty-five pounds—but I always assumed that if I tried to tell anyone, which of us would they believe, a little kid or an adult? I began using every excuse I could think of to stay away from him, but he still managed somehow to get me down to his bed whenever he wanted. I hated my mother for working nights, for not being there, for not being around during most of my life when I needed her, and for not protecting me at all.

Finally, when I was eleven, I developed a tremendous pain in my rectum that didn't go away. It turned out to be a major infection, and while I was sick in bed with it, I finally spilled my guts out to my mother. I figured I would kill him if he tried to hurt her or me, or better yet, tell his probation officer and get him put back in jail. Until that way out occurred to me and I realized that there was a real possibility of getting free of that horrible creature, I could see no way of escaping from the pain other than by running away, and I just didn't think I could take care of myself. Besides, Joy wouldn't have gone with me because I couldn't give her a good reason for leaving.

But somehow I decided that this was it, I wasn't going to take any more of the pain, and when the doctor asked me some questions after he examined my rectum, I blurted out everything. My mother was furious. She kicked Larry out of the house. At first, he refused to go, telling everybody I was a liar and that he would swear on a stack of Bibles that he never touched me. Luckily for me, the school psychologist had become involved in my case, and he called in a social worker and also talked to the probation officer. That was enough. He simply told Larry that if he didn't move out, he was going back to jail. Larry left, cursing and threatening all the way.

My mother divorced him, and though I felt guilty for breaking up her marriage, she assured me that she had had no idea what was going on, that she would have thrown him out right away if she'd known, that she loved me, and that my safety came first.

Situations like this are becoming more common as the divorce rate continues to rise and increasing numbers of children are living with stepparents. Homosexual seduction of a child by his own father is still an aberration with a long history of deep disturbance behind it. Many pederasts look for boys outside their own families. Their own children are a source of ambivalence. In cases such as Herbert's, the stepfather, whose involvement in the family was minimal and whose homosexual bent developed comparatively late in life, was simply making use of what was most readily available. Here, too, the child did not offer any resistance until external forces intervened.

The traumatic effects of incestuous assault on young children may not manifest themselves fully until years later. At the time of the incest, the child appears to be simply passive. Sometimes, however, a child will fight back—most often with suicidal gestures which are transparent, desperate cries for help; more rarely, with a more or less murderous attack on the parent. The next case is an example of a violent reaction which may have taken both directions.

Antoinette

Antoinette was referred to me when I was a consulting psychologist to a suburban school district in an upper-middle-class neighborhood where the median income was $28,000. She was a very attractive fifteen-year-old, well developed for her age, who had been referred to me after she barely survived a mixture of drugs and alcohol. She insisted that it was an accident, but the school was concerned because for some time she had been quiet and withdrawn and seemed depressed. At the same time, as one of her friends put it, "It was like she was walking around with a smoldering volcano inside her." It took several sessions before she trusted me enough to talk at all. Finally, she began, very slowly and painfully.

Two years earlier, when she had just turned thirteen, her father had begun coming into her room after she came home at night to question her about what she had been doing with her friends. The interrogation quickly moved into the next stage—he would physically examine her while warning her that he would kill her if she did anything to "disgrace the family."

Soon this pretense fell away, and he began fingering her and playing with her breasts and anus. "Keep it in the family," he would tell her.

She never thought of protesting because her father, a big, violent man, had been arrested several times previously for assault. He had also been charged a number of times with making improper advances to small children in the school playground. She knew that her father's threats had to be taken seriously.

After a couple of years of these preliminaries—during which she had to fake orgasm—he now demanded that she have intercourse with him, explaining that he knew that all young girls had sexual needs, and that he would take upon himself the responsibility of satisfying them so that the family would not be disgraced by the scandal that would surely ensue if Antoinette were ever to go out with a boy. As in every other case I have seen, he seemed totally ignorant of what was happening to his daughter. Antoinette was normally a very intense child, and her mother apparently did not notice her increasing depression—although it had immediately attracted the attention of the school authorities. She was so frightened, in fact, that for over a year she ceased menstruating.

This caused still greater difficulty with her father, who was convinced that her periods had stopped because she was pregnant and violently accused her of sneaking out of the house behind his back—using this as a pretext to demand that she have intercourse with him. Just then, thanks to medical treatment, her periods returned, and her father became still more insistent: "Now that you've got your period and we know you're not pregnant, I gotta make sure you don't go out whoring around again, because next time you might really get knocked up, you dumb little bitch. So I gotta service you at home." A week later, Antoinette swallowed the pills. Her gesture kept her father away, but only until she returned home from the hospital.

This was where matters stood when Antoinette first came to me. I suggested counseling with her father, which terrified her: "He would kill me if he knew I told you anything about this." She also refused offers to help place her in a foster home, feeling that it would hurt her mother if she left home for no reason. She felt, in short, hopeless and trapped, and all our sessions were dominated by the refrain, "Oh, I wish I were dead. It will kill my mother if she ever finds out about this—why can't I die?" At the same time, she insisted that she was perfectly able to take care of herself.

Antoinette was a gifted student and, despite her problems, managed to graduate from high school at sixteen, and go to an out of state college, as an acceptable means of getting away from her father.

Dr. Judianne Densen-Gerber, who as Director of Odyssey Institute has had a vast experience with victims of early incest, is emphatic about the dangers of a permissive, *laissez-faire* attitude toward this aberration, and vehemently opposes any tendency to accept its being within the range of now permissible sexual expression:

"Incest is no longer a crime in Sweden, but I don't know what that means. I don't know how they're protecting their children. Whether they're going to claim that incest is mental illness rather than a crime, and what they're going to do about it if they do define it as mental illness, I don't know. I really don't care what you call it, I just feel that children shouldn't be abandoned like this.

"There are also all kinds of crazy organizations, like the Paedophiliac Information Exchange, which is based in England and now has branches here and promotes the right of the pederast to seduce children as long as the children consent. I don't know what a 'consenting' child is. How is he supposed to judge what's being done to him? It is outrageous; we no longer give our children time to mature enough to develop healthy attitudes toward sex before they're inundated by adult demands. Sex is after all only one aspect of human development, and if you sexualize a child below the age of ten, or even at eleven or twelve, it becomes too important, and the rest of his growth is neglected.

"It's an unconscionable abuse. . . . In my own practice I

have the hardest time imaginable treating these children who suffer from incest, even more than the kids who are battered, abused, set on fire, and whipped because at least those children don't confuse what's being done to them with love. The parent who sexually uses a child while telling him, 'I love you,' is raising a child who will be afraid to establish rapport, trust, and engagement with anyone else in his life, even with the therapist, because unlike the beaten child, he doesn't seek affection, he fears affection and becomes extremely isolated. Everything in his life is exploitative.

"At Odyssey House, for example, over forty-four percent of the girls who were in trouble because of drugs or prostitution had also been involved in incest as children. After talking with others in the field who also work with prostitutes and drug addicts, or antisocial women in general, I was told that the figures are anywhere from thirty-two percent to fifty percent. I have said during lectures that we think incest in the general population may be as high as five percent—one out of twenty of all women have been incest victims—and I would estimate the number of women in an audience and tell them, 'If there are a hundred women here, I would expect five of you to be incest victims. If you were, would you drop me a note?' and over the years it has consistently ranged from five percent to twelve percent."

My experience confirms Dr. Densen-Gerber's opinion that there is no incestuous relationship without exploitation that leads to the gravest complications later on—of which the stunting of emotional development is only the beginning.

Unfortunately, few incestuous parents will seek help at one of the clinics or counseling centers until they have already been exposed and are being threatened with legal action unless they agree to intensive family therapy. But the fact that these centers exist, that outside help and hope are being extended to both the sick parent and his child victim, has gone a considerable way toward bringing the unthinkable—but no longer rare—crime of incest out of the shadows.

Chapter 6

RUNAWAYS—
FROM WHAT TO WHERE?

They are not bad kids. It is wrong to think that they are bad kids. They are good kids whose only crime is, for the most part, to be cold, hungry and homeless, with no skills, no resources, cut off from jobs or the possibility of getting medical help or public assistance. Since they have nothing to sell, they are easily victimized by the so-called victimless crime of prostitution.

Why do we permit it? Why and how can such a wholesale abuse of children happen in our society? We seem both unable and unwilling to do anything about it.

Prostitution and this loathsome child abuse are big business and are obviously protected. What other reason could explain the apparent immunity with which this blatant, sick, savage destruction of children is carried on in our society?

*—From the testimony of Father
Bruce Ritter before the Senate
Select Committee on Crime,*
—NOVEMBER 14, 1977

When historians of the future study the social dislocation of our time, they may well find its most significant symptom to be the runaway child. Today, in the midst of our supposedly child-centered affluence, at least one million children leave their homes every year.* Whether they choose to flee or are forced to do so, they are headed for a perilous life on the street, where there is virtually no way to live other than by selling themselves into prostitution or pornography.

While both H.H.S. and the F.B.I. keep tabs on runaways, it is the National Runaway Switchboard which provides figures based on firsthand experience. The N.R.S. is a federally funded "hot line" which was established in 1974 under the auspices of Metro-Help, a Chicago-based organization. A child can dial 800-621-4000, N.R.S.'s toll-free phone number, from anywhere in the United States, at any time of the day or night, to get information about places to "crash" for the night or to get help in returning home. The N.R.S. aims to be a "national, neutral channel between kids and their parents or guardians."

In the first year of its operation, about 30,000 calls came in to 800-621-4000. By 1977, three years later, N.R.S. volunteers and staff were fielding 75,000 calls annually. According to the 1979 figures, 200,000 called; 60 percent of the callers were female, 40 percent of them male. The average age was fourteen. More than one third of the callers wanted to reestablish ties with their families. Forty-seven percent said they were staying with a friend; 36 percent said they were "on the road"; the rest said they were independent or staying with relatives. Twenty-nine percent of the youngsters said they had only been away from home for a few days. The N.R.S. reports a racial breakdown of callers as follows: 76.2 percent, white; 14 percent, black; 5 percent, Spanish; and 4.8 percent, other, including Native Americans.

National Runaway Switchboard statistics show that the majority of teenage runaways are white girls with an average age of fourteen. And, according to H.H.S. statistics, most of them are, as Father Bruce Ritter says, "good kids": "Among the [92 percent] serious runners, 54 percent of all runaways were considered nondelinquent, while 38 percent were delinquent." *

Most experts believe that it is inevitable that the chronic runaways will become prostitutes.

In his 1978 study, Professor Louis Lieberman of John Jay College of Criminal Justice, C.C.N.Y., said:

> . . . a dramatic increase in the number of runaways may have contributed to the (suspected) rise in juvenile prostitution. While there are no convincing data to suggest that runaways comprise a significant percentage of the juvenile prostitution population, there are several reasons to believe they do. First, runaways are rarely financially able to sustain themselves, and employment, outside of prostitution, is difficult to locate in addition to jeopardizing their anonymity. The head of the New York City Police Department's Runaway Unit reports that in 1974, 347 runaways were recovered. Most of these runaways became streetwalking prostitutes. A more recent estimate given to us by the New York City Police Department regarding June 1976–June 1977 runaways was about 450. Of these 450, they estimated about 90 percent went into prostitution (both male and female). They further estimated that only a fraction of runaways who go into prostitution were being located.*

Child welfare authorities are becoming alarmed by the apathy of the general public toward the fate of these children. Clearing the streets of prostitutes is a lively political issue, but, as long as they are swept out of sight, nobody seems to care that many of them are as young as nine or ten. Rarely do we offer these children so much as a shelter for one night; only a handful of cities have halfway houses for runaways.

In this respect, at least, conditions have deteriorated since the 1960's, when running away was a common solution to teenage discontent. The flower-child runaways were older (usually over sixteen); most had some sort of value system they upheld as superior to the society from which they were escaping; and a counterculture existed to absorb them. Such centers as Haight-Ashbury in San Francisco, Denver, the East Village in New York City, and the Los Angeles Strip formed an underground society loosely strung together by a culture of drugs, alienation, and antiwar protest which offered these refugees from middle- and upper-income families a rudimentary identity.

In the 1970's drugs remained part of the runaway scene. But the seventies, in turn, contributed an ominous new development. To the runaways of the sixties were added the "walkaway" and the "throwaway" children who do not have to sneak away from home. The "walkaways" are abandoning the scene of a disaster. As one child put it, "My family crumbled all around me, there was nothing to leave. They left me." The "throwaway" children usually come from a home which is technically intact but doesn't want them around any longer. The throwaways form the class of children who are most likely to get picked up by the police runaway squads, since they are looking for rescue. They find, however, when the police get in touch with their parents, that no one wants them back; indeed, if they try to return home, they are often invited to leave again.

Most runaway children do not go directly from their homes to New York City's "Minnesota Strip" or its equivalent; they tend to follow a certain sequence of tentative excursions before making the final jump. For the first few times, they go to a friend's home; next, to the nearest big city; only on the fourth or fifth attempt do they head for New York or Los Angeles. Thus, they give plenty of warning to anyone who might be interested. A persistent undercurrent of all my interviews with runaways was the implication that these earlier departures were a test to see if anyone cared enough to stop them or showed any concern upon their return. It was the lack of response that propelled them toward the definitive leap.

After age twelve, more girls than boys run away; before that, the proportion of boys increases, as the young ones are more likely to become enmeshed in the twilight world of "chickens" and "chicken hawks" (little boys who become the sexual prey of adult pederasts).* The younger the runaway, the worse the prognosis, as might be expected. The longer the children stay on the streets, the more difficult it becomes to reclaim them later—assuming any efforts are made to do so.

But neglect and indifference are only part of the story; some children have good reason to feel that anywhere at all, even the brutal city street, is preferable to where they came from. I interviewed runaways on the streets where they worked; at central bus terminals; in coffee shops, truancy holding centers, halfway houses, and homes of friends. With many, it was not difficult to gain their confidence once they were convinced that I had nothing to do with the police. It was nevertheless almost impossible to get names or ages from even the most forthcoming, so alarmed were they at the prospect of being returned home. This was especially true of the children who were working on the streets as prostitutes, but I quickly discovered that their resistance did not come so much from fear of punishment by their parents as it did from the threat of being forced to return to the same environment which drove them away in the first place, one which put intolerable sexual pressures upon them. Seventy-two percent of young prostitutes and children involved in pornography have experienced incestuous relationships (usually with the father).* Runaways also report a significantly high incidence of early sexual molestation and precocious sexuality.* They will tell extravagant lies to avoid identification if they believe it will mean being shipped back home—lies which express a deep rage at the family's failure to protect them, or at having been abused by one or both parents: "Both my parents were killed a year ago in a plane crash." "My father and mother got blown up in an accident." Some children are angry at one parent for not protecting them from the other.

The runaway problem has reached such proportions that the federal government has finally been compelled to recognize it officially. In October, 1975, Congress passed the Runaway Youth Act:

> The Congress hereby finds that: 1) the number of juveniles that leave and remain away from home without parental permission has increased to alarming proportions, creating a substantial law enforcement problem for the

communities inundated, and significantly endangering young people who are without resources and live on the street: 2) the exact nature of the problem is not well defined because national statistics on the size and profile of the runaway population are not tabulated: 3) many such young people because of their age and situation, are urgently in need of temporary shelter and counseling services.

These services, however, will not be part of the legal system:

> The problem of locating, detaining, and returning runaway children should not be the responsibility of already over-burdened police departments and juvenile justice authorities, and 5) in view of the interstate nature of the problem it is the responsibility of the federal government to develop accurate reporting of the problem nationally and to develop an effective system of temporary care outside the law enforcement structure.*

I hope to make clear in this chapter the nature of this structure outside the law and how ineffectual the current laws are. Nor do I believe there are adequate funds for dealing with the runaway problem. Under the Juvenile Justice and Delinquency Prevention Act of 1974, $10 million was allotted to deal with runaways every year from 1975 to 1977 and, from September 30, 1978, $25 million each year for 1978, 1979, and 1980.* This law is only a minor step in recognizing the severity of the problem faced by American families.

In talking to members of the police runaway squads, one is struck by their concern for these children. The officers are often deeply angered by the tragic waste of young lives they witness daily, and work long hours overtime trying to help youngsters. That help most often must be limited, pathetically, to finding them a safe place to stay for the night. Usually the police can do little because many children fall between the jurisdiction of the juvenile courts (few have been arrested for any crime) and the welfare system. The laws themselves are contradictory and chaotic, varying widely from state to state, and only confuse efforts to help children who have crossed state lines.

One of the agencies first set up to help runaway children in distress was Project Contact, which began in 1968 as part of the Educational Alliance in New York City. It was founded and directed by an energetic man named Robert Meltzer. Meltzer spoke of the peculiar difficulties and dangers he encountered in attempting to hale children out of the pimp system; in some cases he had to renegotiate with the children themselves for their own relief once he had succeeded in buying them back. "Buying kids back from the pimps, as we often did in the early days, was a very hairy scene, let me tell you." The price of a child varied, depending on sex, attractiveness, and age.

One development new to the seventies has been the practice among young girls of selling their unwanted illegitimate babies. "Babies bring a set price of four hundred dollars—white ones, that is," Meltzer said. Some resourceful boys—often themselves runaways—act as "steerers," collecting finder's fees from couples seeking to adopt one of these babies or from the lawyers acting in their behalf. These boys are also paid by pimps for introducing girls into their network; for each young girl that they bring into a pimp's stable, they receive a fee ranging from $200 to $250.

All the agencies which have sprung up, like Meltzer's, to offer shelter and protection to these children are of course well acquainted with the pimps who run the children. But when asked, "Why don't you call in the police?" they invariably reply, as Meltzer did, "We have a problem with it. I know that's a hell of a statement, but you have to understand that if you call the police you destroy your credibility, and the kids stop coming in, too."

Whenever these agencies do feel the need to call upon the police, most of them report a high degree of efficiency, helpfulness, and tact: "They have even worked with us on an unofficial basis, using their presence as a kind of lever, and they really can be very helpful—for example, leaning on a pimp occasionally to release a child when no other action could have been as immediate or as effective. There are, let's say, occasional misunderstandings, but by and large the vice squads and runaway squads do understand the nature of our problems, and they've always made themselves available to us."

A model program, the Youth Assistance Project, was set up in 1976 in New York City by the Port Authority. It was funded at first by the federal government, then, when that money ran out, by the Port Authority of New York and New Jersey. The Port Authority bus terminal is the terminus for runaway children who gravitate to New York from all over the country. Through the project, teams of police officers and social workers patrol the station, hoping to intercept arriving children before they fall into the hands of the pimps, chicken hawks, and pornographers who are continually cruising the area looking for naïve, susceptible, and hungry arrivals.

Until recently, the director of the Port Authority Runaway Squad Police was Sergeant Jose Elique, himself the father of three young children:

"I know what it's like; my own background has been very helpful in relating to these runaway children. I see myself in them, only I was lucky. I survived the drug culture, I survived gang warfare, but I see it still going on to a large extent today, and unfortunately these adolescent children are more prone to listening to their peers than their parents.

"I always tell these children just what I say to my own kids, 'You don't have to believe me, but one day in your life you're going to realize that what your parents are telling you now, their worries and apprehensions, will be yours, because you'll have children of your own—but only if you're lucky.' Some of the kids we pick up we classify as 'throwaway children'; it's an ugly term, but there's no other way to describe them. These kids have been literally ejected from their homes and have absolutely no place to go. Some of them get processed through the juvenile system, but the city unfortunately isn't geared to handle the epidemic problem of these kids. In 1977 alone we had close to thirty-seven hundred juveniles, with one out of every four turning out to be a runaway—not only from New York State, but from everywhere in the United States. And, of course, for every one we pick up, there are probably five or ten we never get to see.

"You see, once we pick them up, we can't interview them right out there on the floor of the Port Authority terminal, so we have to bring them back here to conduct an investigation, so to speak. Often they lie profusely right from the beginning. You have to realize the mentality of a runaway. A kid who has left his home is trying to tell you something—he does not want to be home! He has been arrested—for a crime, as far as he sees—but he still does not want to tell you the truth because he just refuses to go home. Eventually, when they realize that this is the end of the line, that until they tell me who they are and I've verified the information they've given me, they're not going anyplace—then they begin to cooperate.

"When a child first runs away, he may have a few bucks in his pocket, he may even have saved some money, but once it runs out, he has few options. Unfortunately, all the kids seem to flock to this midtown area, which is loaded with all sorts of undesirables, people who are just waiting for the chance to victimize children. When the kids get hungry, they have to eat, and when they get cold, they have to find shelter, so they really don't have too many alternatives. If someone happens to approach them when they're really hungry and down and out and asks them to do something—it could be any number of illegal or degrading immoral acts, for money or drugs—then this child will be much more receptive, no matter how he may have felt about sex and drugs before.

"I just had a girl come in here who arrived on a bus earlier today. She told us that she had been approached by a man who later subjected her to criminal sexual acts. He unlawfully incarcerated her in a hotel room somewhere on this street. She had some information as to his whereabouts, and we're going to go after him.

"With all the peep shows and the tremendous amount of sexually oriented material in every storefront in this area, they can't be closed down—the law can't do anything. People aren't stupid; they say, 'I have my rights, if this is what I want, this is what I do,' and these men go right after what they want. Any guy who wants a ten-year-old boy today, he's likely to have the nerve now to go out and try to purchase one. A few years ago he may have thought, I'd like to do this, but I don't think I'd better because I may really get into trouble.' But now the lid is off, and it's as though something's wrong with him if he doesn't indulge every fantasy he's ever had.

"But for the kid who gets involved in it, it can be a tragedy. If he didn't know what was happening to him, only knew he was hungry and cold, when the truth finally hits him and the dream is over, when the lights no longer excite and he has to eat and get down to basics, what can he do? This is when the kid really gets disillusioned and bitter. But *still* these kids don't want to go home. I can count on the fingers of one hand the kids who walk in and say, 'I'm a runaway, send me home.' One in a thousand might do that. These kids *don't want to go back*, that's why the recidivism rate is as high as it is.

"One problem is that if a kid has been caught here by us and returned home, he remembers, and the next time he runs away he goes out of his way to avoid being caught. Unfortunately, he's learned how to stay out of our hands. We've had children here as young as ten. What's interesting is that the little girls are much tougher—I mean twelve- and thirteen-year-old girls who are actively engaged in prostitution. They will tell you, 'I've been doing this since I was nine,' and unfortunately I have learned to believe them. We just had two girls here last week, thirteen and fourteen. They were both white, Caucasian and Anglo-Saxon, but they spoke Spanish so fluently that, even though it's my native tongue, if I closed my eyes and listened to them, I would have sworn that one of them was Spanish and the other a black woman. They learn to imitate blacks and Hispanics hoping to pass, and some of them get so good at it, it's frightening.

"Just yesterday we had a fourteen-year-old girl come in here, a runaway from out of state. She told us that when she arrived, about four or five days earlier, she'd gone right out on the streets with a couple of girl friends, fourteen and fifteen, had spent a couple of days just hanging around, then they were approached by a man who befriended them, bought them coffee, and offered them a place to stay. They accepted, stayed with him for about two days, then he told them, 'Okay, now you have to pay me back.' And the form of payment he wanted was for them to work for him on the streets as prostitutes.

"Two of them agreed to it—they were in fear for their safety —but this girl who came into my office refused. So he separated her from the others, put her in another room, and sent the other two girls out with two more girls he already had working the streets. Then he beat this girl, he raped her, slapped her around, tortured her, took a straightened wire hanger, and inserted it into her vagina to puncture any of her internal organs that he could reach with it. When she came in here, she was bleeding all over the place, so we took her to the hospital. She didn't even come in here asking for help; we picked her up on the floor of the bus terminal, walking around bleeding. Somehow she had got away from him, he turned his back or something, and she just sneaked away. She supplied us with enough information so that we could go apprehend this guy, and he was arrested.

"I don't know what will happen to him because the courts are strange places when it comes to prosecuting pimps or other sex offenders—nothing much ever happens. You know, what really bothers me about this, the sad part, besides what this girl went through, is that we didn't find the other two girls, her two friends. We went out on patrol very extensively looking for them, but we never did find them. Many of these kids that come here for excitement find that they get much more than they bargained for.

"It's a little different with the boys; for them it's the shame aspect of it. The boys that are involved in the male prostitution trade will tell you, if they tell you anything, 'I'm not a homosexual—*he's* the homosexual, he's paying me to perform an act on me, *I'm* not doing anything.' But deep inside they know that's a lie. I'm talking about the little blond twelve- and thir-teen-year-old boys—these are the kids I personally have had the most contact with.

"Although many of these kids run away and then find them-selves stuck on the street as if by chance, the fact is they're at a crisis in their lives, and we try to intervene at that point and nip it in the bud if we can. It could be a turning point for them. That's what's unique about the Youth Assistance Project here—our social workers counsel the runaways whom we apprehend. In many cases we will counsel the family as a unit because we always try to insist upon the parents coming down here to get their kids in person if it's at all possible. That way we have everybody here together. But if we *don't* succeed in nipping it in the bud—and that's what we're here for—we get some awful tragedies. Just this morning they called to tell me they found some kid's body upstate in a ditch, and two weeks ago a young girl's body, twelve years old, was in pieces in a trunk."

At the other pole of the runaway axis, the Los Angeles Po-lice Department has created its own juvenile vice unit, the only one in the country so far. The pressure of the flood of children and adolescents surging into the city was taxing the regular vice units far beyond their resources. A juvenile unit was pro-posed by Sergeant Lloyd Martin who, after seven years of ser-vice on the regular vice squad, saw the other investigators becoming swamped with the problems of runaway children to the exclusion of all other work. Overcoming some initial re-sistance to funding it, the unit began operations in June, 1977, as the Sexually Exploited Child Unit of the Juvenile Division, under Sergeant Martin's direction.

Sergeant Martin, who is the father of three teenagers, feels that one aspect of the runaway problem, up to now virtually ignored, is particularly urgent. Society has always acknowl-edged the need to protect little girls from sexual molestation, but that little boys are just as vulnerable to sexual exploitation has not been so generally recognized.

"Actually, there are several aspects to the sexual exploitation

of children," Sergeant Martin said, "the first being the child molester, by which I mean an adult, male or female, who receives
sexual gratification from a child. A chicken hawk is an adult
male who receives sexual gratification from little boys only. The
whole area of sexual exploitation includes child prostitution,
where you deal with the pimp, and the model agencies which
service the pornographic magazines. You might have a girl, for
instance, who appears to be eighteen years old but who in fact
is only fourteen, and the model agent procures the girl for this
type of activity knowing perfectly well how young she is.

"The sexually exploited child is a noncomplaining, willing
victim. They don't complain to their parents, they don't come
to the police, and therefore there is no report, and of course no
statistics. We do know that the sexually exploited child is usually either a runaway or a child from a broken home. I think
Senator Birch Bayh's subcommittee on juvenile delinquency
found that we had a million reported runaways in our nation
every year; that's probably eighty-five to ninety percent of the
true number. A lot of children who may have run away three
or four times are nevertheless not reported as runaways.

"None of these kids have any marketable skills, of course,
and the only way they can survive is by prostituting themselves;
they live by pulling up their dresses or pulling down their
pants. I don't know of a soul who takes runaways in off the
street without getting something in return, and it's usually sex.
The chicken hawk looks for the child from a broken home, or
a runaway, so he can move in and play the father role. An ideal
situation for a chicken hawk would be a broken home with just
a mother and five boys.

"I'm talking more about boys than girls because in our society when we say 'child molester,' everybody thinks of a dirty
old man with a trench coat and a sack of jelly beans saying with
a leer, 'Candy, little girl?' That's not the way it happens anymore, but still nobody thinks about little boys, although in my
opinion at least as many young boys are being sexually molested
out there as girls, or even more today. The figures for this area
show that it's between seventy and seventy-five percent boys

to twenty-five percent girls, which comes as a surprise
people. I recently arrested a guy who told me he'd
Hollywood for eight years, and in that time he'd had five thousand different boys, mostly at his home. Another man, a sixty-
two-year-old chicken hawk, is the nicest guy I ever met in my
life. He told me he'd had a boy a day for thirty years. So you
can see that the number of children who pass through the hands
of all the chicken hawks in the area is something really phe-
nomenal.

"The way I spot them, I notice somebody who seems to be
paying more attention to a child than a normal parent would—
that's always a giveaway. They spend hours hanging out where
the kids do, they seek employment around them, they volunteer
to work for welfare groups or social service agencies that get
a lot of kids asking for help. They tend to be very specific in
their requirements as to age, body size, and type, and you'll
usually find, ironically, that the hawk or molester is that particular child's best friend.

"When I first went after them and the porno producers and
the pimps, I would ask them 'How many children in the Los
Angeles area are being sexually exploited?' Taking an average,
we came up with a figure of at least thirty thousand a year in
the city alone. It came out in the paper that at least thirty
thousand children under eighteen were involved in the sex industry here, but now I think that's a conservative figure. But I
don't like to play the numbers game anymore; what I say now
is that if there's one child in Los Angeles who's being sexually
exploited, sexually abused, then we should take strong action.
Last year alone, we arrested over a hundred adults who were
sexually abusing children.

"By the time the child is over fourteen, you're talking about
an accomplice; they're considered accomplices, and you need
corroboration for a conviction because just on their testimony
alone—when you can get them to testify—you cannot convict
anybody. The willing victim is a difficult situation. What you
really need for corroboration is somebody else actually witnessing the sex act, but obviously this is very difficult. But because

of the aggressiveness of these men and the number of children they go through, surprisingly often you get a situation where somebody did see it. Or you may have a child not necessarily seeing the sex act itself, but sitting in the other room when the man takes the other child in the bedroom, and sometimes that's accepted as corroboration. Also, most child molesters and chicken hawks like to photograph their victims, and that can be used in court.

"What we do know is that the number of these adults and their victims is colossal. In late September, 1976, we started a task force against child molesters, and that first month alone we identified over three hundred people who were sexually involved with children in the Los Angeles area. That got into the papers, people became concerned and wrote letters, and in July, 1977, we became a permanent unit, with me in charge.

"The maximum time right now in the state of California that a person convicted of crimes against a child can be imprisoned for is three years. For the second offense, it's four years, and for the third through the hundredth offense, five years. The most important fact about sex offenders against children is that I've never yet seen one who changed his ways. All of them are recidivists, and the minute they're released, they go right back to their same old habits and haunts. As far as I know, there is no treatment for them. On the other hand, I know of no qualified psychologist or psychiatrist who can treat the willing victim. We know how to handle forced victims of incest and physical abuse because that gets brought to the attention of the police department and then to the social workers and so forth, but the willing victims don't complain.

"You see, when a chicken hawk picks a child, *he wants that child*, and he'll go to any amount of trouble to get him. And let's say it's a broken-home situation, the child's got nothing, then the chicken hawk suddenly comes into his life, pays all kinds of attention to him twenty-four hours a day, and now that child's got everything—I mean the ultimate. Then he gets a little older, and just as suddenly he's the wrong age—let's say he's now ten and the hawk only likes eight- or nine-year-olds—

then he gets dropped down to nothing again. That's exactly how you destroy a kid—by dumping him. Once you take away a person's self-respect, what's left? Once you do that to a person, what can he be in our society except a criminal? He doesn't care who he hurts because he's been so badly hurt himself, he's been destroyed.

"I've talked to at least a thousand chicken hawks and child molesters and probably another thousand victims, and there's almost nothing we can do. We're helpless if the child refuses to testify against the hawk, as he usually does. Another thing that doesn't make life any easier for us is the number of organizations now that openly advocate child sex—the Paedophiliac Information Exchange, the Child Sexuality Circle in San Diego, Better Life, Hermes, operating out of Chicago, and the Guyon Society here in Los Angeles—all of these groups are promoting sex with children. The latest thing now is father-son sex clubs, and of course there again—especially there—you don't get any complaining victims. There is no violation of the law; it must be proven that someone actually did it before we could step in; and since we have freedom of speech in this country, they can say anything they want to and get away with it.

"I first got involved in 1973 when I was working on the vice squad, and we found a consistent pattern: One particular child would be seduced, that child would procure two more, those two would find four, so it spread out very fast, just from that single episode. We began to feel that we were soon going to be facing a problem that was increasing like wildfire, a geometric progression. We're the only unit of its kind, but the exploiters of children don't live only here in Los Angeles. The first case I ever handled, we ended up going up to Redwood City and serving a search warrant there, then to San Francisco, and finally to Concord, where a schoolteacher was procuring boys for this particular suspect—so it's not a localized problem.

"I see our morality sinking and our family structure going down as well. I was on the Merv Griffin show a little while ago with Robert Blake, the actor, and he said we should have a place for these kids to go and get love. Of course he's right, but who in the hell are we going to hire to supply that? How do you buy love? I know that this unit is not going to stop child pornography in Los Angeles; we'll never be able to do that as long as there's one camera and one man who gets sexual gratification from a child.

"Other cities have not really faced up to the problem. They tell me it doesn't exist where they are; they say, 'It's too bad you have such a serious problem in Los Angeles. We feel sorry for you.' But they've got exactly the same problem themselves —every city does. Look at Boise, Idaho, just a few years ago— they simply refuse to recognize it." *

This frustration at the public's failure to recognize rampant sexual abuse of children as an undeniable fact of life was echoed by Glen Sousa, Supervising Investigator of prostitution for the Los Angeles Police Department:

"Our experience has been over the past few years that the girls on the street are getting younger and younger; approximately twenty-five percent of our arrests for prostitution are juveniles under eighteen. With children that age, there seem to be more boys than girls getting arrested, but one reason for that may be the fact that you can tell a boy's age more accurately. A girl can get away with presenting herself as much older than she is. But even allowing for that, thirty percent of our prostitutes in Los Angeles are young males; in Hollywood it's as high as fifty percent. And that's just the street boys— there are a lot we never see on the street at all; they work out of a call circuit for a directory service. Highland Avenue in Los Angeles, east of Hollywood Boulevard, is called the 'meat block.' It's predominantly boys, but runaway girls can be sheltered there, too. Various people shelter them—mostly exploiters and degenerates, although sometimes a sympathetic soul will shelter them without asking for anything in return. But that's rare.

"Nowadays these children come from all over—not only geographically but from every class. I've handled prostitutes from social backgrounds that included executives' families, professional families, some very wealthy families. It's not only a lower-class profile anymore."

In San Francisco, sometimes called the "gay capital of America," an even higher proportion of the younger prostitutes are boys, according to Police Captain George Eimil:

"In the city of San Francisco last year there were three thousand arrests for prostitution, including all ages, male and female—and you must remember that San Francisco is a small city, we only have six hundred thousand people. In the younger groups, from ten to sixteen, the proportion is approximately sixty percent boys to forty percent girls. One place was working ten or twelve boys out on the streets, besides using them for pornographic films and photographs. They were also being sent out of the state for prostitution—the client would pay for an airline ticket, and they'd fly anywhere in the country. You begin to realize these kids can be an important industry in themselves. We've found that most of their parents have just given up; they leave them alone, let them come here and do whatever they want to. They feel they can't stop them.

"Our big problem is that in 1976 they changed the law so that a runaway arrested in California is not kept under locked conditions. He's taken up to a detention facility—the Youth Guidance Center, an unlocked facility—which means that we pick them up and they just walk out. They can't be kept there, so they're never returned to their parents. Almost the minute we pick them up they're back out on the street unless we can prove specific acts of prostitution. No matter what age. If you have a six-year-old runaway, the sad state of the law is that he can walk right out of the place. And anyone having sex with a child under fourteen is committing a felony, but with any age over fourteen, it's called 'unlawful sexual conduct,' with a much lighter sentence.

"In this area we've got a couple of hundred amateur pimps. As soon as a girl gets off the Greyhound bus here, she's approached by some guy who's an aspiring pimp. He's never done it in his whole life, but he's seen the way these guys operate and he wants to imitate them. Our policewomen down there have made many arrests for pimping. The guys try to turn them on the minute they appear, thinking they just got into town. Pimping has become such a standard occupation, it even has its trainees."

It is clear from these interviews that most of the professionals who come into contact with these children through our legal or social welfare institutions are deeply stirred by the seriousness of the problem, but at the same time they feel helpless to deal with it—perhaps because they realize too well that at their level the only help they can offer is so transitory as to be almost meaningless.

No one is more bitterly eloquent on the subject of society's ultimate indifference to its "throwaway" children than Father Bruce Ritter, an angry, impassioned Franciscan priest, formerly a medieval scholar. Almost singlehandedly, with little political or church support, he has made a "clean, well-lighted place" of an old building on Eighth Avenue and Forty-fourth Street in the heart of New York City's brutal commercial-sex world.

Here any child under twenty-one who is in trouble can stay for a night or two. In its first year almost 5,000 children sought help at Under 21, as Father Ritter's center is called. Of those, 900 were under fifteen; 1,200 between sixteen and seventeen; and 2,900 were between eighteen and twenty-one. Between 60 and 70 percent of the children have been involved in prostitution. A trained staff provides counseling, shelter, and meals.

Father Ritter tells how he got involved in helping runaways over ten years ago:

"My students at Fordham challenged me to put my beliefs into action, so I went to work in one of the poorest parishes in New York, on the Lower East Side. Very late one night I heard a knock at my door, and there were six little kids standing outside. It was bitter cold and snowing hard, and they asked if they could come in and sleep on my floor. Of course I said yes, gave them some food and blankets, and they lay right down in a row on my floor and went to sleep. The next morning one of the younger kids went out for a few minutes and came back with four more. 'This is our family,' he told me, and I learned that these particular ten children—the oldest was sixteen—came from all over the country and had been living together in one of the abandoned buildings on my block, taking care of each other. The previous night the junkies had burned them out because they wanted to pimp them and exploit them sexually, and these kids had already had quite enough of that. They'd spent several days before arriving in the East Village in Yonkers, where a couple had taken them in, but the price they had to pay was to appear in a pornographic movie, which they did. They got out of that scene as soon as they could, came down here, and then got burned out.

"Well, I couldn't find any place for them in the child welfare system. To do that, you pretty much have to have them arrested first and I couldn't do that, so I just kept them. I got some old bunk beds and the kids lived there in the apartment with me. I intended it to be temporary, I had no desire to achieve instant fatherhood, but that was the beginning of Covenant House because those kids had absolutely nowhere to go, nobody wanted them. They were truly desperate—and society didn't even recognize their need.

"The problem of urban nomadism is certainly increasing; there are many reasons for that, but an important one is a change in the law about ten years ago eradicating the category of wayward minor from the statutes. Now the law permits children here in New York State, once they reach their sixteenth birthday, to 'emancipate' themselves. They can literally walk away from their homes, and it is almost impossible legally to get them back. It can only be done by taking out a writ of habeas corpus in the Supreme Court, and even then a jury trial will be held to decide whether or not in fact the child is 'self-emancipated,' so it's an impossible procedure.

"The problem of child pornography is directly related to prostitution, which is the inevitable result of homeless, hungry children wandering the streets. I've never yet met a kid involved in pornography who wasn't also prostituting himself. Our center right now has about sixty kids in it, most of them into prostitution, as young as thirteen, fourteen, fifteen. A lot of the lost children we have here end up in the sex trade—from my experience I would estimate two thirds of them; slightly more boys than girls.

"Our district attorney, Mr. _____, stoutly maintains that prostitution is a victimless crime, and yet in the last three years, almost two hundred prostitutes have been murdered in this city, including recently a twelve-year-old. She had stayed in our center at one point. Then we had Gail Alexander, seventeen years old; her body was cut up in a dozen pieces.

"What we're doing is only a stopgap, obviously. This is big business we're talking about; both the real estate industry and the people in organized crime control the pornography trade. The fact is that the sex industry, which in a ten-block radius around this point alone is making a billion and a half dollars a year, is protected by our police, our politicians, our judges. Judges will not sentence, prosecutors will not prosecute, police will not enforce, because we as a society have decided that this really perverse thing is an adult zone, there's no harm in it. Yet most of the people who are used in this so-called adult zone are adolescents, some of them retarded, and many of the adults who use them are vicious, cruel people.

"There are eight hundred pimps working this area alone, and they control thousands and thousands of girls. At least six of them run call services—you can pay for these kids with your MasterCard. They're really telephone answering services, and they arrange everything between the client and the child prostitute. The word on the street these days, as the pimps say sardonically, is 'Johns prefer chickens.' And the pimps prefer to use the call services; they can risk sending their chickens to apartments and offices and homes because they can verify phone numbers and addresses. A lot of the hungry kids on the street will sell themselves for five or ten dollars, but twenty dollars is the going price, and a call boy can get forty-five dollars, up to one hundred dollars, or even two hundred dollars.

"I've been threatened many times for speaking up, and a lot of knives have been held at me, but I have no choice when

I've seen what happens to a kid over a period of time. The worst part of it is that children have no understanding of consequences. They haven't developed any kind of insight, while attitudes form very quickly. This means that if you put a kid in the sex industry, he's going to split himself in two. For a while he's going to stay inside one half of his head and decide, 'What I am over here is good and that's me, and what I do over there is something else.' But gradually the two sides begin to merge, and the attitudes almost invariably follow the activity, not vice versa. We used to think that the kid got into the industry because of bad attitudes and then healed when he stopped, but that's not so—it's pretty much always the other way around. A kid gets into prostitution because he has to survive, he has no place to go; and then once he's involved, the attitudes that justify it take shape. Sometimes they even reach the point where the kid starts proselytizing. He is now hooked.

"Some of them can be saved; about twelve to fifteen percent go home, but a large proportion stay with the sex industry. If a kid has been on the street for three years hustling up and down Eighth Avenue, you know he's not going to make it. He dies. Often he dies physically, but I mean that he almost always dies emotionally. There is a kid in the center right now, a beautiful kid, seventeen, can't read or write. He's been on the street three years now, and I guess he's jumped in a thousand cars and slept with a thousand men. He's an alcoholic, too, and he asked me the other day, 'Bruce, can you give me one good reason why I shouldn't jump off the Brooklyn Bridge?' And I couldn't think of any. I lied to him; I lied. I made up reasons that sounded good, but I suspect he knew I was lying. A beautiful kid, a very bright kid, too, and he's not going to make it, he's got no future.

"We have another boy, he used to be nice but not anymore; he's no longer even good-looking. He's been a hustler since he was at least fourteen—a go-go boy. He dances on top of a bar in the Village. The johns like him, they always stick a five-dollar bill in his jockstrap—when he wears a jockstrap. Every now and then he gets an engagement at one of the male burlesque houses—like the Ram Rod, four performances a night—

but he makes most of his money servicing the customers. He lives in the Continental Baths; the management gives him a cheap room there. Sixteen years old.

"We have in our files hundreds and hundreds of cases of kids brutalized, beaten, tortured, and raped by their pimps; and yet prostitution is still called a victimless crime. And the increase in the demand for these kids is our own doing; our society has stimulated the demand for the supply. I think it's true that there always has to be something under the counter, and thirty years ago what was under the counter were stick drawings and some very modest hard-core pornography. It was highly illegal, and you were considered pretty sick if you didn't keep it out in the garage somewhere buried under a pile of old tires. Gradually, under the umbrella of the First Amendment, we permitted that stuff to come out from hiding and sit right there on the shelf. Later the hard-core porn and the bestiality and the sadomasochism came out on the shelf, with the child pornography still under the counter; then, when that went out in the open, underneath were the snuff films; and it's stayed that way now for the last couple of years. People can openly and without any embarrassment ask for films or magazines showing a six-year-old child having sex with another six-year-old or with an adult. It's not in any way illegal.

"Some of the pimps I've met, even, aren't any older than fifteen or sixteen. I've got a list here of about eight hundred pimps, just for laughs—everybody around here knows who they are, but nobody touches them—and the only amusing thing about this whole business is some of their nicknames: Buffalo, Brown Sugar, Big Boy, Bird Dog, Big Time, Buck Butch, Boo Boo, Black Sam, Beau Ray, Blue Jesus, Big Slim, Blood, Big John, Baby Ray, Bad Marvin, Bo Peep, Buddy Red, Baby Brother, Boozie, Baby James, Cowboy, Cornbread, Champagne. You can see from that the fantasy life, the self-created myths that are at work here."

Many studies examine the relationship between pimp and prostitute, detailing the brutality and exploitation involved. But it is worth noting here that when the prostitute is a child, the relationship takes on father-daughter aspects:

> He is providing something that normal society had taken away from these women. They have condemned her so that the only alternative for her is either that of a lesbian relationship for emotional satisfaction or that of the pimp relationship. The pimp in essence does promise to provide help for the women and bail in case there is a legal problem. But in essence what it comes down to is he is providing just an emotional relationship, something that she has to settle with.*

People like Father Ritter are unhappily aware that their efforts to rescue a few runaway children can do little except publicize the seriousness of the problem. They all feel that the most essential point to get across is that we must stop thinking of the sexual abuse of children as an aberration; we must recognize it as an inevitable consequence of an increasingly sexualized society which is frantically seeking release from its profound and widespread frustrations.

Father Ritter, the police, and the social welfare agencies see most of these children at the end point of a process that has been set in motion much earlier. When one hears the children speak for themselves, their awareness seems to float in and out of focus. Sometimes they are sharply conscious of themselves as victims; at other times they seem stoically accepting of whatever may happen to them; at still other times the events they are describing seem to have happened to someone else, as though they have depersonalized their experiences as a defense against intolerable anger and pain.

Here is Ruth, who left home for good at the age of twelve:

"My mother remarried when I was six. Her husband began taking a special interest in me when I was about nine and got my first period. I would be lying down on the couch watching television after dinner, and he'd lie down next to me, start fondling me, and masturbate himself while my mother was in the kitchen. I had no idea at all then what was going on. Then he began wanting to make sure I was getting myself clean when I washed or showered, and at nine or ten I didn't mind too much having him watch me, but he would play with himself at the same time.

"As I got older, he began to accuse me of doing this or that in school, in the school closet with boys, although I never did anything with anybody. And he was always criticizing the way I dressed; he hated me to wear miniskirts. While all of this was going on, he used to threaten me constantly. If I ever said anything to my mother, he'd see to it that I was very sorry, and I guess she never did know much about what was going on. He was the king of the house, the supreme authority, and it was a big ego trip for him. Here he is in his late fifties, and suddenly there's a young girl in his life, along with his new wife.

"As he became more aggressive and demanding, I began to resist, and we slapped each other around quite a bit because I would always fight back—at some point I realized that what he was doing to me wasn't right. And sometimes he would really smack me around. They weren't actually all that bad, the beatings; they looked worse than they were because my nose bled very easily, so there would be blood all over the place and my clothes would be all ripped off. If my mother happened to come in and see what was happening, she'd get slapped around, too, and it would be even worse for me after that.

"This continued until I was around twelve; then one day when my mother wasn't home, it got really bad. Finally, in the thick of it, he said, 'I'm going to fuck you!' We'd been having an argument, and he said, 'I'm really going to fuck you, you know!' And he started after me. Stupidly, instead of running outside, I ran upstairs to my room. He chased me as if he was going to kill me, and I really became hysterical. My jeans got ripped, but he didn't rape me—not that time. But it was obvious that sooner or later he would.

"A week before my thirteenth birthday, my mother finally got the message, and left him and took me to the home of a friend. But we only stayed there for a couple of weeks. She ended up going back to him because, as she explained to me, he was a good man, he did take care of us, and nobody's perfect. She's a very weak woman, and anyway she'd been out of work for a while and didn't have any money. When I told her I wasn't going to go with her, she wanted to know what I was going to do instead. 'I don't know,' I said, 'but I'm going anywhere but back to him,' and I walked out the door. That was the first time I ran away.

"I had twenty dollars and a change of clothes, and I was only thirteen. I got on a bus not even knowing where it was heading, only that wherever it went it would take me away from home. On the bus I met a guy who was going to the hospital to steal some syringes to sell for dope. He was a junkie but an okay guy, and he let me stay with him. A week later I called my girl friend, and we arranged to meet in a park near her house, but I never got there because I hitched a ride and the guy who gave me a lift raped me. I'd had sex with the junkie, but that was no big deal, he was too busy trying to hustle. And, of course, I was using no birth control; in fact, I had no conception of sex at all. All I knew was what my stepfather had been trying to do to me, so this rape was really my first experience. And as a runaway, I couldn't even report it to the cops.

"I went back to my friend's house, called my mother and stepfather, and they said, 'Either you come home or we'll call the police.' 'Well, I'm not coming home,' I told them. I didn't think they'd want the police coming around, especially my stepfather, but they did call the cops. He wanted me back under his control.

"So I got sent to Juvenile Court, and while I was getting booked they told me that if they took me in with all the lesbians and bad people in there, and me so young, it would really mess me up. The cop who was booking me said this. But I said, 'I don't care, I'm going anyway. I'm not going home, I've just really made up my mind.' It was better in jail than back home with him.

"I stayed there for a week. The first day I thought I was going to die. I woke up to hear someone screaming, and there I was locked into this cell; I didn't know what was happening. I started screaming myself, 'Let me out of here!' and banging on the wall. But there was nothing anybody could do; the probation officer had to wait for a foster home, and that takes time. In the meantime, they didn't want to keep me in Juvenile Hall because I wasn't really a delinquent. So far I've just been a victim, both at home and out on the streets.

"So I got sent home again. But now whenever he hit me, it was instant hate. I got really scared. I couldn't stand him anymore, and after a few weeks I split again. I was too scared to stay with him. I went back to the junkie—I didn't know where else to go. This was in an all-black section in the San Francisco Bay area, and I stood out starkly. I had never taken drugs before, but all he gave me was some marijuana, and only because I asked if I could try it. He told me all the other stuff was just not any good, and if he ever saw me taking it, he'd kill me. But I did sell for him, and I was also holding the dope so he wouldn't be arrested for it; if I got caught, the rap wouldn't be too heavy on me. I began carrying the knife, too, the switchblade knife.

"One night I couldn't get back into the hotel where we were staying because he was out selling. I didn't have a key. He always had to sneak me in because it was obvious that I was a minor. I'm petite now, but at thirteen I really looked little. I had no dope on me at the time, but I did have the switchblade knife and some pills. Anyway, I couldn't get in, and I was standing at the phone booth trying to call him when the cops came patrolling. I was the only white person there. They must have realized then that I was a runaway, and I had these pills and the switchblade. They took me into the room and said, 'Do you have anything on you? Because if you do, you'd better get rid of it,' and one cop said, 'I won't say anything about it, I'll just ignore it.' So I got rid of everything and gave them the switchblade, and they took me down to Juvenile Hall for the second time. They didn't charge me with anything, though; it was really very nice of them.

"I was only being held as a runaway now. I guess I was lucky, but even just for being a runaway they kept me there for 151 days. And after that I still couldn't go home. I had the same probation officer, so she knew my situation and she was just as ineffective as she'd been before. I was too advanced now to be in Girls' Home; after all, I'd been experienced on the streets, but one of my uncles read about a convent and decided that was the place for me. They had a good residential school run by the nuns. You had to go to church every morning. It was a very nice place, with five or six cottages where we lived. That was where I got the news about my grandmother dying. She was the only person who understood or loved me. She'd taken care of me when my parents first split.

"I spent eighteen months at the convent, and they tried brainwashing me, programming me, whatever it is they're supposed to do, until I supposedly got my head straight. It had barbed wire and chicken wire and everything else except guards, and they went by the point system. If you put on too much makeup, if you dressed wrong, if you talked in church, that meant your time was extended. The earliest possible time you could get out was after four months, and there was no way I could make that. I kept blowing it, especially after my grandmother died.

Then one day, instead of carrying books, I took my regular clothes and changed out of the convent uniform in the bathroom. As I was approaching the front door, this old nun was wheeling a very old man in a wheelchair. I said, 'Can you let me out?' very politely because the gate was locked. But I had a pair of scissors—not dull scissors either—and I was going to do something, I was determined to get out of there. I was absolutely ready to kill her, but she let me out right away. Outside I ran into a nurse who knew me, but she didn't try to stop me either.

"So I got to San Francisco. I was completely lost, walking up and down the street. I walked for three hours, and it was getting very cold. I ended up in the Fillmore district. I always seemed to gravitate to the black section of any town; they're the ones who are going to pick you up first anyway—and finally someone came along who did. He didn't mess with me, though. He was an older man and he was with me, but the next morning I just left. I had ten dollars stashed in my boots.

"Outside I ran into another junkie, but this one was going to turn me out on the street and make me into a prostitute—fourteen, I was then. That was some year I had at fourteen, wasn't it? He took me on a shopping spree, bought me all kinds of clothes, grown-up clothes that made me look sexy, like a little baby doll. He got me high-heeled shoes and everything; he spent about three hundred dollars on me just in one day, in fact. That was when I realized he wanted to turn me out.

"We took everything back to his place, and then he said, 'I have to take care of business,' and he got a friend to come in and watch me. This friend, John, wanted to get a grab at me before I went out to work on the streets, so I said to him, 'Get me out of here, and I'll be with you.' 'All right,' he said and took me to his cousin's place, so that when the first pimp came back, I had split with all my clothes and everything. John had prepared some story for him, so I conned him, too. He had to go back to explain to the first guy that I had run off. Now the cousin's after me. So I said, 'All right' to him, too; he was older and didn't look as if he was going to force anything on me. I asked him, 'Just take me to the subway station across the Bay to familiar ground, okay?' So he did, and I left with all the clothes.

"After I got away from them, I turned myself back in to the convent. During the first weeks I had been gone, I just shacked up with whoever I could; I didn't know anything about turning tricks. I slept with these guys just for a place to sleep and some bread. When I came back to the convent, I talked to the head shrink, who put me in the infirmary and gave me tranquilizers to calm me down. But I was still determined not to stay there; it was just that I had nowhere to go.

"A couple of the girls there started a riot to get out, and we held up the sewing teacher. I held a pair of scissors on her.

We were just going to tie her up and maybe stick a pair of scissors to her throat and say, 'Okay, you're getting us out of here.' But the butch gym teacher saw us and stopped us. They charged us with assault and battery, but later they dropped the charges. They considered me very dangerous after that, though, and put me in the county girls' home. I changed during that time; they switched my probation officer, so it was like another close friend rejecting me because I could talk to the first probation officer, but I couldn't talk to the second one. I had her for a year or two. They tried family counseling; they tried everything, nothing worked. By this time I had been in and out of Juvenile Hall about ten times, and all my charges were runaways. They never caught me doing anything, although they were always suspicious. My file was about six inches thick, what with my psychological tests and my record.

"Then they sent me to the State Youth Authority, and I guess that's the last stop. I went through a thirty-day observation period, then they brought me in front of the board, who said, 'We're going to put you into Ventura School for Girls.' They had nowhere else to put me; I wasn't a junkie yet, so I couldn't go into a drug program. They had security guards at Ventura with walkie-talkies, and if you fucked up they put you on medication. I went to school there, but I never learned anything. I got straight A's, but I was still a defiant young lady. Finally, the head psychologists there said, 'Let her go.'

"By this time I was sixteen, and again they sent me back to San Francisco. One of the girls I was really close with in Ventura got released at about the same time. She was a junkie with a pimp, so she called me up. While I was standing in front of a movie house waiting to meet her, I ran into another drug dealer in a Toyota. He was flashing all kinds of money at me, but I just ignored him. Finally, I hooked up with him. He got me a baby-sitting job that paid fifty dollars a week, and I could keep what I hustled. Besides baby-sitting, I drove around with him in his Cadillac, and I'd count his money as he made his stops and collected it. He also had girls working for him dealing dope, and in massage parlors, too. That was when I started turning tricks officially. It was great fun. He had connections in the Virgin Islands, and we spent some time there and traveled all over the country.

"I decided I liked this kind of life, that it really suited me. But I also decided after a while that when I got my head together, I really was going to give up hooking. It's painful. I was pregnant at fourteen and a half and had to get an abortion, which I had to arrange and pay for myself with the help of some friends, and that kind of thing hurts a lot—it hurts physically and emotionally. The doctor gave me a local anesthetic, and I was awake the whole time, which is really depressing. I could hear the suction machine going. They turned up the music after they turned it on, but I still could hear it, and meanwhile the guy's taking a vacation in Puerto Rico. But he helped me pay for it.

"Since then, I've kind of knocked around with different guys going back and forth; and now, at seventeen, I've had it all. I've been a junkie, I've worked massage parlors, I've worked the streets, I've worked out-call. And I must say it's been a very wearing kind of life. I know for sure that when I'm a mother, I'm going to watch my kids and care about them, and not let what happened to me happen to them."

Chapter 7

FEARS AND FANTASIES

We have seen what actually happens to runaways once they reach their destination—whether it be New York, Chicago, or Los Angeles. And we have seen F.B.I., H.H.S., and National Runaway Switchboard figures on how many children there are and what age, sex, and race categories they fall into. Experts such as Father Bruce Ritter of Covenant House and Under 21 ⚥ estimate that as many as 70 percent of all "chronic" or "serious" runners will end up in prostitution and/or pornography. Dr. Judianne Densen-Gerber of Odyssey House in New York agrees. She believes that child prostitution has increased 1,000 ⚥ percent and that it involves one million children, some of them as young as six.* From these facts, figures, and testimonies emerges an unpleasant picture of our society as one in which adults increasingly view children as sex objects.

What about our children? How do they view the outside world of strange adults and unfamiliar situations? What do they know about street life? How much of what they "know" is fact, how much of it fantasy? Here we explore the vision conjured up by children based in part on direct experience within their own families; in part on whatever they have absorbed from movies, newspapers, magazines, books, pop music, and television—especially television; and in part on rumors circulated by peers.

We see the valid concern of mental health professionals who

have confirmed the findings of Drahman and Thomas (1975). They have found that children exposed to media violence also become more tolerant of aggression in real-life settings. Furthermore, as the toleration effect develops, children perceive violence as a commonplace part of everyday life and not worthy of any special attention.

To find out how children perceive sexual danger and violence, and how that perception evolves as they mature, I undertook a research project involving 5,000 children aged five to sixteen, in kindergarten through the eighth grade. Both girls (2,640) and boys (2,360) participated. They represented five states—eastern, western, and southern. All of them were living at home at the time, although a few had run away and returned home previously. They came from middle-class families in either large cities or suburbs. (Not from rural areas, however. The experience of children living in the country differs so much from that of city or suburban children that another approach would be more appropriate for them.) The study was conducted from 1976 to 1980.

It is impossible to get most school administrators to allow students to be asked certain straightforward questions about running away, sex, and violence. It is hard also to get children to talk or write freely about these subjects. After some initial experimentation, I found a set of questions—composition topics —which satisfied administrators and evoked deeply personal responses from children. All the questions are phrased in a negative way, which is consonant with children's reluctance to admit knowledge of sex.

The topics students were asked to respond to (by dictation to a teacher for the very young children in kindergarten and grades one and two; in their own writing for the other children) were as follows:

Kindergarten/Grades 1 and 2   Why I Should Not Take Candy or a Ride from a Stranger

Grades 3–5   Why I Shouldn't Run Away from Home—What Are the Dangers?

Grades 6–8   Mary had an argument with her parents. She ran away to the Central Bus Terminal. She met a man named Slim. What are the dangers facing Mary?

The teachers who took dictation were asked to encourage children to express themselves freely. Likewise, the teachers and volunteers trained to administer the project for older children were instructed to present the questions in a neutral manner and to receive replies without judgmental comment or bodily signals.

Following are extracts from children's compositions, along with interpretations and commentary on the differences in response from different grade levels.

Kindergarten, First Grade

WHY I SHOULD NOT TAKE CANDY OR A RIDE FROM A STRANGER

Seventy-eight percent of this group responded with warnings that the candy might contain poison. Seven percent indicated that something might be wrong with the candy, saying, "It might not be good for you" or "There may be something in it." Some of the children said that the candy might contain drugs, alcohol, or needles. Five percent said simply, "It's just not nice" or "It's a bad thing to do" or "I wouldn't take it because I don't know him." Six percent did not know why they should not take the candy.

Almost all the children focused on the risks inherent in the candy itself; only 4 percent understood that this was a transaction involving a person with an ulterior motive and that an obligation would be incurred if the candy were accepted. The following replies are representative (these children are between the ages of four years ten months, and seven years):

"He might make you go somewhere with him."

"He might take you to his house and not let you go when it is time to go home."

"Strangers are bad people. They could get their guns and shoot you."

One sophisticated child responded, "He might be trying to fool you with something. My mommy told me there is a lot of sick people in the world."

One more naïve child, a first grader, asked, "What's a stranger?"

Except for these few, however, none in this group understood that the source of potential danger was more likely to lie with the candy giver than with the candy. If the stranger were to offer to eat some of the candy with the child as a guarantee that it had not been poisoned, the child's defense would crumble. At this age, four to six, the responsibility is clearly the parents' to protect their children. Apart from whatever instruction is given the children, in case the parent or a known adult is not around, children must be supervised and guided until they are old enough to fend for themselves more effectively.

Grade Two (Same Question)

DON—AGE 7½—PRIVATE DAY SCHOOL

You should not take candy from strangers because it may be poison. Any store that has open candy I will not have it. If I was playing and I found a piece of candy I will not eat it. When I go to the library I will give it to the lady, I will not eat it.

ALICE—7

It might poison you or it might put you to sleep, it could hurt you. They put medicine in the candy.

Second graders' responses are fairly close to those of the kindergartners and first graders. Seventy percent of this group cited poison as the chief danger in taking the candy. In this group there is a preoccupation with cleanliness: "It may have been on the ground" or "It may be dirty." Fifteen percent indicated that the candy giver, the stranger (always a man), also posed a danger.

Some of these children offer concrete advice about what to do in this situation: run. Avoidance and flight are the only defenses a child this age has against a menacing adult.

MELODY—7½

You should not take candy from strangers because it might be dirty. And strangers might take you away from your home too. If they try to grab you run away.

Grade Three
Why I Shouldn't Run Away from Home— What Are the Dangers?

At this stage children's awareness of danger is at a point where many of their compositions earnestly exhort other children not to be tempted by enticements from strange adults. Particularly significant here is that only 4 percent of the children thought to ask another adult for help when in trouble. These middle-class children seem either afraid of the police or ignorant of their role as potential helpers.

Although food wasn't mentioned in this question, many of the children inserted it in their responses; the lure of food is apparent.

Patrick—Age 8—Suburban Public School

It is dangerous to run away from home because you might get kidnapped for a month. Some stranger might bring you home for lunch and give you bad food. Somebody might make you rob a bank. Somebody might try to run you over with a car.

Some of the children showed an effort to control the situation by listing or compartmentalizing.

Billy—Age 8½—Suburban Public School

Sunday you run away. Monday you get hit by a Sunday driver. Tuesday you get kidnapped. Wednesday you get shot. Thursday you get killed. Friday you are found. Saturday you are berried.

A few side with parents, delivering a stern moral lecture.

Darlene—Age 8—Private Day School

Running away is very dangerous. Some kids just don't know how to take it serious. When they get in a little argument with their parents they think right away, oh, now it's time to run away. They shouldn't do that because when they get hurt it's not their parents' fault it's their fault, all their fault. But when they get hurt they think it's their parents' fault. The kids that get hurt blaim it on their parents for getting mad at them.

For the first time, we see that girls and boys differ in their responses. Third-grade girls are more practical than boys.

Sherry—Age 9—Midwestern Public School

It is dangerous to run away from home because if it is summertime, you are wareing summer clothes and when it's cold you could freeze. If it's wintertime when it gets hot you will get very hot in winter close. You money supply does not last very long, and when you have no money you have no clos, no food, you die. And your mother and father will be worried sick. Besides, ware will you go?

Some compositions begin to show that children have not only read about runaways, but also have had friends who ran away . . . or have run away themselves.

Jane—Age 8½—Western Suburban Public School

On the news there's a lot of reports that people get kidnapped. Once there was a little girl kidnapped in my camp.

There are killers going around. Don't run away. My friends and I ran away because my brother beat me up. My mother was worried. She called the police up and cars were looking for me. So don't run away from home. Mothers get worried and sad. If your little and you can't cross a street then you are in trouble alright. You will get punished and beaten when you get home.

Grade Four (Same Question)

This is probably the most volatile group in that, of all the grades, kindergarten through eighth, the fourth graders harbored the most elaborate fantasies of destructive violence. Often these fantasies were only minimally related to the stimulus, but once they were triggered, they poured out. It is with the fourth graders that this study shows how early the fascination with violence begins, how solidly it is implanted, and how quickly it becomes eroticized, developing into a more and more open connection with sex in the prepubescent and pubescent years.

A pervasive theme with these children is fear of starvation, of being neglected by adults. It often heads the list of calamities which could befall a runaway.

Daniel—Age 10—Eastern Private School

It is dangerous to run away from home because you could starve to death. And your mother and father will get worried. And you might get erested by the police department. You could get hit by a car. Or you might get mugged. You might get kidnapped. You might get shot. . . . And you could get lost. . . . You might get robed. . . . You might get sick. . . . You might get poisoned. . . .

Although 20 percent of grade-four girls are developing breasts and 12 percent are menstruating, only 3 percent of them were able to articulate a sexual threat.* Also, there is little difference between the responses of girls and boys on this level.

Of the girls who mentioned sex, most referred to a situation in which a man has taken advantage.

Lana—Age 9—Southern Day School

Because a man might come by and pull you in his car and take you somewhere. Like to a house which no one lives in. Then they will keep you there. Then your mother would get worried, and call the police. But the police can't find you. They tell your mother and she cries. You escape and get out of the cellar and onto the rode. You run as fast as you can. The man tries to catch you, but he can't. The police find you and ask you questions like "what did he look like, where is his hideout?" And things like that. Then you go to the house and catch him. He's put in jail. The policeman brings you back to your mother. She is glad to see you. She hugs you and kisses you. The next day you find your name in the paper. You are proud of yourself.

In the very few fourth-grade compositions which mention sex explicitly, it is always linked with being raped and killed.

Jarlene—Age 9½—Western Public School

It is dangerous to run away from home because you can get hit by a car or let's say you are walking down the street and a car full of boys comes by and they stop and tell you to get in and if you do they can rape you and kill you.

Grade Five (Same Question)

The fifth-grade compositions show a slight drop in the amount of unmotivated violence. Children's fantasies here move from the role of victim to that of participant. Also, they begin to write about family discord and to mention money. Some compositions show only partially repressed sexual excitement. Bear in mind that by the fifth grade, almost 35 percent of the girls are developing breasts and 26 percent have begun to menstruate.* It is no longer possible for these children—boys or girls—to ignore their sexuality.

Fred—Age 10—Eastern Public School

Don't ever hitchhike either, it may be dangerous. The people that are in the car may be a lady or a man. They're both dangerous because they do bad things to you.

Terry—Age 10½—Boarding School

It is dangerous to accept rides from strangers or pick up a suspicious looking character. It is alright if you know the person. But if he is a stranger be on alert at all times. If you stop for a hitchhiker and he tries to force his way in, roll up your windows tight and start honking repeatedly. If you have a hitchhiker in your car don't leave the car running. Take the keys with you or ask him to come with you. Many times when you see a hitchhiker ask for his credentials and run your hand up and down his body. When you see a hitchhiker in front of your store don't leave the car running. He might have been waiting for a chance to get a free ride. It's a very common reason why there are so many people who are fatalities.

Stacy—Age 11—Eastern City, Private School

Because he might have a knife in his hand. He may strangle you under a tunnel. Anyway it's spooky. If he's ugly run. If he's cute, well, run also.

Grade Six
Mary had an argument with her parents. She ran away to the Central Bus Terminal. She met a man named Slim. What are the dangers facing Mary?

Sixth-grade children show a sophistication. Now 55 percent of the girls have developed breasts and 48 percent have begun to menstruate.* For many of the boys, masturbation and/or nocturnal emissions are common.* Both boys and girls are influenced by the rock culture of older teenagers, lyrics of which often contain explicit sexual references. Some of these children have begun to use drugs and smoke marijuana.* All these developments are evident in the following excerpts. These children show ambivalence over leaving home; excitement and fear almost balance out in their writing.

Antoine—Age 12—Midwestern Public School

The guy Slim might try to take Mary's money away from her and might try to do something like beat her up or something else. She might end in a home if they get her for running away.

She might starve and run out of money. She might not get a job to support her. She might get real sick and go to the hospital and die. A religious group might take her and brainwash her. Where would she live when she would run out of money to pay rent or the hotel in the streets. And if she tried to get a ride somewhere she would have to hitchhike and might be mugged by the guy in the car and robbed.

And end up like a bum or something.

Wilma—Age 12—Private Day School

Mary might think that he's her only friend and he might be a murderer, if he finds out that Mary thinks that he's her only friend whom she could talk to by her telling him that he will probably find a way to get her somewhere where usually nobody goes, by trying to con her to go with him.

Mary did tell him about what happened and didn't miss a thing. That gave him the key to strike!

People called him Slim because he always liked slim girls and he killed the rest that were a little over slim and made them slim with his knife.

Mary was a little overweight and he asked her that after the bus stops would she go for a little walk. And she answered yes. The bus stopped and when they went for a walk he said he had to leave and so he started his stuff, he cut some of her side, when she made a loud scream and ran as fast as she could. He through his knife at her, but he missed.

She had enough money to go back home. Her parents were glad to see her and she thought it was great to be home.

Grade Seven (Same Topic)

By the seventh grade, physical maturity is well under way. Only a small minority of seventh-grade girls have not yet begun to menstruate.* Children are about three years ahead of the previous generation developmentally.* There is a certain openness about sexual feelings and actions that is new, too, especially among girls. Sex and violence are linked by these children. Violent fantasies they have absorbed, including matricide and patricide, bondage and slavery scenarios, are described. The street has a certain allure. Children seem to be aware of venereal disease, although they may not call it that. They also have begun to understand the pimp-prostitute relationship.

Manny—Age 13—Boarding School, New England

The dangers of Mary meeting a stranger are number 1: she could be kidnapped and held for ransom. Number 2 she would be offered a ride in Slim's car and then he could take her to a deserted area and kill her, leaving her dead where he killed her. Number 3, he could offer her a ride then take her for the ride, then rape her, and strangle her and stab her. And put her in a bay and dump her in a lake or any other place. Number 4 he could offer some kind of food that has poison in it and number 5 sexually abuse her in some way. Number 6 he could make her become a hooker. Number 7 he could say to her that he has a job for her and make her pose in pornographic or blue films or magazines, that show her body naked. Or he could make her pregnant. If she should be 13 it would be a burden for her to take care of a young baby, her mother maybe could care . . . take care of her baby. But if not, she would have to go through the experience of going through an abortion. Or he would give her drugs and make her become an addict. Mary would go through many dangers of this so called man Slim.

Clarisse—Age 13—Eastern Boarding School

Slim could be a pimp, and he would make her a prostitute. She could be killed by a psycho or could be sent to jail. He would hit her if she disobeyed. Slim would make her take drugs and take an overdose and die from the drugs. She would take birth control pills and if she forgot to take one she could have a baby without a husband. She could get a disease from someone and spread it to all the people she would have contact with and all the people could die and she could die. If she gets put to jail she could be beaten very badly by the guards. If she tells who the pimp is she could be killed by the pimp or any of his helpers. I'm assuming she is a teenager.

Grade Eight (Same Question)

In the eighth-grade writings, we see some themes which have shown up in almost all the lower grades: concern with food and fear of starvation and concern with money. These children, however, understand the financial arrangement between pimps and prostitutes, which the younger children do not. These more experienced children may have more of a grasp on reality, but they are no less caught up in the fantasy of running away. Drug use is more common among these thirteen- and fourteen-year-olds than it was among sixth graders.

Jeremy—Age 14—Western Urban Junior High School

Mary could get raped by this guy Slim and she could get kidnapped and held for ransom and then she would probably die anyway. And if Slim wasn't a rapist she might go to some other city or state with no money and she'd have to take the chance of being caught. And if she didn't get any food she could die. And then she would have to eat out of garbage cans. And she could get food poisons in her body. I mean any way you look at it, she either should go home or she's got a million to one chance that she will live.

Julius—Age 13—Eastern Day School

Mary was a 13 year old girl. She was a pretty girl, but her life with her family was not good after that night. Mary was at a party with some new friends she had met. She knew them only from school. That night while she was there they all gathered around this one guy who was a junkie. He was spaced out and was offering anyone anything they wanted. Mary wanted to be with the group so they finally got her to smoke a joint. On the way home she blacked out and was found the next day by the cops. Her parents were furious with her and grounded her for a month. She didn't think she committed such a crime so she ran away to the Port Authority Bus Terminal. There she met a man named Slim. He asked her what she was doing here and she told him she had run away. He handed her a card and left her saying call me if you have any trouble. She lasted only a few days on the money she had brought so she called the number. He told her he knew a way she could get money and to meet him on Eighth Avenue at 2:00. When she got there he told her she could work for him. She knew what was in store for her and when she refused the offer he beat her up and left her in an alley all bruised. The next day she begged for money until she had enough for bus fare home. Finally she got enough and when she got home she was grounded for a year and that was stupid. She would have been better off if she'd stayed at home.

Conclusions

The compositions in this study illustrate the evolution of a child's concept of danger, from the infantile persecutory fantasies, coupled with admonitions from parents, to the paranoid projections of third, fourth, and fifth grades. In grades six through eight, a developing, if still somewhat sensational, sense of reality is added. Overall the children do not seem assured that they can turn to the family for protection; the older ones feel a push and pull when it comes to the idea of leaving home. Violence has become central to these children's lives and is directly linked with sexuality.

After carefully reviewing the literature and our own research techniques, we realized that new approaches would have to be developed if the violence and sex connection were to be elicited. There was an awareness of the fact that this had eluded other researchers. The challenge was certainly there. Would we succeed in exposing the hitherto deeply hidden and perhaps even unconscious association between sexuality and violence in American children? Poor and blue-collar children were relatively free to express violent fantasies, but middle-class children, our target population, were not. By extensively restructuring the questions and the format in which children responded we were able specifically to elicit responses of violence and sex fantasies from middle-class children. For the first time, what other serious researchers had long suspected but could not tap into came tumbling out in these compositions.

What is the source of this violence in these children's consciousness? There are many influences on their minds, of course, but one of the strongest may be television. Much research has been done in this field: Drabman and Thomas suggested that children exposed to media violence also may become more tolerant of aggression in real-life settings;* and Liebert and Baron suggested that children engage in general forms of aggression as a result of viewing violence.* Liefer and Roberts also provided evidence that young children often cannot distinguish between reality and fantasy violence.*

Many experts, such as Walling, Corder-Bolz, and O'Bryant,* and Horton and Santogrossi,* propose that parents watch television with children and supplement viewing intake with discussion. Parents can express their feelings about the violence being shown, ask children questions about the characters or plots, and present nonviolent alternatives.

That there is a very direct connection between violence on television and young children's fears was corroborated recently in a study sponsored by the Foundation for Child Development and researched by Temple University's Institute for Survey Research in Philadelphia.* That there is even a correlational relationship between violence and how much television a child is exposed to is seen in this study, which revealed that heavy television viewers were twice as likely to be scared often.

Nicholas Zill, the director of the project, said, "The survey reinforced the belief that television violence should be checked in some big way, not just with a family hour or *Sesame Street*. The F.C.C. is a disaster area in its regulation of television."

Chapter 8

CHILD SEX EXPLOITATION –HOMOSEXUAL AND HETEROSEXUAL

I. Chickens and Hawks

An alarming development on the sex scene of the seventies was the increasingly aggressive pursuit of very young boys by seemingly respectable older men. Pederasty, or pedophilia, certainly is not new in human experience, but in the last decade those who practice it have become militantly politicized. The brazenness with which some pedophiles operate has scandalized Middle America.

One of the first cases to come to public attention was the so-called Revere Case in Revere, Massachusetts.* The discovery of a large call-boy operation there shocked residents of the city and state. Over 250 boys were available for sex anywhere in the Massachusetts area for fifty dollars and up. The purveyors: a child psychiatrist, headmasters of exclusive New England schools, and administrators of state institutions responsible for safeguarding institutionalized boys. What shocked people was that the adults involved—either as purveyors or as clients—were not peculiar ne'er-do-wells or drifters; they were solid citizens, respected members of the community.

Revere, however, it turned out, was just one branch of a national network with headquarters in Houston, Texas.* From there hawks can order chickens by telephone from anywhere in the country. The operators claim that within half an hour a boy can be on the caller's doorstep, provided the caller's credit card clears.

Other cases made headlines, keeping pedophilia in the public eye. One of the more sensational cases involved John Gacy of Des Plaines, Illinois.* The bodies of thirty-three boys he had "befriended" were discovered concealed in or under Gacy's house. In another case sexual exploitation of young boys was connected with kidnapping. In January, 1980, Ronald Devyner was arrested in upstate New York on the charge of kidnapping two boys aged eleven and fifteen.* Devyner, who previously had been imprisoned for molesting children, often wore a clerical habit and referred to himself as "Father Ron," and he claims that he is a real eastern rite priest. According to the F.B.I., he is part of a loosely knit ring of forty men who dress as clergymen, correspond with each other, make pornographic movies, and exchange boys for sexual purposes. Investigators believe that the ring worked the entire East Coast of the United States and Montreal, Canada, where they held a convention in June, 1979.

In his book *For Money or Love* Robin Lloyd reports on another indication of how extensive the pedophiliac network has become.* A publication—*Where the Young Ones Are*—which was compiled by one of the pedophiliac groups, lists where young boys can be found in every state. It gives a city-by-city rundown of beaches, bus stops, playgrounds, amusement arcades, schools, and so on. The cheaply produced, mimeographed book costs twenty-five dollars a copy and sold over 100,000 copies within a few months of publication.

Far from cringing in shame, many of the men involved in the "boys for hire" game are demanding respectability. They have formed advocate groups such as the Guyon Society, whose motto is "Sex before eight, or then it's too late," or the Paedophiliac Information Exchange, which has headquarters in London and branches in the United States and other countries. The newest organization is one which grew up in response to the Revere Case. It's called N.A.M.B.L.A., which stands for North American Man-Boy Love Association.

Since the laws are against pedophilia, these organizations are mounting campaigns to change the laws. Their target is the age of consent laws, to permit sex between adults and children. The agitation for changing the laws has caused an uneasy division within the gay rights movement. The conservative majority of homosexuals fear that forcing the issue of sex with children would result in a violent backlash that would wipe out all the gains made toward acceptance of adult homosexual unions.* However, an increasingly vocal faction of gay activists is advocating legalization of man-boy sex.

Most of the rhetoric in the debate, which has surfaced recently in conferences on "man-boy love" in Boston and New York and in the editorial pages of gay activist publications, has centered around the question of the sexual "rights" of children. Since the pedophiliac organizations are among the very few which have openly articulated a case for sexual relations between adults and children, it is interesting to see how they present their argument.

It goes:

(1) Children are doubly oppressed: Their sexuality, which is fully developed from a very early age, is harshly repressed by a hypocritical and punitive moral code imposed by puritanical heterosexual parents. (The rhetoric of the movement reflexively equates heterosexuality with "uptightness" and inhibition.) Furthermore, physical brutality toward children is the norm in heterosexual homes.

(2) All the pedophile asks, on the other hand, is the opportunity to lavish upon these boys the affection, tenderness, and loving concern their hostile homes deny them.*

For example, David Thorstad, a militant spokesman for the pedophiliac movement, writing in *Gay Community News*, asserts:

> The gay liberation movement is fighting not merely for the rights of adults to engage freely in homoerotic acts, but also for the millions of our society's children to enjoy a free sexual life . . . and [for] the rights of children to control their own bodies.

At a time when abuse of children by their parents is

epidemic, it is ironic that it is men who *love* boys who are made into the ultimate criminal. In view of the facts about child abuse—revealed by the heterosexuals themselves—it is not only absurd to charge gay men who share their sexuality with boys as "child molesters," it is also a deliberate deception designed to divert attention away from the failure of the family institution and of society at large to raise their children to be the unthinking heterosexual robots that have become the ideal embraced by priests, politicians, psychiatrists, and other instruments of the status quo.*

Thorstad's argument for "cross-generational" (or "intergenerational") sex, in the antiseptic language of the movement, was immediately challenged by a lesbian columnist, Nancy Walker, who countered with a direct hit at its weakest point:

> The issue is not whether we should be fighting for the rights of small children to explore their sexual potential. They will inevitably do that. Let Thorstad and his confreres at least say what the real issue is: that they want to fuck children. . . . "Repeal all age of consent laws! Freedom of sexual expression for all!" is the cover-up slogan for men whose only interest is their own sexual gratification. . . .
>
> Prepubescent children are not taboo because this is a sex negative society . . . but because they can be physically hurt and *may* be psychologically injured as well by sexual intimacy with adults. I would not be at all averse to laws that allowed children to experiment with one another. They do that anyway, as I recall.*

This, of course, is the crux. The "sexual rights of children," insofar as they also involve adults, are not rights belonging to the children at all, but only to adults who want to make use of them sexually. The pedophiliac slogan is aimed against laws intended to protect children from exploitation. As Nancy Walker shrewdly points out, the only legitimate interpretation of Thorstad's phrase "rights of children to enjoy a free sexual life" would be the right of children to free sexual play *among them-selves*, but this is an issue which is of no interest whatsoever to pedophiles. As one adult member of the Gay Youth Movement said, with unmistakable emphasis, "The end of the age of re-pression is too long overdue. In the never-never land these men live in now, they are very prone to blackmail and harm. We must protect them. . . . *These men find these boys gratifying, and society has no right to repress these kids*" (italics added).

Prorepeal activists are fond of stressing that they never have to approach a boy; the boys eagerly seek them out, all they have to do is show up in a car. What this proves, according to one pedophile (who wanted to remain anonymous), is that

"Kids below ten have sexual feelings, and they should not be suppressed, just because we live in a puritanical, ambivalent society. Young children don't just have some sexual feelings, they have more sex than adults. They don't know what to do with it. They are bursting with sexuality. There is more raw, primitive, joyful lust in boys of seven, eight, and nine than in adults. Society wants these kids to suppress it all, or maybe just play with peers, or themselves, but when older men, who under-stand them and could help them enjoy their bodies, try to give them some warmth and a good role model to identify with, everyone gets uptight."

But the studies of children who habitually have sexual rela-tions with adults show that they almost always come from severely troubled homes.* They are not driven by the urgency of an overwhelming sexual need; there is nothing "joyful" in their "lust"; the paradisiacal vision of burgeoning boys in bloom is the wish fulfillment of a pedophile. What truth there is in the pedophiles' case lies in the fact that most of the boys they have contact with are escaping from families in the process of dissolution, and have turned to prostitution not only for money, but also primarily to seek the protection, however momentary, of a surrogate father. Sex is their bargaining power, not their need. With it they buy a material and emotional security—albeit short-lived and illusory.

But the alliance is usually cruelly curtailed. Most pedophiles are extremely narrow and specific in their sexual preferences; many live long and full sexual lives without ever having a single encounter with anyone over fifteen, thirteen, or ten, depending on their tastes. And it is the rigidity of this sexual choice that causes much of the harm to the child in these relationships. A boy at the age of nine is suddenly taken up by an older man who becomes his all in all—father, lover, friend, mentor—and who encourages an absolute faith and trust. But when the boy reaches the awkward age of thirteen or fifteen, or whatever the limit of his appeal may be to that particular man, he will just as abruptly be jettisoned, returned to where he was found. As one man who prefers brief encounters in hotel rooms told us, "None of these boys could do very much for me in the long term. I mean, what would I do with them when they became thirteen, fourteen, fifteen, and started developing muscles and facial hair?"

But most pedophiles say that playing the father role is part of the appeal. They prefer to see themselves as the salvation of innumerable boys whose own fathers were cruel, indifferent, or absent. As proof that the relationship is entirely beneficial to the boys, they like to point out that many who have passed through their hands grow up to become happily heterosexual husbands and fathers. A professor who has recently retired to become a spokesman for the pederast movement contends:

"All boys have a need for a fathering figure, and there's no way of telling when they're that young which of them will remain gay and which will become straight. I don't suppose that the boy is homosexual, or anything else, at that age. The relationships I'm talking about have nothing to do with sexual orientation, and a very great deal to do with affection and love, mutual love. And I think that every boy has a need for that.

"I've never had a boy move in with me; he would have to be a runaway to do that. I've had a boy spend a week or so with me during the summer, let's say, or over Christmas vacation, but always with the idea that they were living with their parents and still in school.

"When they reach a certain age, it is my experience that

the boy makes the initial decision, if not the final decision, to end the relationship. I have had boys leave me to explore the world a little more; they don't want any more ties to me. On the other hand, I've also had boys stay with me until they were twenty-one or twenty-two, right through college. I'm sure I've helped them, academically; I can't say for sure about socially." *

Most authorities, however, would disagree with the assertion that it is the boy who leaves; the consensus confirms the experience of Sergeant Lloyd Martin, Director of the Sexually Exploited Child Unit of the Juvenile Division in Los Angeles. He says that in by far the majority of cases, the adult initiates the break. The younger the boys—the farther down the pedophile's preference reaches—the more likely this is to be true. A man whose taste is for boys of ten or eleven is far more likely to abandon them than they are to leave him. In any event, when a sexual liaison between a child and an older man ends, whether hours, months, or years later, it is not the child's needs which are being met.

According to Dr. William Prendergast, a psychologist working in the New Jersey sex offenders' center who has worked with hundreds of pedophiles who have gotten into trouble with the law, the origins of an exclusive sexual interest in children lie in an unresolved traumatic experience in the pedophile's own childhood:

"Like the battered children who become battering parents, these men who have been molested in their childhood end up as adult child molesters. Usually the experience itself may have been pleasurable, but they got caught and were badly punished for it, and this is what fixes them in their need. The crisis occurred, they were found out, they got rejected for what they had done, so they try to recreate it to find out why, what happened, is this what love is?

"The difference between the man who uses little boys and the one who uses little girls is that the former is a much more frightened individual. He knows what to do with a male, but he's terrified of females; while the one who uses little girls knows what to do but is afraid of failing with an adult female.

The pedophile, in my experience, is much more frightened and passive than the other; the guilt is much more internalized.

"We don't try to change the man who insists he wants only to be involved sexually with males, but we do insist that he change the object of his choice. If he wants to remain homosexual, that's okay, but not with the children. It's not easy, because they're deeply afraid of adult relationships, but we can't let them go on abusing children—because it *is* abuse, there's no doubt about it. A child is simply not old enough to make a decision; I don't care if he says he likes it! He is not old enough to know what kind of choice he is making, or what label society will put on him, what the price tag will be later on.

"How do we really know what these children's reactions are? If we followed the pedophile line of reasoning, why don't we also say that children should have the right to get married, to vote in elections, to drink, and to drive cars? Because they're not yet capable of judgment; that's why they need protection. I feel very strongly about this, because the men I see here are themselves casualties of this scene."

Just how a pedophile goes about fulfilling his fantasies depends on how actively he needs to realize them. Dr. Maurice Yaffe, Senior Clinical Psychologist at Guy's Hospital in London, believes that "it is likely that only a proportion of those whose preferred sexual fantasy is pedophilic in content will have had any actual contact with a young boy or girl." *

However, we also talked to three men whose pedophiliac inclinations are both conscious and highly active, each of whom in his own fashion pursues his fantasies as openly as society permits. Leo, thirty-three, is a successful salesman who lives alone but spends most of his time on the road. "I tried marriage," he said, "I yielded to pressure to make it in the straight world, and all I'm left with now is a heavy alimony and child support for my wife and two daughters." Leo feels that if it weren't for his job, which gives him limitless mobility, the outlook would be bleak. "I love my daughters, but we can only be so close. I have my world and they have theirs. Thank goodness I travel about constantly so I get some perquisites—otherwise I would be living a rather mundane, cloistered life.

"When I arrive at a city on my itinerary, the first thing I do is check into my hotel, have a leisurely lunch or dinner, and then, if I know anyone in town, decide whether I want to make a few calls to boys I'm already friendly with or make some new friends. Usually I'll decide to get in the car and go cruising. Just about every sizable American city has cruising areas, and I know all the ones in my territory, which pretty much covers the eastern seaboard. I'll cruise the local bus stop first, then head for the penny arcade or the bowling alley—wherever they hang out. Inevitably I'll find a boy. When I look over the pickings, I go for the aesthetic type. I prefer them clean-cut, about thirteen or fourteen, just starting their growth spurt, sincere and bookish.

"If we pretend I'm just giving him a lift, there's a good deal of nonverbal communication from the moment he gets in—things like how far away from me he sits, how he looks at me, whether our hands touch. Then we negotiate the price. Usually the kid comes out with something he needs, like a new tire for his bike—that's ten dollars—or a new shirt or a pair of pants for twenty dollars or so. After that things move pretty quickly. I'm not interested in prolonging it—as soon as I've got my money's worth I say good night. Sometimes, if I'm interested in seeing the boy again, I'll take his number before I drop him off just in case I hit a dry spell the next time I'm in town, although that hasn't happened yet. But most of the boys I deal with aren't really very much interested beyond the evening any more than I am.

"If I'm satisfied, I then drive back to my hotel, have a few drinks, and call it a night. Or sometimes, if the evening is still young and the kid wasn't enough for me, I'll go out and find another.

"I feel that my life is filled with a great deal of excitement. I'm always in action, busy, going after what I want. I have no desire at all to settle down, now or ever. This for me is the best of all possible worlds."

Charles, forty-six, is an architect who has lived happily with his lover, Henry, also in his forties, for the past four years. "But I find that, while I love Henry very much and we care for each other very deeply, quite often I need a little more excitement, and excitement for me means the young ones. I go for the kids about nine or ten who hang around the downtown area, the amusement arcades, the movie theaters—you find them everywhere. I travel a little, and when I'm away I always make sure I have a room where I can entertain if I decide to bring a boy back with me. I go for both boys alone and group scenes.

"Henry gets very upset with me sometimes; he feels I'm not acting mature. But everyone has his own thing, and this happens to be mine. There's something irresistible about young boys just before they start blooming in their adolescence, while they still look like little boys. Their innocence is an absolute turn-on for me. These kids are warm, affectionate, and trusting. I love teaching them, and most of them learn very quickly—they love to turn on with me, whether we're smoking grass or doing a bit of coke. I'm good to them, too. Most of them have never had a father who cares about them, and many haven't had a warm meal since they can remember. I don't believe all the propaganda, all the fuss society is making about these boys being hurt. I've never hurt anyone—just the opposite.

"My goodness, I could have adopted twenty-five or fifty of these kids along the way if I hadn't had Henry, but I don't consider that becoming a father at my age would do very much for me, and anyway what would I do with them when they got too old for me, like twelve or thirteen? I'd have to part with them, and partings for me have always been very painful.

"No, I find that the quick affair, the stolen love in the night is the most exciting. Some of the best affairs I've had have been the quickest—in the men's room of the amusement arcades. It's fast action and thrills I'm looking for from these kids; I've got love at home."

Charles's frank indifference to the fate of the boys he enjoys is as guiltless as that of any man who hires a prostitute. The innocence is the "turn-on," but his imagination never extends so far as to feel any sort of responsibility for protecting it because that would extinguish the excitement. The pedophiliac fantasy, like most sexual deviations—and like the pornographic ideal—always seeks a fulfillment that is without consequences. It is this that reveals the false pieties of the "man-boy love" movement: The pedophile's gratification depends upon being able to see the child solely as an object for his enjoyment, whose needs, if they are considered at all, exactly match his own —exclusively and infinitely sexual, with no awkward spillover into reality.

Unlike Leo and Charles, Robert, a thirty-six-year-old midwestern marketing manager, has taken boys to live with him and talks at length about the power of love, but an attitude of sexual consumerism dominates his emotional life, too:

"What I really think, quite frankly, is that there aren't enough men like us who genuinely care for boys—I mean who really take them in and love them. You may think that's an odd thing to say, but you must admit there just aren't enough loving or caring people anywhere in the world today, and especially those who really love and pay attention to these boys.

"I think I know something about boys; my sex life began when I was eleven, with some of the kids on my baseball team. If you figure that since then I've had at least two or three different boys every month for the past twenty-five years, you can see that I'm entitled to consider myself an expert.

"I'm very concerned about the gay youth situation—they're a neglected group. I think the gay community has a responsibility to poor and minority children. These kids get kicked around by everybody because most of the would-be middle-class, so-called respectable gays want to avoid being identified with them; they're afraid of what society would think if gay groups acknowledged an interest in boys. But intergenerational sex is coming, whether you like it or not. Society is just going to have to accept it and make the best of it because the trend is all that way. I do a fair amount of traveling, so I can tell you that this is not a uniquely American thing, either—far from it. In the Scandinavian countries, for instance, they're much more open about it; some of them have done away altogether with age of consent laws. There are boys all over the world who need the kind of love that only men like us can give them.

"Some people don't take these kids seriously, but I've had them living with me, and I consider myself an ideal father. I'm very masculine, as you can see; there's nothing faggoty about me. I can't stand screaming queens, and I'm certainly not the dirty old man hanging around outside the school offering candy to little kids. I keep my business strictly private.

"I live alone, unless I happen to have a boy with me, and the longest I have done that for is a few years. I do belong to a small social-club kind of thing with a few friends of mine. We meet occasionally and enjoy being together with our boys.

"When I go out, I know exactly where to go to get what I want, although I enjoy the chase, too. That's always an important part of any game, isn't it? But I don't think of it as just a conquest, I regard it as making friends. I find, frankly, that the younger kids have fewer hang-ups and inhibitions. For me almost the most exciting part is that moment of truth when you've finally got involved and you say to yourself, 'This is it,' and you both know what's going to happen. Well, I find that this is a dual process, that kids eleven, ten, nine, even younger, know exactly what they want, too. They have their own way of letting you know that they've selected you. They'll sort of gravitate toward you, snuggling up while at the same time they talk looking away as though distracted, but always loud enough for you to hear.

"That's when I make my pick, and it can be anything from a quickie to a boy like Rick, who lived with me for three very happy years. But that's another story."

Tony, now fifteen, left his Texas home three years ago, worked as a homosexual prostitute for a few months in Houston, then came to New York City, where he is now a successful East Side hustler. He works sometimes through an "agency," an answering service that sends him out on call; sometimes he cruises bars or even the street. He sees himself as a cool businessman, indifferent to his clients, and is quick to tell you that he has a girl friend, although his feelings about her have recently become somewhat ambivalent.

Most chickens will deny that they are homosexual and would have you believe they do everything for money and nothing from any inclination of their own. To some extent this is the classic defensive posture of the prostitute, but in young boys the need for denial goes deeper. Few boy prostitutes are as clear about their sexual identity as the pedophiliac proselytizers would like to think.

Some boys, especially the younger ones, even deny that what they do with an adult man—unless it involves penetration—has anything to do with sex at all. In his book on boy prostitution, *For Money or Love*, Robin Lloyd quotes a deputy district attorney in Los Angeles:

> "We had a case here where the adult admitted to having oral sex with a twelve year old. I spent two hours with the youngster talking about baseball and a hundred other general things to put him at ease. I then asked him if he had sexual relations with the adult in question. The boy emphatically denied it! He seemed genuinely shocked at the suggestion. When I told him the adult had already confessed to eight separate incidents, the boy shrugged and said, 'Oh, that! Sure, he blew me a few times, but we didn't have any sex.'"

Tony, although proud of his detached professionalism, also expresses contempt for chickens who deny that they are gay: "I think that's a lot of bullshit. I take money from these guys, and I like it. And most of the other kids I see that are in this, I can tell you they're really getting off on it, too. I have to admit there've been a couple of times when I'd give a guy a break myself when I thought he was good-looking. There are certain guys I can really get turned on to, you know what I mean? Most of the ones who come on to me are fat, greasy old men in expensive suits, and I find them a drag, but business is business. I hardly ever turn anybody down, but some guys I just find awfully repulsive.

"Sometimes I'm lucky, though, and I'll get a guy who's really built, and we do a whole bunch of stuff. Depending on what he wants and how I feel, I can be the aggressor or I can be the guy who takes it. I can go either way."

Tony is considering accepting one of several proposals he has received to settle down and live with a client, passing as his nephew or son, just as a female prostitute dreams of escape through marrying one of her johns: "So far I've resisted because I really like the excitement of the cruise and the different faces, and I don't want to be tied down to one guy. If I met a rich old man who'd be a good sugar daddy to me, I just might do it, but I wouldn't let him start hassling me about going back to school or doing something with my life.

"A lot of guys want to know how you got into it and where you're from and where you think you're going. I can't stand all that talk about love and staying together—I think that's a crock of shit. These guys want to get laid, or they want to get fucked or blown or they want to blow me—that I can understand, and it's fast, it's over and on to the next one—but I'm really not into this love bullshit. Sex is what these guys want and sex is what I can give them, but love has nothing to do with it."

Tony sees little future for his relationship with his girl friend: "I've been feeling less interested in this girl. I think it's a real bitch that here these guys are paying me, and this little cunt expects me to spend my hard-earned bread on her."

One reason for his cooling off seems to be the excitement of being admired by male connoisseurs: "I'm very well-built, and all the guys keep telling me, 'Wow, are you hung!' At first, I didn't know what the hell they were talking about—I was always very sensitive about my penis—but now I guess I can be proud of the fact that I'm well-endowed. It's funny, my girl friends never seemed to really appreciate it, but size is always important to these fags. I'm skinny and I look very young, so most of them are surprised when I take my pants off. These guys practically take out rulers. They're always rating your performance, too. Almost everybody I've been with has asked me how good he was, and made comments about how good I was."

Tony's future is obscure, although it now seems unlikely that he will achieve—or choose—the resolution reached by Ned, now twenty-two, who, while never a full-time male prostitute, in his early teens had "quite a bit of activity with gay men," beginning with his eighth-grade English teacher:

"He invited me to a play, and of course I was flattered; who wouldn't be, in junior high school? Then he started asking me over to his house, and after a while we became friendly. There was a lot of hugging and touching, and before I knew it I was having sex with him. It felt good, although also it felt very funny to be doing it with a man. I'd always had lots of girl friends and in fact prided myself on having gone steady more than anybody else in my class. The whole time I was fooling around with fags, in fact—about six or seven years—I never gave up girls. I always had both.

"My teacher introduced me to a couple of other men who were very nice and didn't really ask very much except to suck my penis. I used to wonder what they were getting out of it. I was prepared to refuse if they wanted me to start going down on them or anything, but they seemed perfectly happy with that, and they'd take me a lot of places I'd never have got to otherwise, and spent a lot of money on me.

"I was ashamed of it, though; I couldn't tell any of my friends about it. I resisted being with any of them for longer than an evening. My teacher used to invite me to go away with him in the summer or to spend weekends up in his cottage in the country. I felt things might get too heavy, beyond what I could handle, so I never went.

"Through it all I was living at home. My parents just thought it was wonderful, simply terrific that a teacher was interested in me to that extent. He used to call the house, come over, talk things over with my parents and me, giving us advice and all, and they thought he was simply great. I think he enjoyed the game, the challenge of impressing my parents with his respectability. The really funny thing is that my parents are tremendously conservative, and whenever there was anything in the paper about homosexuals, they'd make derogatory comments. My teacher just nodded sympathetically, he never argued with them.

"The guys always asked me if there weren't any other boys I knew they could invite over, but I kept that part of my life very separate. My best friend knew—he was the only person I ever told about it—but he thought I was a little queer, so I stopped talking about it even to him. It wasn't always sex either; these guys seemed to enjoy just being around young kids. Sometimes we never even took our clothes off. They'd have lots of parties with older men and young boys, with the best booze, lots of good food, terrific pot—it sure impressed me as a kid. I can't say I ever felt exploited at all. Nobody ever forced me, although I did get so I wanted to please them a whole lot.

"There was one period when I was about sixteen or seventeen when I really began to wonder, am I going to go straight or am I going to end up being a fruitcake? Let's face it, I was a horny kid. I think if there'd been even a machine that touched me in the right place, I'd have been able to get off. I honestly think I preferred masturbating, that with my hand there was less conflict than having the kind of sex I did with those guys. I never really understood what they were talking about when they'd go on and on about loving and caring. It felt good, what they were doing to me, but it was nothing more than a mechanical release.

"But it does shake you up when you think about what happened, and you find yourself getting an erection. Not that I ever looked at a guy's body and went crazy. It never did anything for me, but I would get very angry at myself for getting turned on thinking of the experience I'd had with this man because it scared me when I'd find myself going over and over it in my mind. I figured if I'm thinking about gays and finding it a turn-on, then maybe I'm a fag, too.

"It didn't work out that way, though. Just about that time—maybe because I *was* so scared—I began to stay away from the bars and parties where I knew I'd meet these people. That was four or five years ago, and now I never think about it anymore. I'm engaged now—we're getting married in a few months—and my sex life with my fiancée is perfectly adequate. I've had other girls, too, and it's always been fine. For me the whole thing with the guys was much more the companionship; I don't think of myself as a homosexual at all. I'm pretty sure that today I'm none the worse for it, but I'm also glad it's all behind me. I just want to forget about it altogether."

Ned's case is a good example of the sort of outcome pedophiliac apologists like to cite in support of their claim that sexual relations with older men never convert a boy who is not already a confirmed homosexual. It is clear, though, that some sort of seduction is taking place, whatever form the persuasion takes. In Ned's case he was dazzled by the luxurious world his passive availability opened to him. The child is being bought. He always knows it, too. Pedophiles may impress themselves with the higher values of love, but the boys are never deceived.

II. Baby Pros

> Between the age limits of nine and fourteen there occur maidens who, to certain bewitched travelers, twice or many many times older than they, reveal their true nature which is not human, but nymphic (that is, demoniac); and these chosen creatures I propose to designate as "nymphets."
> —*Lolita*, VLADIMIR NABOKOV

In the 1950's, when *Lolita* was published, the story of Humbert Humbert and his insatiable appetite for "nymphets" provoked great controversy. Humbert was viewed as lascivious and immoral; his seduction of a coy thirteen-year-old was out of step with the mores of the time. In the seventies the film *Pretty Baby* portrayed the same theme, this time based on the story of photographer E. J. Bellocq and his fascination with an exquisite child prostitute of twelve. Not only was the film more readily accepted than *Lolita* had been, but also its leading lady, Brooke Shields, is one of the acclaimed child stars of the decade. The sexualization of young children is one of the results of changes in sexual attitudes during the seventies.

Historically, children have always been sexually exploited, but they were children of the slave class or of the lower class of their society. Today we have middle-class and upper-class girls becoming prostitutes—"baby pros." Dr. Dorothy Bracey, Director of the Criminal Justice Center in New York City, reports in her study "Juvenile Prostitution in Midtown Manhattan" that there are many part-time, experienced young prostitutes from affluent suburbs who make forays into the city:

> Of the out-of-town teenagers we studied, the majority presently turning tricks in New York have either had prior experience as prostitutes or at least have had serious flirtations with the idea of sex for money. The total innocent who is corrupted by the evil city is not a commonplace figure in midtown Manhattan.*

The New York Port Authority Runaway Squad has labeled these children "Weekend Warriors." * They are children who live with their families in the suburbs or in middle- or upper-income residential areas of Manhattan, attend school regularly, and work as prostitutes on selected weekends. Many of them are wealthy children who have no need for money. They prostitute themselves to relieve the boredom of their everyday lives, for kicks. The dangers of this development are many. For one thing, these girls serve as role models for classmates, bringing word about the commercial-sex world back to their schools in the "bedroom" communities of metropolitan New York and other big cities. Dr. Bracey says:

> It is unknown to what extent this is a widespread phenomenon, but it does have some interesting implications regarding the spread of juvenile prostitution in the middle class. . . . the presence of these part-time prostitutes in the middle class provides the opportunity to an ever-in-

creasing number of middle-class girls to learn prostitution. If this is true, juvenile prostitution may become a matter of direct concern to white, middle-class parents to a much greater extent than is presently true.*

Their socioeconomic and cultural backgrounds make the Weekend Warriors different from other juvenile prostitutes. They are better educated, generally do not have pimps, and can mingle with an upper-crust clientele. In addition, they convey their sexual expertise to peers back home and act as recruiters of prostitutes like themselves. Bryan pointed out that there is an apprenticeship system through which girls are taught by a peer how to be successful call girls.* Bryan did his study in Chicago, but it is applicable to prostitution operations in New York or Minnesota or Kansas or California.

An unsettling aspect of the problem of baby pros is that they apparently are frequently used by people in high places for gratification. *A Sexual Profile of Men in Power* showed that the use of children by men who are highly successful in government is not unusual.* Precisely how many cases of this there are is unknown, but Sam Janus and Barbara Bess found that of 5,000 clients of prostitutes in their study, 60 percent were men in politics.* Of course, not all the prostitutes were juveniles, but we do know that, as Dr. Dorothy Bracey reports in her study, police often do not list a prostitute as a juvenile. She believes that juveniles are not accurately represented in arrest statistics.*

Child prostitutes are used in other countries, too. Roman Polanski, the movie director who was arrested for having relations with a thirteen-year-old girl, maintained that only in the United States were people so prudish. Indeed, there is evidence that child prostitution is involved in international politics. Jack Anderson reported in his New York *Daily News* column of December 20, 1977, that he knew the "sordid details of a story that would revolt the world." He told of the sexual abuse of girls aged eight to fourteen by the top leaders of a South American government.

And there has long been international trafficking in young girls, in some of which the United States is involved. *The New York Times* of March 27, 1977, reported on Mexican children who cross the border into California to engage in various criminal activities, including prostitution. These children are sometimes taken to San Diego, where they are "sold" to a purchaser who then owns the child. Children reportedly have been sold for $300 to $800, depending on the child's age (the younger, the higher the price) and attractiveness. It is speculated that some of these children are used in the pornographic film business. Most of them move as itinerants back and forth across the Mexico—United States border.

Within our borders we have the infamous Minnesota–New York connection, the pipeline which channels juvenile prostitutes from Minnesota and other midwestern collecting points to New York City. Al Pahlmquist, the police officer who runs Midwest Challenge, a rehabilitation center for drug users and prostitutes in Minneapoils, claims that as many as 400 girls a year are shipped to the East. What keeps this pipeline in operation is the great amount of money involved and the ready buyers and sellers at either end.

Many men have claimed that extramarital sex with a prostitute doesn't count, that it doesn't constitute being unfaithful to their wives. Having no emotional tie to the prostitute, they say the experience is not as guilt-producing as an affair would be. The same goes for child prostitutes. Whatever residue of restraint or compunction a man may feel about engaging in sex with a child is reduced when the girl is a prostitute. A prostitute has "been around." Her cool attitude appeals to many men. The young prostitutes have a certain nonchalance all their own. This attraction to nubile young women is encouraged by magazines such as *Penthouse* and *Hustler*, which push innocence as sexiness. And, too, the increased practice of group sex may have removed some of the age barriers; intergenerational sex became more acceptable after the sixties.

The future for the child caught up in child prostitution is a grim one. It takes its toll immediately and long-range. Federal

Bureau of Investigation crime statistics show that 70 percent of the women now serving time for felonies were first arrested for prostitution.* C.A.T., a feminist prostitute organization in Los Angeles headed by Dr. Lois Lane, takes this realistic stand: "Prostitution is viewed as a social problem contributing to a wide variety of social problems, including drugs. . . . since prostitution is frowned upon by society and is an illegal profession, it is extremely difficult for a woman to find a legitimate occupation when she leaves the life." *

Secondly, as a child, the young prostitute suffers. She loses the growing time needed to mature, to develop a self-image, to value herself. Young girls who enter the sex market have trouble seeing themselves as desirable in any way other than as a commodity, a sex object.

In Los Angeles, according to police statistics, it appears that there is an even greater market for chickens than there is for female child prostitutes, but elsewhere both the supply and the demand for young girls—"baby pros"—still far outstrip those for boys.* In talking to some of the girls' clients, one is struck by a strong sense of deep hostility along with a view of women as a negative influence in the men's choice of sexual object. The terror of women becomes unmistakable when they talk of young women aged twenty or twenty-five as being "over the hill."

Like homosexuals, these men seem to be pursuing some ideal whose qualities they project upon the actual child. Unlike homosexuals, they vehemently reject any "father-daughter" relationship. A compelling reason for seeking out very young girls as sexual partners is the terror of advancing age and particularly of being boxed into a husband-father social role that seems all limitation and no possibility. A child, who has no past, seems to provide the momentary illusion that by possessing her, one is at the beginning of one's own life when every road is open.

Sometimes, too, one glimpses a poignant nostalgia for a little girl loved long ago when both were children, the senses and emotions painfully acute, and consummation impossible.

Again we talked to three men, Don, Jack, and Bernard, all

faithful clients of baby pros, and to a fourteen-year-old prostitute, Brandy:

BERNARD: It's absurd even to ask, why do I go for young girls? Why, this whole damn society is built around youth and nothing but. The shrinks have been doing us a great injustice, making mature men who go for young girls feel like freaks. Look at all the millions of dollars that are spent in this country by old bags trying to make themselves look young—everything from getting their boobs lifted to rearranging their faces, just so they can try to look young. So why should I feel like a pervert for going for somebody who really *is* young?

JACK: For me it's the sense of innocence, purity, and sincerity. I've had girls, frankly, as young as ten, and I've got to tell you that some of them would knock your eye out. My preference is for girls at just that age where they start budding, if you know what I mean. I find it just irresistible. Sometimes you get a little girl who is right on the brink, with those beautiful, tiny, firm breasts and a firm, clean body with no sagging or folds or wrinkles—it's an absolute turn-on for me. Anyone who looks at Brandy knows that this is youth and this is quality. There's a freshness and a vitality in this kid that no old lady in her thirties can match. Even though I'm thirty-six and divorced and she could be my daughter, she isn't, and that's what makes it for me.

DON: Some people are surprised at the fact that I have just turned forty and am interested in girls less than half my age. But to me and to a great many other men I know, a young kid—and by young I'm talking about eleven, twelve, thirteen, fourteen—who knows what she's got and enjoys her body and enjoys making a man feel happy is a treasure. Maybe it reminds me of the little girls I used to love, and maybe what I'm doing now is only what I always wanted to do with them, I don't know. My marriage is a good one, and occasionally my wife and I do get it on, and when we do, it's okay. But there's a world of difference between the kind of sex you get in a marriage and what you can have with a young kid.

BRANDY: I got started at a party at one of my girl friends'. There was a lot of good dope, and I got really stoned. Then this older guy, about thirty-five, came on to me, and we got it on, and afterward he asked me if I would do a favor for him. He had this client who he owed a favor to, and he asked me if I would go out with him and be nice to him, for $100. The idea excited me right off the bat. The other man, his client, was really nice; he even gave me a $20 tip. I was only twelve then, but I looked older. I was ready to tell him I was seventeen, but he never asked.

BERNARD: There is absolutely nothing wrong with a man being able to get his pleasure wherever he wants. I'm not hurting anybody. I pay my tab. I'm kind to these girls; I'm not like some of the freaks I hear about that beat up on them. I'm well aware of all the different revolutions that have been going on in this country, the sexual revolution and the feminist revolution and the gay revolution, and I see no reason at all why I should justify my particular preference for young, early pubescent girls.

DON: I find that the young kids today are very different from even five or ten years ago. There's much more enthusiasm, there's a lot of passion; you know they're not faking it like so many older women. I find in these kids a warmth and sincerity I can't seem to find anywhere else.

In my business I have to entertain a lot. I have yet to find a salesman or a buyer that's going to ask a kid to bring along her birth certificate and turn her down if she's under sixteen.

JACK: I've had a good deal of experience—I spent many years in the armed forces in a lot of different places—and I find that in other countries they aren't as hung up about the purity of youth as Americans seem to be. I think it's a disgrace, the fuss everyone made about Roman Polanski and that thirteen-year-old girl. To me what's important is the kid was willing and he was willing, so what's the big deal? He even paid her well for her time. That kid wasn't a virgin. I'm not talking about using any kind of force; I'm talking about a girl who knows what she likes. If she likes older men, that's terrific.

She's getting what she wants, and I'm getting what I want.

BERNARD: I think that even though a lot of people were shocked when *Lolita* came out, it really hit a very sensitive nerve in our society, simply because everyone knew that that's where it's at: Men are interested in young women, *very* young. To me a girl of thirteen or fourteen is every bit a woman. As a matter of fact, I understand that there are kids who start getting their menstrual periods at the age of nine or ten. Well, I'm from the South and I follow our old maxim, "If they're big enough, they're old enough." It's a two-way street—the kid can say no just as well as I can. But it certainly is a hell of a lot nicer and a hell of a lot more rewarding when we both say yes.

DON: I guess eroticism is a very personal thing. For many guys the kind of thing I'm doing right now with Brandy and her friends might have been just a masturbation fantasy. Maybe they even used that fantasy to be able to make it with their wives, I don't know. What I do know is that I've found myself to be much freer and much more able to really get into the substance of sex with a zest I thought I had left behind years ago. There's something very rejuvenating about being with a young kid; for a little while at least, time and space are suspended. Suddenly, I feel young again and I feel good. For one thing, there isn't the criticism or the demands that older women are so notorious for. I frankly wish I had been born into this generation instead of into the inhibited World War II generation.

BERNARD: It's not just the firmness of the flesh and the fact that nothing is sagging. It's also that the kid still has a sparkle, that she still has some idealism, that she's going to be doing something with her life. It's an upbeat experience for me, not like these tired old whores. Being with somebody young is definitely exciting, and being with somebody young and also sexy is absolutely the greatest for me.

Everything is easier with kids. You don't get any of the nasty sarcasm that some of the old broads dish out. I mean, an old hooker can really cut you to pieces. And hookers get old so early. I've known girls in their twenties who can be very nasty and very bitter; life is passing them by. I'd rather be with some-body at the beginning of the voyage. These kids are still on the carrousel; they're going to catch the brass ring. They're excited and they want to please me, and I certainly am inter-ested in pleasing them.

DON: I also enjoy women in their twenties and thirties, but nowhere near as much as a young kid with her wits about her and that basic animal sensuality that only kids have. They can be so happy with just little things that would seem laughable to an adult. I like to think it brings out the kid in me, too. And certainly since I discovered them, I've found that my sex life has improved and increased; it's a much more important part of my life now.

JACK: I don't like to pussyfoot; I think if the truth be told, any guy would rather have a young kid than a woman. I be-lieve that this starts right from the time when you're young yourself and you find that these young kids who tease you and wave it in front of you are getting off on your being turned on by their little bodies.

I've found that if you're gentle and you listen to what these kids need and you're tender, they love to be taught by an ex-perienced man. There's a thrill in being the first guy to do all kinds of things with a girl that I don't think anything else can replace.

BERNARD: From a physical standpoint, there's no question about why it's a turn-on. From an emotional standpoint, there's just much more sense of comfort. These kids don't look to criti-cize or compare you negatively with anyone else. I know that maybe it's a bit of a father thing, but let's face it—every man that's twenty years older than a girl is bound to have people making some kind of father comparison, but I think it's stupid. I'm nobody's father, and certainly not these girls' father, al-though I've helped a great many of them, and I think I'm very nice to them.

JACK: This kid looks up to me. I'm somebody special in her life, and she makes me feel like her teacher. There's a lot young girls have to learn, you know, and I helped her to get set up in her apartment here when she called on me. I always find that she's very grateful and appreciative for anything I've shown her, not like some of these jaded old ladies—and I mean they can be jaded at twenty-five or thirty.

BRANDY: I notice that some of them will talk about their daughters, say that I remind them of their daughter or of somebody they've gone with who was young a long time ago, and that really turns them on. I've even had guys who told me they have trouble making it with older ladies, like over twenty-five, but that they have no trouble with a young girl.

What I find they like is when I act a combination of innocent —pretending that they're teaching me—and sophisticated but appreciative. I don't know why but they like it that way. All these guys want to play teacher; they really get off on teaching me things. Don't any of them realize that I may have done them before? Anyway, they don't ask and I don't tell them. I just give them all my attention, and make my eyes round with concentration on them, and I "ooh" and "aah" a lot, and they're happy.

JACK: My own experience is that if I let myself go with what feels good to me, then I not only enjoy it more, I can appreciate my partner more. Certainly Brandy is nobody's fool. This is not only a pretty girl but also a very bright girl. This is a young lady who has her eyes and ears open and knows the score. This kid knows more about turning men on than probably most girls twice her age.

DON: I must say that it's probably not for everyone, though. A man has to know who he is and what he wants from the world. Some guys tell me—and I find this strange—that when they're with a young kid, they fantasize that it's their daughter. I think that's sick. When you have to start using fantasies with young kids, you may as well give up the whole show. But I think that when the two of you agree, provided you both know what you're agreeing to, then you have the best it can possibly be.

BERNARD: I find that call girls are getting younger and younger anyway, and if I'm paying my money, I might as well get what I want. You're going to find that the tendency in the next few years is absolutely toward younger kids. It's beginning to come out in the open now, and it's going to become more and more accepted. I may be a bit early in this, but I'm definitely more of a trend-setter than a freak.

Only partly concealed under the defensive rhetoric, according to Dr. Robert E. Gould, Professor of Psychiatry and Associate Director of the Family Life Division of New York Medical College, is a barely contained "performance anxiety" and a terror of comparison. Bernard was explicit about this.

"The pedophile with a child," says Dr. Gould, "can feel that the threat to his mastery is minimal. He is much more comfortable dealing with someone who is completely outside his sphere of competition, and the best way to be sure of this is by restricting yourself to virgins or children. I suspect that with many men it doesn't much matter whether it's a boy or a girl, as long as it's someone who is incapable of making judgments based on experience.

"The power factor also plays an important role. They must be dominant, which doesn't necessarily mean sadistic; they can be very kind and loving, as so many of them say they are. But unquestionably they must feel themselves to be the initiators, the stronger, the more masterful. If their usual life experience has made them feel weak and inadequate with their wives or friends, then they need this one area in which they can prove themselves to be dominant, superior, and in control."

One might suspect hidden motives behind the pedophile's object choice from the contradictions that animate his perception of the child: She is innocent, not "jaded," and looks eagerly to be taught; at the same time, she already "knows" more about how to please a man than any of the "old bags" of twenty-five or thirty will ever learn. The paradoxes are resolved when it is understood that this vision serves the need to maintain an illusion of control. The child is a pure sexual being with no independent will or judgment (hence the "innocence"), but she also has desires (if she were perceived as innocent even of sexual impulse, the client would have to see himself as a sadist or rapist), and what she wants exactly corresponds to what the client wants (as is the case with the homosexual pedophile). In short, she serves as an idealized projection of his sexual will.

Many men who are actively pursuing this new sexual ideal have somewhat more difficulty than do Jack, Don, and Bernard in subduing a sense of guilt. Some deal with it by laying the responsibility on the insistent seductiveness of the "new generation." George, who teaches in an expensive prep school and has had a variety of sexual experiences with his female students, said, with some uneasiness, "If anybody had told me when I was in college or graduate school that I would one day be talking freely about having sexual relations with junior high school girls—my own students—I would have said they were crazy. My own sense of morality is still intact, I think; what I believe has happened is that this society, and especially this new generation, has revolutionized attitudes so much that these kids just don't experience the hang-ups that we did.

"Sex for many of these kids is simply a pleasurable thing. And, in fact, I do feel that for most of them it's a far safer and more desirable outlet than drugs."

George first succumbed when he began moonlighting as a tutor after school in students' homes:

"It was a pretty short time before I found myself having sex with one of these girls, but I went through a great deal of agony first. No, I wasn't going to have intercourse. I spent a tremendous amount of time just fondling and touching them, feeling that I was helping them to orgasm, thinking that probably it was good for them. Sometimes the kid would insist at first that she also wanted to do something for me, so we would move on to mutual masturbation and later to oral sex.

"I always had a real hang-up about penetration and intercourse. With everything else I could justify to myself having fun and making the kid feel good, but I always had hanging over my head the danger of pregnancy. I guess that shows the generational difference right there, doesn't it? These kids never worry about it at all. I have students in my classes as young as twelve and thirteen who are on the Pill. But I only had relations with a few students—I'm not going to let this become any promiscuous or gang-bang scene. I like to consider myself a sensitive person; I feel that I helped these children.

"They all know I'm not married, and at the beginning of the school year when I have new classes, I always get a tremendous number of crushes, which calm down rather quickly. It's after that that a few girls persist in making contact with me, either having me over to tutor them or inviting me to dinner with their moms. They have very effective ways of seeking out my companionship.

"At this point I'm always very careful to make sure that if I do have an affair with a kid, she's one who can handle it. First of all, I make sure that she wants it as well—she practically has to seduce me before I'll go to bed with her. And although by now I've gotten over my hang-up about penetration, I always have condoms with me just in case the kid is not on the Pill, although most of them are—some since the age of eleven.

"I feel that I'm moving with the times, and that this kind of socialization is not to be criticized so much as who the socialization is with; as I said, I'm not going to pick a kid who'll be troubled about it afterward. I think I'm a good person and that I contribute to these kids' lives; and I must tell you quite frankly that they have enriched mine as well. I frankly admit I like the freshness, the innovativeness, the excitement that these kids bring to bed. In fact, it often happens when I've been involved for a while with a kid that she'll tell me about her girl friend who also wants to make it with me, or perhaps she suggests we should all make it together. I always turn these invitations down. I'm not looking for any kind of orgy; I'm not out to become the Pied Piper of seduction. What I do have is what I feel is a meaningful relationship with the girls I'm involved with. None of them have been hurt, and many I'm sure have found pleasure.

"I'll never forget one kid who was very depressed, alone

all the time, hadn't seen her father for years—a very pretty child, but moody and lost in her own thoughts. When she and I became involved, initially we spent months when I would just listen to her talk about herself, which she badly needed to do. Then I noticed that gleam in her eye, you know what I mean? That gleam that told me she was excited and getting interested in something more than just my being a good listener. From there we moved to an affectionate, then to a passionate relationship.

"If I had it to do over again, the only thing I would change is I'd probably get involved with these kids much earlier. I never should have ruled them out for so long just because they're young."

George's discomfort, such as it is, at what he is doing stems from a vestigial sense that he is, after all, in a position of trust which, even by today's standards, he is violating. George knows how to "pick" his objects, he can manipulate the social situation, he ingratiates himself with parents before he moves. But essentially his impulses and his rationale for yielding to them are the same as those of a man we'll call Fred, a middle-aged caretaker in an elementary school whose case made headlines recently in the local newspapers:

"This isn't anything that I'm particularly proud of, but I gotta tell you that when I see all these movies and television shows they put on these days, I don't think I'm doing anything so terrible. Mind you, I'm not justifying, but I don't really hurt any of these kids. They like me, they come to me. I'm a custodian, so there's always some kids wandering around the lost-and-found looking for things. And every so often I get this urge. They're so pretty, and I don't think they realize that even at eight or nine they have this animal magnetism about them.

"Look, I'm fifty-eight years old now, and I've been doing this for a good long time—I'm ashamed to tell you how long. And I find that kids nowadays are maturing earlier, and I don't think I hurt them. I try to control myself. I'm a churchgoer and I pray for forgiveness, but I find that I just can't help myself sometimes. I look at these kids, they dress very sexy, some of them at nine or ten are developed even, and they have that kind of daring look in their eye. All I do is, I just fondle them and play with them a little bit, and then I leave them go. In all the years, I haven't hurt anybody.

"I don't think what I do is bad for them—I don't really know anymore what's good or bad—but my own feeling is, no, I'm not proud of it. I would be very upset if anybody did this with any of my kids. I have two daughters, and one of them was molested when she was a kid, and I was pretty upset about it at the time. But kids today get over it quickly, they forget very fast, so what the hell?

"I don't want you to think I'm proud of what I do; it's just that every so often I feel these urges coming on. And it's a strange coincidence that whenever I feel one of these urges, there's always some little kid looking very cute, walking around the place shaking her little ass."

The first child who complained to her parents about Fred was ignored by the school authorities, although Fred was sent to me for a psychological evaluation. My recommendation that he receive psychiatric treatment was also ignored. When the parents of a second and then a third child complained, a scandal erupted and threw the whole school administration into a defensive tizzy. Finally, Fred was fired, but no further action was taken, and, in fact, he was almost immediately afterward hired as custodian at a parochial school nearby.

On the whole, child molesters are not taken very seriously; they are seldom convicted, and when they are, sentences are mild.* Many authorities agree with Dr. Gould, who believes that while sexual relations between adults and children are always based on coercion, ". . . much of the talk about the lasting trauma is somewhat exaggerated. In my experience a child who is pretty well together in other respects and is doing well in the world, getting along with his parents and in school, will not be permanently harmed. Like any other single unpleasant experience, it will not have lasting effects unless the child is borderline to begin with. In that case, a strong precipitating factor like seduction or molestation can make a difference, but it tends to get blown out of proportion to its real importance.

"I've seen a number of children I would characterize as casualties of the sexual revolution, but I also saw many children before that who were damaged by the hypocrisy and the depression and the guilt."

In my own experience, children who have premature relations with adults, whether they are forced or not, often suffer a prolonged trauma, which manifests itself in disturbed sleep and appetite, persistent nightmares, trouble at school. It seems unquestionable still that while free sexual play among children of the same age is harmless and perhaps even to be encouraged, sexual relations of any sort between children and adults are *always* an unwarranted interference with the normal process of growth and can only hurt the child.

The most important "right" of a child is the right to develop at his or her own pace and in his or her own time, to be as free as possible from the emotional demands of the adult world.

Chapter 9

BOYS ARE . . . GIRLS ARE . . .

One of the most far-reaching contributions of psychoanalysis has been the discovery that children are intensely sexual beings with an erotic life that is expressed in both activity and fantasy. Most of what we know about the sexuality of children, however, has come to us indirectly, either recovered retrospectively from the memories of adults who were undergoing analytic treatment or from a few case histories of children who were being treated for phobias and anxiety states.

Such case histories are limited in number and scope. What is missing in them, and what has been generally unavailable until now, is information about the sexual feelings, attitudes, knowledge, and experience of normal children, acquired directly from them and in sufficient quantity that we can begin to see some general patterns and trends. The present study is an attempt to fill this gap. My data was obtained from interviews and from compositions and projective drawings by some 9,500 schoolchildren. Most of this material was gathered between 1976 and 1980 from children of kindergarten age through the ninth grade in public and private schools in ten states.

Although I had the cooperation of parents and school administrators, I nevertheless met some of the same problems mentioned in the chapters entitled "A Decade of Change" and "Fears and Fantasies": how to create an atmosphere in which children could feel confidence and trust. I found that the children were least constrained if the compositions were assigned by student teachers, graduate students, or even a regular teacher from another class, and this is the practice I followed when the project took its final form.

I also found that direct questions were much less productive than those phrased in such a way that the children could hide behind an appearance of denial. For example, asking them to tell what they knew about sex or to discuss the sexual content in films they might have seen seemed to dry them up. But if the same questions were put negatively, asking why they should *not* see X-rated movies, for example, the children communicated freely.

Children know all too well that direct questions, although apparently neutral, usually imply an expected "correct" response, which the child can only guess at. Such phrasing places the child in a dilemma as to whether the way to approval is to say nothing and appear innocently ignorant, or to show off his or her knowledge. In this study I was not interested in discovering how young children meet adult expectations, but in finding out how much they really knew and what their true feelings were about sex. It was therefore essential that the questions stimulate the child's interest, provoke the fullest possible response, and allow the child to feel safe from judgment while responding.

In addition to negatives, seemingly insignificant variations in phrasing made the difference between a guarded, minimal response and a composition which showed verve, wit, and an obvious pleasure in talking openly about what probably had only been guiltily whispered before. For instance, "What do you like about boys (girls)?" sometimes seemed to arouse suspicion, while "What is a boy (girl)?" and "What do you most dislike about boys (girls)?" usually produced colorful, delighted replies. Making it possible for the children to deny any interest in the opposite sex even while responding freed them to express themselves unrestrainedly.

Because their curiosity so often meets a rebuff from adults, most children harbor an ambivalence that colors all expressions of their experiences of and feelings about sex. The following composition illustrates this very clearly in its passive hostility tinged with sarcasm:

Lloyd (Grade Five)

WHERE I LEARNED ABOUT SEX

I learned about it in the street, from my friends, and in dirty books. I think when I get married I will tell my children about lays, blows and humps etc. I think you should learn about things like that at home not the way I learned them. This are the facts of life your son (daughter) will have to learn about them thinks sooner or later. A girl would have to know about periods and what to do when they get one and not have to go crying to there mother saying my _____ is bleeding, my _____ is bleeding.

In this composition there are two aspects to the anxiety, which is pronounced. In spite of his swagger, Lloyd wants to show compliance with the values of authority ("dirty books . . . I think you should learn about things like that at home not the way I learned them") at the same time he conveys his resentment at having these values forced upon him. He also is letting us see something of his terror at the enigma of female sexuality.

The next composition is a typical example of another common preoccupation among children: their isolation and alienation from adults, and their anger at being rebuked—or, worse, ignored—when they try to reach out:

Theresa (Grade Seven)

SEX EDUCATION

It all started when I was 11, my girlfriend had just started to menstruate and she was only 10! Since I lived with my aunt and uncle who are both in their late seventies my aunt when I asked her said just keep clean or made some other excuse to get off that, to her embarrassing topic of sex. Well anyway my girlfriend told me everything, and when I say everything I mean everything, love, marriage, intercourse, how to get children, breast feeding, felt-up, laid, masturbation, menstruation, shaving, and how to be more feminine.

Well anyway I really could not believe she knew all this and I knew nothing whatsoever, but she had books her mother sent away for and some she had sent away for. She showed me everything just like it was should I say mother or aunt should have. Well by that time I was 12 and she was 11 and that August I started menstruating, and since we go away for the summer I couldn't wait to tell her. But I just couldn't tell my aunt I have got my period. I buy my own napkins, belts and my pants with my allowance. The only one that knows is my friend. I guess this is not right but I cannot help it. I just hate my aunt when it comes to this subject of sex.

The infamous "generation gap" begins with the breakdown in communication between parents and children on sexual questions, particularly when the children are seeking concrete information and reassurance. Too often they get neither. This may be because the parents associate sex with guilt and shame. Amy Dwelley notes this attitudinal problem in her article "Sex Interests of the Pre-School Child":

Many adults, including even parents and teachers, may not be fully aware of the extent to which a pre-school child may be interested in sex. This could be because some adults feel the subject is shameful and degrading and therefore a child in its complete innocence could not have "evil thoughts" such as sex curiosities imply.*

If such parental attitudes make themselves felt very early, the child will not only feel uncomfortable with sex as an abstract unknown, but also with his or her sexual development. He or she will turn to peers for information.

It is important for parents to overcome their discomfort, to fight any urge to transmit negative feelings about sex, and to take the initiative when children begin to inquire about it without being invasive. They should encourage healthy discussion of sex. Some say it is dangerous not to do so. In *The Innocent Child*, Hugo Beigel says, "The ignorance of a four-, five-, or six-year-old child may appear very cute to some adults, but actually it is a perilous state. . . . If therefore, a child of five has never asked questions about sex differences or reproduction, something should be done about it." * Children will absorb only what they are ready for at a particular time. There is a sensitive but vital link between a child's right to privacy and his or her need to know.

While the parents who block their children's efforts to discover their sexuality with peers and who protest loudly against sex education in the schools present one extreme, we now have another group of overzealous parents. They are the ones who foist information upon children who have not asked for it and are not prepared to receive it, in the misguided belief that this is the way to prevent neuroses later on. We describe the manipulative strategies of some such parents in the chapters entitled "Family Sex Games" and "Our Children Today." Neither group of parents does its children any good. Children need protection, privacy, and safety, and then benign neglect to discover themselves at their pace with their peers.

In this survey of children's attitudes toward sex, we will consider two grades together—kindergarten and first grade, second grade and third grade, and so on—since developmental differences can be seen more clearly in two-year blocks of time.

Kindergarten and Grade One

By the time a child enters kindergarten, he or she has probably already attended a nursery school or a day-care center. Whatever the child has been taught by parents has therefore already been adulterated by contact with other children, and now that the child is five or six, he or she is ready to begin integrating information received from peers, teachers, and the media.

The central, indeed the obsessive, sexual concern of children of kindergarten age is, "Where do babies come from, and how do they get out?" They have learned the functional use of the genitals as passageways for elimination, and almost all know that the babies grow "in the stomach." Some assume that the babies get out through the anus, since other solid matter emerges there, while others favor the "zipper" theory, the idea that the doctor opens up the mother's stomach as though it had a zipper fastening, and painlessly removes the baby from the belly. The notion that the baby comes out of the vagina is frightening to many children, especially to girls, who cannot imagine how their small bodies could possibly expand enough to contain and then eject anything as big as a baby.

Curiosity on this subject is rampant and frequently obsessive. Some children ritualistically act out scenarios of childbirth as a way of mastering their fears, while others become anxious that their own bowel movements may at any time produce a baby. And this fear is not confined to girls.

Almost all children have grasped the fact that the baby lives in the mother's stomach. A variety of ideas circulate as to how it comes out, but very few young children know how it got there in the first place. Most parents will answer questions concerning pregnancy and birth, especially if the child already has had some experience with the arrival of younger siblings, but not many will discuss conception with children this young. At kindergarten age some children somehow understand that both a man and a woman are needed to "make babies," but why and how escape them.

Research has shown conclusively that gender identity in the individual is quite solidly established by the age of two or three, but it is usually not until kindergarten that children think of each other as possessing gender.* When they do think of the opposite sex as such, it is for their essential role in the creation of babies; but first come falling in love and getting married. Children often enter kindergarten with very firm ideas about romantic love, marriage, and babies following each other in due course—ideas drawn directly from their primary identification with their parents. Contact with other children soon modifies these as interest expands to include playmates as well as potential love partners.

Many studies, such as Tavris and Offir's in 1977, show that males at all ages engage in more physical aggression, including fantasy aggression and play aggression, than females do.* This difference shows up when boys and girls begin to play with each other at school, where they are placed together for long periods of time and their play interests and aggressive needs become blatantly clear to them for the first time; thus the complaints in some of the kindergarten and first-grade compositions about the behavior of the opposite sex.

The first competitive envy of peers who are more popular or who become leaders emerges now, and anxiety over status can reach tormenting heights even this early. Many of the following compositions ridicule and demean the opposite sex as a way of expressing deep anxieties, although a good deal of self-deprecation occurs as well. Embryonic feminine protest and early homosexual ideation also can be seen in the products of both boys and girls. But the first two grades are above all excited at spending most of the day in the company of other children, and at having taken the first step toward becoming grown-up:

Kenny (Grade One)

WHAT IS A MAN?

A man is a grownup boy. He is someone who likes to play with kids. He gets married to some girl he likes.

Randy (Grade One)

WHAT IS A MAN?

A man is a big and tall and strong working fellow. He earns the money for your family.

In differentiating men from women, girls already give a clearer, more detailed account than boys do:

Leslie (Kindergarten) (Girl)

Girls have long hair. Girls have ribbons in their hair. Girls wear stockings. Boys wear pants. Boys have tie shoes. Girls have pocketbooks. Girls wear blouses. Boys wear shirts. Girls have dishes. Boys wear blue sweaters. Girls wear all color sweaters.

As Tuddenham pointed out in a study of sex differences among grade school children, even in the primary grades, children conceive of each other with the stereotypical view of adults. Boys are seen as aggressive, daring, and frightening. Girls are thought of as docile and timid:*

Robert (Kindergarten)

Boys aren't supposed to hit girls, except when they are married. There is not much difference between boys and girls. Boys make friends faster, and yes I like girls. Stacy I must like because she is the one who is going to marry me, because she is my friend.

Carol (Kindergarten)

Boys have short hair. Girls have long hair. Girls wear sunglasses. Boys wear regular glasses—they can't see very good. I like boys because they are my friends. Girls also have trouble with boys because boys can beat people up. I like my brothers. It is nice to be a girl because they look pretty. And I need a pink crayon to draw a girl.

While we kept the composition questions general ("What is a boy/girl?"), our interviewers asked some kindergarten children specifically how they could tell boy babies from girl babies. Although several of the children had younger brothers and sisters, they denied any knowledge of the genital difference, offering instead such safe answers as "Girl babies are bigger," or "Boys cry more." This denial of genital awareness persists for a long time, even while the same children are keenly conscious of sex differences and talk freely of prospective marriage partners and the babies they expect to produce themselves.

By first grade some openly erotic interest begins to appear.

It is fascinating to see how a child of this age who wants to express envy of the opposite sex, or to disguise interest as dislike, will often use a sibling as a concrete example of the hatefulness of boys or girls; while the child expressing affectionate or erotic feelings toward the opposite sex will speak only in generalities:

Louis (Kindergarten)

Do you like girls?

I would like a girl to kiss me. I like girls. They are good to boys. They are beautiful. I would give them a big kiss. Then they would kiss me again. I would have fun and enjoy it.

Jody (Grade One)

Do you like boys?

Yes I do like boys, when they kiss. I don't like boys when they kick.

Crystal (Grade One)

Do you like boys?

I don't like boys because they are mean, and they fight with girls. My brother is mean and says curses. I like to go to sleep with him, my brother, because he's my brother.

Barry (Grade One)

Do you like girls?

I like girls sometimes. I like it when they give you a box of candy, but then I have to return it because you can't accept candy from strangers. I don't like girls because they make trouble, they trip you.

Diane (Grade One)

Do you like boys?

I like boys. I have a boyfriend. I think he's nice looking.

I like his attitude, he helps me, I like to be chased. I don't like my brother, he is a pest, he hits me and pulls my hair.

Grades Two and Three

By this time most children can read. Middle-class children tend to read above grade level; even among those this young there will be some who can read at seventh-grade level.* This means they can and do absorb information from advertisements, magazines, and books which are not meant for them and which may use language of adult pornography.

With the age span from the beginning of Grade Two through the end of Grade Three running from seven to almost ten years, there are also growth disparities. A few girls by the third grade are developing breasts, and since the average age for the onset of puberty is now twelve, some ten- and even nine-year-old girls are already menstruating; this is no longer a biological rarity.* And as the age at which menstruation first occurs continues to drop, so does the age at which girls' curiosity about boys becomes openly expressed, while boys their age, who lag a little behind, are still masking their interest in girls as disdain.

Until now, too, boys and girls have been about equal in physical strength and have played together as a matter of course. But with this tendency toward extremely early maturation, the differences in muscular development and endurance appear much earlier, too, with the result that girls as young as eight or nine already may have lost the interest in competitive sports with boys that a generation ago would have absorbed much of their playtime.

Studies, such as those by Terman and Miles and by Looft, have shown that boys this age are attracted to occupations involving danger, excitement, and physical activity.* They want to be athletes, police officers, doctors, and astronauts. Their behavior may show imitation of their perception of the behavior of their idols. For example, an eight-year-old boy may mimic the stance and swagger of a police officer or a cowboy or a football player.*

Fears of inadequacy in the struggle for status now begin to crystallize around the sense of inferiority vis-à-vis the opposite sex, emerging as a resentment of "showing off"—"I would like girls better if they didn't show off all the time." Whereas pre-school and kindergarten children conceive of gender as a fixed state of being, second and third graders are compelled to realize that being a boy or a girl is also a matter of continually affirming one's sexual identity through one's behavior. The constraints imposed by parents and other authority figures weigh more heavily as the indulgence granted little children begins to give way to more rigorous and sex-defined standards. This is the time of the first classic injury to the self-respect of little girls:

"You mustn't sit all sprawled out like that."

"But Johnny sits that way and you never say anything."

"He's a boy; he can sit any way he likes. You keep your knees together like a young lady."

But at the same time that parental pressures increase, an opposing force begins to be felt—the powerful influence of peer pressure. In the first two years of school, by far the strongest, if not the only, authority comes from parents; by the second and third grades, the approval of other children counts for almost as much. Some children begin living almost double lives, with one persona for school—usually the side that is all bravado, pushing hard for independence and a sense of mastery—and quite a different one at home, where the child may still be the sweet-tempered, pampered baby. For boys, as Greenson points out, this means disidentifying with the mother and going on to identify with the father.*

And while by now almost all children know where babies come from and have a pretty good idea of how they got there, they still shy away from the notion that they themselves were created that way by their own parents.

Some second and third graders are beginning to take a "romantic" interest in each other, and many will talk at length about their girl friends or boyfriends with a wealth of physical detail. Very conspicuous here is the emphasis on the sense of smell—that primary and most primitively aphrodisiac of all the senses—but it is usually mentioned negatively, with a great show of disgust at "smelly boys" or girls who "use stinky perfumes." A tremendous amount of energy goes into the repression and denial of very strong emotions, especially by boys who "hate" girls with a vehemence equal to the helplessness they feel at the force of their own feelings:

Lizette (Grade Two)

WHAT I DON'T LIKE ABOUT BOYS

I don't like boys because they don't take baths. Also I don't like them because they are nasty, horrible monsters and their mouths stink. Also they are dumb and stingy. They like to kiss too much.

Cynthia (Grade Two)

WHAT I DON'T LIKE ABOUT BOYS

Boys are nasty, they like to kiss girls. They ask you for dates every day. They are sissies. They don't take you on dates! Boys are nasty, but girls are not like that. They are worth nothing. My brother has a girl friend, and I have a boyfriend. Boys are very nasty. Why do girls have to go with boys?

The next composition is unusual in that it puts in writing what ordinarily only produces private giggling among boys. Both the excitement and the anxiety which generate it are very obvious:

Roy (Grade Two)

GIRLS

Andrea is shite head, yes, a very fine fuck head. Her tishie fell off, and all the piss came out and then her fannie split in half and poo poo and it mixed up and it was a diarrea.

The next two boys are eager to show their understanding

of present and future social roles, and to exhibit their compliance with what will be expected of them:

Leonard (Grade Two)

WHAT IS A GIRL?

Girls play with dolls and dollhouses. They wear dresses and perfume before a date. Girls have high heals on there shoes. Girls like to get married and boys don't. They don't rastle, fight or do dangoures things. A girl likes to look pretty and boys look hansome. They wear lipstick and hairspray. Girls wear makeup, bracelets, necklaces and beads. The girls have the baby in their stomach.

Mike (Grade Three)

GIRLS

Girls are weaker than boys. We hate them when we are young, and love them when we are old. Some look good and some are fat. Some are fickle and some have nice personalities. P.S. I have more to say when I am older.

The following girls' compositions show the beginnings of awareness of what it means to be defined as the "other," the "opposite sex":

Danielle (Grade Three)

BOYS ARE . . .

Boys think they are so cute but when a girl comes to school looking beautiful they whistle and when the girl turns they start laughing. And when a boy falls in love they chase you all over the world.

Roberta (Grade Three)

WHAT I LIKE ABOUT BOYS

I like boys because sometimes they give me the gum out of the baseball cards. Boys are good. A boy plays ruff, like tackel football and boys play with trucks. I do not, I like to play with boys because most boys do not cheat when they play. Boys wear ties when the get dressed up, and they wear tuck seddoes. Boys wear after shave like High Karate and Black Belt. Boys shave and girls don't. Boys wear only a bottom to their bathing suits. But they are not great, and I hate boys.

Grades Four and Five

These children range in age from nine through eleven. They have an accurate grasp of the biological facts of life, and some even possess very detailed information about deviant sexual practices. Many children now express more or less open curiosity about their parents' sex lives, although they may, at the same time, be reluctant to accept the idea that their parents are sexual beings.

Fourth and fifth graders can read almost anything, and they also are, of course, avid consumers of television programs, so much so that they have even been credited with the ability to make and unmake adult stars. A large part of Farrah Fawcett's success was attributed to her popularity with boys under ten.*

In general, boys of this age worship the same adult sex symbols as teenagers do—movie and television actresses, pop singers, and some young female teachers as well. And, in imitation of the older boys, these children claim to look at the same female features—breasts, hips, legs, and face (in that order). Boys will concede now that they like to look at attractive girls, well-dressed and carefully made up and coiffed.

In general, children have tended over the past decade to become more self-consciously aware of themselves as aesthetic and even sexual objects than they have ever been before. This is one important area in which innocence seems to have departed forever. Part of the blame must go to the eagerness with which television and print advertisers have seized on the possibilities for exploitation of this lucrative new market of pre-teenage children. Children today have been "educated" to view themselves as important consumers whose opinions and tastes are anxiously solicited.

By the end of the fifth grade, more than 40 percent of the girls will have begun menstruating, and 58 percent are beginning to develop breasts.* Not only is this happening earlier, but in some families it is being talked about much more openly—and not just in confidence with the mother, but with father and siblings as well. Many middle-class families are proud of having "demystified" sex, a process which features explicit clinical discusions where nothing is withheld. It has been my experience that parent-child sex discussions like these, in which there are "no holds barred," can be very invasive and seductive. There is a great need for children to maintain private inner lives whose boundaries are respected by parents. These areas, not surprisingly, generally include a child's sexual development. As we have seen in the chapter on Family Sex Games, so-called "openness" is often destructive to a child's emotional growth. In many cases there is a symbolic "I'll show you mine if you show me yours," and in some situations it is not symbolic at all but very blatant. The "mystery" that children attach to their "secret" worlds helps to establish the beginnings of a unique and personal identity. This feeling of control over one's private life indeed leads to the successful mastering of other areas of development as well. Privacy is vital if children are ever to be able to feel whole, competent, and at peace. Society already impinges so much on children and is so overinvolved in their budding sexuality that loving parents serve their children best by protecting them from undue pressure and invasion, even from themselves.

A nine- to twelve-year-old boy may say he has, for example, already "gone steady" twice, a girl, two-and-a-half times— "going steady" meaning an enduring relationship of anywhere from half an hour to six months.* Brother-sister incest, too, seems to be on the increase in this age group.* This incestuous trend is part of a relaxation of previously entrenched taboos which have gradually, over the past decade or so, been losing their power to inhibit. In general, brother-sister sex play is considered the least exploitative if the children are close in age. It becomes a matter for concern when the brother is five to ten years older than the sister. Another symptom of the trend toward early sexual involvement, of course, is the 80,000 cases of pregnancy in girls under twelve that were reported in the United States in 1979.

Children in the ten-to-twelve age group who are sexually active tend to reverse the usual process and begin using contraception only after they have already become pregnant at least once.* Part of the reason for this is simple ignorance, but some of it must be attributed to ambivalence, a partially conscious wish to bear a child. We explored this in the chapter on child mothers.

The complexity of the birth control issue may be seen in the case of a thirteen-year-old girl who was going steady with a fifteen-year-old boy and was receiving instruction in birth control at a gynecological clinic for children in New York. The doctor (our informant) gave her a two-month supply of birth control pills and told her to come back when she had used them up. At the end of the two months, the girl reappeared, bringing two girl friends with her. They explained that notwithstanding the careful instructions given to the first girl by the gynecologist, they had decided to divide the pills among them, each girl taking one pill every third day for the two-month period. The gynecologist, upon examining the girls, discovered that all three of them were pregnant. It is episodes like this which have led public health officials recently to agitate for mandatory sex-education classes in the fourth and fifth grades.

This mysterious behavior also owes something to the fact that the boyfriends of these girls are usually older, more experienced, and more sexually aggressive than they are, The sanctions against premarital sex for girls have largely disappeared. Whatever freedom from frustration and repression this has brought, it has left them with fewer defenses against unwelcome sexual demands. Younger girls find it especially hard to say "no," or even "wait," if the boy is at all insistent. Contraceptive measures, especially if one is too young to have a very developed sense of cause and effect, tend to be neglected.

Another cause contributing to the high incidence of pregnancy seems to be the current fashion for rejecting anything that is not "natural," both because it may be physically harmful and on the theory that it interferes with spontaneity.

Finally, great numbers of young children are already habitual users of drugs—mostly marijuana, but also amphetamines, barbiturates, and even cocaine. Surveys in Maine and Maryland, for example, showed that one out of every six youngsters in *all grades* in high school smoked grass daily.* In her research on marijuana use, Elisabeth Coleman Brynner found that we now have a new breed of marijuana users that includes eight- and ten-year-old children and is very different from the flower children of the sixties.

The parents of many of the children who wrote the following compositions and whom we interviewed were members of the "counterculture," that first generation of middle-class drug users, and a number of these children have told us not only that they smoke marijuana themselves, but that their parents supply them with it. An additional 8 percent of the children we interviewed along with their parents told us that the latter supplied not only marijuana but Quaaludes, cocaine, LSD, and "uppers." These parents offered two main arguments in justification: "You can't stop it; everyone else is doing it. It's better for me to control the supply so I know they're getting decent stuff instead of that junk they pick up on the street," and "Drugs never did me any harm, they're organic substances. I like to see my kids turn on and it makes me feel good to turn on with them." With such parents (even though they may be a minority) condoning the use of drugs, the liberated sex and drug culture of the young adults of the sixties has made its way down through teenagers to young children.

The nine- to twelve-year-old group is the one in which boys first begin to show homosexual trends, which may or may not become fixed and permanent. The most recent studies show that 90 percent of adult male homosexuals were confirmed in this sexual identity by the age of twelve.*

Girls of this age are allowed more latitude for ambiguous behavior. They can have "crushes" on other girls and on their female teachers; they can go in for pajama parties, the sharing of clothes and beds, and indiscriminate physical contact without attracting any particular attention. Female homosexuality has never been taken as seriously, nor its preliminary signals suppressed as harshly, as has male homosexuality.

The next composition clearly shows some of the sexual ambivalence that is still characteristic of this age:

Heide (Grade Five)

WHAT I THINK ABOUT BOYS

I like boys because since I moved here I haven't a friend yet that likes to run and race with me. They always walk. Boys like to run, so do I. I like to wear pants like boys do, boys aren't always mean. They can be nice if they want to and if you give them a chance and understand their heads like I do. The girls don't give them a chance. I'm a tomboy. I guess that's why my family is mostly men and boys. But some boys are bullies. I don't like bullies. Also boys are gentlemen sometimes. It's good to be a nice gentleman. But almost every boy is messy. But I'm not messy.

In contrast to Heide's spunkiness is the resignation of the next composition, which has accepted subordination as the inevitable fate of women:

Hope (Grade Five)

WHAT IS A BOY?

A boy is a human being that all girls need. Besides God created man first. Many people say the man is the leader. If it weren't for boys and men ladies and girls wouldn't be able to have children. Every woman or girl needs a man or boy. As people say every woman or girl follows their man or boy and pretends to like it. Some girls pretend not to like boys but deep down inside they really like them and when the little ones grow up they will learn. That's what a boy is to me.

Fourth graders, as I also showed in the chapter entitled "Fears and Fantasies," are the most given to violent fantasy, which they will weave into any narrative and exuberantly incorporate into any description of their lives:

Stephen (Grade Four)

GIRLS

I like some girls because my mother was one and without her I couldn't be born. Girls make the world fun but sometimes to me, girls are a bit funny. They try to take advantage of you especially when they are bigger than you, but most of all I think that girls are very dangerous in that if they don't like you and they cook for you they can poison you or they can put something in the clothes that can make you feel you're going to die, or stab you in your sleep. We'd be better off without the girls that are not grown. They are lucky because when they grow up they don't have to go to war, because they can't shoot a gun and they wouldn't try to.

In the next composition, every female role—mother, future wife, present attractive nuisance—is cataloged with the cockiness and comic self-assurance that is typical of fourth-grade boys. Fourth graders see, with a clarity they never have again, the entire adult world as inherently improbable and preposterous, and they can sometimes mimic its pretensions to devastating effect:

Allen (Grade Four)

WHAT A GIRL MEANS TO ME

A girl means a disagreement
A girl means washing the dishes

A girl means a high bill
A girl means getting up out of your seat
A girl means getting yourself polluted
A girl means getting a shot
A girl means eating cauliflour
A girl means getting a lousy supper
A girl means a marriage
A girl means a divorce
A girl means a kiss
A girl means a coody shot
A girl means answering the question I am pretty
A girl means watching her TV programs
A girl means listening to her radio
A girl means getting called on when you don't know
the answer
A girl means not getting called on when you do know
the answer
A girl means walking to school
A girl means no lift to school
A girl means do this when you're doing that
A girl means being screamed at
A girl means no TV
A girl means do your housework!
A girl means did you practice your saxophone?
A girl means a late dinner
A girl means don't touch
A girl means no curses
A girl means you get germs
A girl means spanking you and then saying I am sorry
A girl means a billion dollar kid to take care of
A girl means no candy and no popcorn either
A girl means a teacher
A girl means killing yourself
A girl means buy it with your own money
A girl means no!!

Matthew (Grade Five)

WHAT I THINK OF GIRLS

They talk too much. Sometimes they are nice, but that's only once in every 5 million years. Girls are sick because every morning when they wake up they put on tons and tons of makeup and they are in the bathroom for at least two hours. They talk on the telephone too much. They only where their clothes once and then they throw them in the closet to rot. They have to buy every record that comes out. They are always talking about clothes. When they are little girls they have to have every doll, toys, and games. When they see something they start spending money like it grows on trees. The only good thing about them is when they do something nice for someone and that isn't very often.

Fourth-grade girls have the same violent impulses as the boys do, and they are less restrained in expressing their feelings toward boys aggressively. Their excitement is closer to the surface, and most of their "hostility" is really a way of practicing a primitive form of relatedness:

Brenda (Grade Four)

WHAT IS A BOY?

What is a boy. A boy is sometimes bad and sometimes good but not all the time. Some boys are nasty, all the boys in my class are. Every girl they see they think they can get. They'll be running after us, and they also come into the girls' bathroom. All the boys in my class are ugly. Maybe a little bit of them are handsome, but not all of them. The boys in my class think the girls like them. I got a boy that sits next to me who is a bug. I don't want to say his name because he might think I like him, but I don't. If you wear a dress in my class the boys will try to feel your legs. If I wear a dress and a boy tries to feel my legs I will kill them. That's why boys are bad. Like they say what will boys do without girls? I don't know and do not want to.

I know what I will do without boys, have fun, but not so much, but it will be fun. Some day I would like to punch them right in the eye till their pants fall down. And they are liars.

The next two girls have more than made their peace with the conventional feminine role; it gives them obvious pleasure:

Beatrice (Grade Five)

Boys

Boys are pretty good. At least they are most of the time. All girls in my class say they hate boys except that's ridiculous because for instance there are dances every other Saturday night and there wouldn't be any girls there if they despised boys. Also, this year there is a lot more teasing about romance, which almost proves that the opposite sex has become a main interest.

The boy that I sit next to always sticks nails in me, steals my junk, writes on my desk, pulls up my dress, calls me up with dumb recordings, and gets me in trouble (not on purpose). I really think it is fun even though I always end up getting yelled at. I would rather sit next to a boy than a girl, anyway. Boys must like girls too, because they always tease them. Girls mature faster than boys too so they say.

Brenda's battles and antagonism, however, are more typical of girls this age than the complacency of Beatrice.

The last composition in this group expresses the boys' equivalent of this acceptance; girls have become manageable, at least as a concept:

Gerald (Grade Four)

WHAT IS A GIRL?

A girl is a member of the female sex. A girl turns into a woman and has children. She has to marry to get a baby.

Women have things men don't. Girls have more energy. They say girls mature faster than boys. Girls have long hair with a beautiful figure.

What is a girl? A girl is a woman who goes through changes. Girls grow to become women. Girls are foxy, sexy, cute, beautiful and pretty. I like girls a lot.

Grades Six and Seven

These grades, the beginning of junior high school including ages eleven through thirteen, are considered by teachers and school administrators to be the hardest to handle; inhibitions against overt sexual behavior and aggressiveness in general have lessened. As Maj-Britt Rosenbaum said, in a paper presented to the American Psychiatric Association, "At no time in life does a body change as rapidly and as dramatically as during adolescence, taxing the adaptive capacity of the ego. Suddenly the formerly so familiar body looks and acts differently and also evokes new reactions." * Only 12 percent of the girls have not yet begun to menstruate.* Eighty-eight percent of the children in this age group have seen R-rated films; 15 percent have seen at least one X-rated film.*

The Kinsey Report of 1953 found that only 35 percent of women who had graduated from college had ever masturbated, while among working-class women an insignificant number had ever done so. Today 35 percent of sixth-grade girls have experimented with self-arousal, while 91 percent have had some sort of sexual contact with boys ("fooling around").*

By thirteen or fourteen, boys have "gone steady" an average of four times, girls six times.* At this age "going steady" is likely to mean that intercourse, or physical intimacy that comes close to it, has occurred. However, the boundaries between the state of virginity and its absence are now mostly blurred. The "going all the way" of previous generations is a term that has virtually lost all meaning, as sexual initiation has lost its momentousness along with most of its mystery. Together with the developmental trend whose rule of thumb is that today's twelve- to fourteen-year-olds are about six years ahead in their social and physical development of children that age in the late 1950's, this means that some degree of sexual activity is the rule rather than the exception among urban children in their early teens, and that it is a matter-of-fact experience for them rather than any sort of profound awakening.*

In statistical support of this phenomenon is the fact that while venereal disease is increasing to epidemic proportions among the population in general, the fastest growth of all is among children between eleven and fourteen.* Over 1,500,000 cases are being reported annually in the eleven-to-sixteen age group.* Since gonorrhea is asymptomatic in its early stages in women, it is suspected that the ratio of unreported to reported cases is as high as three to one.* There are more cases of venereal disease among children this age than there are of measles.* A possible reason for this, in addition to the much greater exposure, is the increased use of birth control pills instead of condoms, which give some protection against venereal disease.

Although the birth rate in general is declining to an all-time low, illegitimate births are on the increase and rising fastest of all among white girls from ten to fourteen.* Pregnancy rates among white girls in their early teens are increasing two and a half times faster than for minority children of the same age.*

According to the next composition, these children, or some of them, still carry the sexual guilt that was supposed to have evaporated twenty years ago:

Helen (Grade Seven)

Boys

　　Today's teenage boys have certain ideas on what girls should and should not do and even know how to do. For example if you're seeing a boy he may want to have sexual intercourse or touch you in some way and you may agree that you love each other and there is nothing wrong with it. If he finds out or if he thinks that you're experienced, he looks at you as "that kind of girl!" They all want to think that they're the first and only boy you've ever made it with. Also it's okay if you mess around with them but when it comes to marriage all of a sudden they want a virgin. If I could change things I'd put us on equal footing, morality is morality, no matter what sex you are. Either it is right or wrong. Not right for one and wrong for another.

In many of the compositions by children in this age group, it is striking how often the girls express a wish for boys to be "nicer," that is, to exhibit less of the traditional masculine aggressiveness. It seems that the boys are not unreceptive to such attitudes. As Mirra Komarovsky found, "Some machismo elements are questioned by young men. Moreover, the ideal of masculinity now includes some qualities such as patience, sensitivity, and artistic appreciation."* The next composition is a good example of a boy at the age of cowboys, gangbusters, baseball, and girl-hating acquiescing to the desire expressed by Helen and others. He is unafraid of giving lyrical expression to very vulnerable feelings of sensual need:

Joseph (Grade Six)

GIRLS ARE

A girl is a feminine person. She should be soft and nice. A girl is a person who should have nice shining hair and wear pretty dresses. A girl should have a soft complexion and should have nice shaped eyes and a nice mouth. A girl should have the things that she needs to be a girl. A girl is beautiful like a flower in bloom. A girl is gentle as a bird. A girl is someone you can fall in love with. A girl can be attractive. Girls are very smart. A girl is energetic. You can talk to girls when they are in trouble. A girl is someone you can kiss at times to make them feel better. Some girls are very shapely figurewise. If a girl hangs around boys all the time she will act like a boy, if she hangs around girls she will act like a girl.

Girls now are trying out a series of social postures and roles in a search for one they can feel at ease in. Early physical maturation together with the social demands on this generation to grow up fast means heavy pressures from within and from without to establish workable relations with the opposite sex and little time to explore what this means. The girl who wrote the next composition is still seeking an identity of her own; at the same time, she is busy experimenting with attitudes toward boys and ways of being comfortable with them:

Yolande (Grade Six)

BOYS ARE

A boy is a mate, a friend, a companion. Some boys are unattractive and smart or sometimes it's vice versa. But sometimes you get lucky, and the boy is cute and smart. Sometimes boys know or think they're cute and try to act like they're too good for you. Some boys are *male chauvinist pigs*. They think girls sometimes are just made for them. For instance you go with a boy and he tells you he's going with about two other girls. Then you say oh, since you can date other girls, I can go out with other guys. Then he says you can't do that. You say why not? He tries to think of an answer. He says because you're a girl. Some boys swear they're smart but don't know a thing. Some boys think we girls are a sex object. That's what a boy is. And some of the things I said go for girls too.

At each grade level, we found some children who felt at odds with their gender. Some were simply floundering miserably, while others were struggling to come to terms with their sexual identity. The next composition is by a child who is obviously under great pressure to accept what she urgently feels to be the drastic limitations of being a girl:

Toni (Grade Six)

BOYS

Boys are more fun to play around with than girls. Girls stink when it comes to playing! Boys are not like girls, they are funny and will talk to you. I have liked boys and boys' toys and games ever since I was in second grade. It would be more fun to have gym with them. I hate wearing dresses and being very gentle. I like being R-O-U-G-H! It is not fun to be taught to only stick around with girls and having slumber parties. But parents are so strict they won't let you have a boy-girl party or anything of the sort. Boys get real cool bikes and get to egg houses on Halloween. I have trailed behind them. But girls are alright I guess if you have to be one. I wish I was a boy. But I guess being a girl isn't that bad!

Toni's composition, and others by both boys and girls in this age group, show how the sex-role identification process began changing in the seventies. Wesley and Wesley (1977) argue that "women must become more masculine and men more feminine to be able to lead satisfactory lives within the structure of today's society."

For these later grades we added the question, "Where did you learn about sex?" because the providers of sex information tend to carry their own value systems. Most of the children said they favored sex education in school, since their parents, who they felt should have taught them, for one reason or another had shirked this obligation. The following girl's composition, however, makes an exception of parochial schools:

Constance (Grade Seven)

SEX EDUCATION

I got most of my sex knowledge from my parents and my girlfriends outside from school. I think that sex should be taught in your homes and by your friends. At home you can get a better understanding from your parents because your parents went thru it. Your friends can give you a better understanding. I don't think sex education should be taught in Catholic schools because the nuns do not know what sex is like. Sometimes if you get sex from your friends they will tell you the wrong meaning but sex is usually a good thing. I know and realize all about the sexual intercourse between male and female sexes. I know about the time of pregnancy, menstruation, etc. I think the terms blow, raw, meat, dick, etc. are very vulgar.

Boys also prefer school as the source of sex education, even while claiming that they already know all about it anyway. What they are actually looking for is confirmation, not the basic facts; very few children learn anything substantially new to them about sex in classes, but they need to receive reassurance about these facts from someone in authority whom they trust. This is especially important now that sex has been brought into the realm of advanced medical technology; an accurate understanding of the mechanism of contraception, for instance, seems to be beyond the grasp of many teenagers.

Sex-education classes can also be vitally important, in the absence of guidance from parents, in setting limits and standards of behavior for children who at this age feel helpless to do so for themselves. Children cannot be expected during this period of extremely rapid growth also to assume the responsibility of self-direction. They look instinctively to adults for help, and when they fail to receive it, feel betrayed. The following composition is explicit about this:

Paul (Grade Seven)

SEX EDUCATION

I think I know a lot about sex. I know how to make children. I know what the sift is. I know what a scumbag is. I jerk off. I know what a blow job is. I know girls have periods once a month. I learned it from bits of information from the outside, but wish my parents would tell me to make everything clear but I think they will tell me pretty soon since I am just 14 years old. When I get older I think my children should learn in school.

Grades Eight and Nine

This group includes an age range from thirteen through fifteen. For many of these children, this is a crossroads, separating those who plan to go to college from those for whom high school is the end of the line. With the latter, antisocial and self-destructive behavior begins now; some drop out of school altogether only to face an abyss of boredom that, without any further education to pull them out of the unskilled labor market, may be the beginning of a lifetime of deadening apathy. This is the time when the drug problem can become serious, when earlier tentative experimentation may develop into an addiction. The scoring (acquisition), the preparation, and the shooting up give rootless, bored children a structure for their time.

By the age of sixteen in most states, even fifteen in some, children can drive—which means not only mobility but privacy. For many the only place they have to be alone is in the car, which is soon converted into a mobile bedroom. For this age group, 275,000 pregnancies are reported annually, and probably at least double that number of abortions are performed.*

Untreated venereal disease, especially the asymptomatic gonorrhea which has already become epidemic among younger children, is showing up now at a later stage in its course when the symptoms become obvious—one of its consequences sometimes being a permanent sterility in girls.* (Gonorrhea in boys produces unmistakable symptoms very early; boys are therefore more likely to be treated before irreversible damage has been done to the reproductive organs.)

What makes life most difficult for this age group is the completion or near-completion of physical development—the girls especially looking and acting like mature women—which con-

ceals a massive insecurity and a sense of being pushed too rapidly toward crucial decisions that will affect the whole course
of their lives. Simultaneously, these young people can be irri-
table with parents and teachers who see that they are still not
capable of running their own lives and tell them so. Dr. Maj-Britt
Rosenbaum was aware of this:

> I have been struck repeatedly by the pseudo-liberated
> facade that so many even very sexually active girls present.
> They may profess the most liberated viewpoints—blissfully
> unaware that their unconscious lags behind. It later makes
> itself heard, nowadays seemingly much less in terms of
> guilt, but in terms of confusion, or "scrambled brains," as
> one girl put it, after an especially intensive period of
> searching for sexual partners.*

Both boys and girls now attract sexual attention from older
men and women. Girls may suddenly find themselves with
older men whom they cannot handle as easily as the boys they
go to school with. Recently, too, older women have been freeing themselves from the social restraints which placed teenage
boys out of bounds to them. As a result some boys also are
finding themselves in situations with women where they are in
way over their heads, grappling with emotions they cannot
control.

The homosexual tendency, where it exists, has been consoli-
dated by this time; homosexual boys by the age of fourteen
have accumulated considerably more sexual experience than
have heterosexual boys of that age, thanks in part to the existence of a vigorous homosexual subculture with a receptive
social structure.*

At the same time, however, "going steady" has begun to lose
some of its appeal. Instead, one hears more about the importance of "hanging out" with one person, sleeping together on
a casual basis but with no "pressures" or "demands" on either
side, and only minimal "involvement." This is the social-thera-
peutic language of the sixties, with its view of sexuality as a

passionless, cooled-down, easygoing, healthy, painless exercise in "interpersonal relations." The seventies saw this style affect even the moment of sexual initiation among young teenagers, a moment that seems to have lost some of the terror and wonder that previous generations invested in it.

Despite the prevailing blandness, however, there are still some marked differences between boys and girls in their social relationships. Girls of this age are more interested in doing things in groups; boys prefer either to be alone with a girl or with only one other couple. Boys, when talking about what attracts them, put much more emphasis on the physical features seen in isolation from each other (breasts, face, buttocks, legs). Girls tend to see the whole person, body and "personality," together; if they do separate the body from the total being, they still see it as a whole, not an assembly of parts.

The first composition in this age group is a good example of a very matter-of-fact approach to sex:

Camille (Grade Nine)

BOYS ARE

I think sex is taken very much for granted these days. Once you reach the age of 11 I think kids should be taught about it. When I was in sixth grade I was curious so I hung around with the wrong kind, and got something out of it. Often I went to the library and looked it up. Some boys I know have nothing on their mind but sex. Sex is beautiful if you take it in the right sense, but if you don't, it can be very dangerous. I think it's okay to have a boyfriend once you know what sex is all about. Every time I asked my parents they told me I'm too young. Now I'm going on 14 and I'm pretty sure I know everything. Sex should be taught in every school, Catholic and public in sixth grade and up, no lower.

The next composition, although it seems to express a greater intensity, gets most of its energy from this boy's view of sex as an instrument of rebellion against his parents:

Stanford (Grade Eight)

SEX EDUCATION

I think that sex education should be taught in three places, in school, home, and outside the home. I think the only reason parents don't groove on sex education is because they are scared what you might find out and that they will lose supreme power over you as a parent. Where I found out about my sex was in the street, my friends and I really get it altogether when we talk about sex and how it really grabs onto people and gives them outrageous feelings. The information I know is how to stamp out virginity, masturbate, get blow jobs, get hard-ons, and get a lay off a girl or maybe get her so high that she will end up pregnant.

The next two compositions show girls coping with the question of how to deal with the issue of male dominance and female submissiveness:

Linda (Grade Eight)

WHAT I LIKE ABOUT BOYS

What I like about boys. I like boys who are gorgeous. Also with a great personality. Personality counts more than anything else in the world, and especially if a boy has a really *strong* personality. Anyway what would I do without a boy? Boys should be easy to talk to, at least I think so and have manners but not be square. Boy do I hate square boys. But on the other hand boys are murder. They beat me up, pretending to flirt and to play around with me, but I wind up with black and blue marks on my arms, on my legs, and other places I can't mention here. No, but some of the boys I stay with are nice but they are all taken already. But I honestly hope I really find a really sweet strong boy who is really an earthy guy. He should have a good sense of humor, and he has to be a little crazy like me.

Agnes (Grade Eight)

DATING

The teenage boy that everyone knows and wants to go out with is a sex fiend. Sex is the game and they try to cop anything that they can from a girl. The guy with a car has his roving bedroom, and he tries anything anywhere. Most guys also try the pickup act to get a piece here and there. The only thing a girl can do is play hard to get and be expert at self defense. Lucky for me I took karate. The female has to know the male weak spot—balls. A little action, puts him out of condition as well as in pain to stop him.

Finally, I reproduce a group of compositions which offer a mélange of received ideas, compliance with convention, complacency at living in such "enlightened" times, even an unabashed admission of incestuous impulses. This selection is inconclusive, far from exhaustive, but perhaps suggestive of the range of responses from teenagers to our invitation to ponder the fascinating subject of sex:

Ginny (Grade Eight)

BOYS

Well I feel that sex is a natural part of life today. In the past sex wasn't considered as it is today. It really depends on the personality or background of a person to judge if sex is a correct thing. Well me, as a person, I think that short skirts and see-through blouses are fine, but I wouldn't go near to having a boy touch my personal places on my body unless I knew him fairly well. I know that my mother would think the opposite.

Tim (Grade Nine)

DATING

Dating is generally a boring staid way of getting to know someone. It's also a pain in its formalities. For me

I try to regard a girl more as a person to be with than a date. My sexual relations follow in the same pattern. If I feel like kissing a girl or touching her I do, whether I know her well or not. I may know someone for months and never touch her. For me the only fun sex is honest sex, and thank goodness there are some honest girls around. Not too many but there are some. The only time I ever indulge myself in a girl which I have no feeling for is if I'm high, which is fairly often. Not often enough however, I don't often find anyone I really like so I'm usually high as hell. If I follow my physical drive with a girl I don't like, I really don't enjoy it.

Eddie (Grade Eight)

GIRLS

Most girls are fags. But some you can do stuff with. These are the fun girls. There are a few unmentionable things that I like to do with them. But the girls you can do things with really are the best. For instance you can go to the nearest whorehouse which is not too far from school and get laid, when you get stoned, but the girls who are the opposite are really bad. They are a bunch of flat little dogs. But that is not my fault. The ones over 14 are the best. But under that are shrags that's because they're my age. Take my sister she has the best build and the most beautiful body and is cute. Boy I envy my sister's boyfriend, and I know just what they do, because I also watch them. I guess I'd better sign off here.

Saul (Grade Nine)

WHAT DO I WANT IN A DATE?

When I'm out with a girl, that I like, I like her for various reasons. One of the important ones is looks. Therefore I do want to touch the girl I'm out with. Unless she bores me. I go for a non pretentious girl with good looks, and a good build. However, I find few to meet my high standards. According to Masters and Johnson all girls are latent harlots. It is this concept that keeps me going.

If Freud had not developed the concept of a latency period, children's need for it is so great that it would have to be invented again for the 1980's. While precocity is often valued in our society, anyone reading these compositions cannot fail to realize that this precocity is the result of pressure. In many instances these children are coerced into competitive sexual performance. As recent research on adults demonstrates, they, too, are often trapped by performance expectations.

What is missing for children today is a breathing space, a time of life to enjoy childhood unhampered by adult needs. There is a need for freedom and personal development without the external world looking over their shoulders and judging them by adult standards. This will inevitably occur at some later stage. Children need the opportunity to have "pal" relationships and be able to be close to peers of their own sex. In this way they gain support, feel a sense of unity with their peers, and can face the stresses of sex and socialization in a stronger, more natural way. There is much to be said for team games and fun and play in the carefree manner that only children can have. Robbed of this period of life, children too quickly mimic adult behaviors, denying their childhood mores. It is increasingly rare these days for children to have this leisure time and not be rushed into instant adulthood.

Even areas of growth and development for young children become too quickly labeled sexual in adult terms, and then they take on the seriousness connected with this term. It takes wise, loving, and compassionate parents to protect children from outside pressures for sexual precociousness, and to love and appreciate their children for who they are, not for what they can do.

In a fascinating way, we are witnessing what I call "adult latency." This can be found among the newest burgeoning cult groups. The chief characteristic these cults share is the prohibition of premarital sex. Here we see a population of young adults in their late teens and early twenties simply giving up their sexuality. We also see here the ready willingness to give these authoritarian forces in their new world complete veto power over their sexuality, providing them with relief from what had been for them an anxiety-ridden area. The cults are keenly aware of this and actively solicit young people drifting around college campuses, as well as refugees from the drug culture, most of whom had burned themselves out in their previously promiscuous lives. Suddenly, it appears, these young people, who are in their sexual prime, are willing to give up this allegedly "free" living and casual sex. Why? The answer seems to lie in the fact that in childhood they were not allowed time for the original latency period. Thus, they become sexual beings early and lustily but without a sense of peace and comfort.

Psychoanalysis has pointed out that children have an erotic life of their own, but we must add that for healthy personal development, appropriate time must be permitted for it to emerge at its own pace. We must observe the children's calendar, not our own.

Chapter 10

OUR CHILDREN TODAY

Now we come to what is perhaps the most important question of all: Has there been a real change in the sexual life of so-called "normal" children—the children who belong to no deviant population, whose physical and mental development are proceeding as expected? And if there has been a change, how has it affected them, and what are its implications for their future and ours? Are we raising a generation of children who, as some visionaries believe, can teach us to live with the exhilarating prospect of true sexual freedom for everyone? Or are we due for a reaction, a swing back from the extremes of "liberation," which already may have become discernible in a recently observed trend toward a "new asexuality"?

Some of the people who work closely with young teenagers feel that the change has more to do with what gets talked about, and that the apparent enormous increase in sexual activity is largely illusory; others believe that the sexual revolution has indeed filtered down over the past generation from young adults to older adolescents to children. Certainly evidence for making such a case is not hard to come by. According to a report issued by the House Select Committee on Population in 1979, one in every five American children aged thirteen and fourteen has had sexual intercourse.*

But everyone agrees that whether or not they are acting on what they say, middle-class children are no more emotionally mature now than they were in the 1950's or at any other time in the past. Their knowingness, their often astonishingly articulate awareness, and their facility at self-analysis are nothing more than the contemporary style of psychic defense—masks that cover the same agonizing insecurities and fears that have always beset adolescents.

They may, in fact, experience even more severe anxiety than their counterparts of twenty or thirty years ago. For one thing, their families may not stay intact long enough for them to grow up in them. With a divorce rate approaching 50 percent, more and more children are developing a precocious alertness to signs of tension between their parents, and an anxious sensitivity to the frailty of the bonds holding today's families together.* If some children seem to be shrewd manipulators, underneath they are neither as self-possessed nor as detached as they appear. Their sexual acting out, which appears to be the result of a new sexual sophistication and pragmatism, can often be ascribed to an angry, hurt, vengeful, frightened response to a family situation that is no longer supportive but has in some way turned threatening.

Peer pressure, the pervasive use of inhibition-lowering drugs, and the proliferation of sexual messages from television, movies, songs, and print media together have far less effect on children, most psychologists agree, than do disturbances within the family. Even if the family is intact, a child who acts out sexually at a young age is usually found to be responding to some pressure, covert or overt, from within the home. These pressures can take a variety of forms, depending on the family structure, as we shall see.

To begin with, the most fundamental disturbance to a child is, of course, the trauma of divorce, of the sudden loss of structure provided by two parents who reinforce each other in the meting out of love and discipline. Dr. Virginia Sadock, Director of the Program in Human Sexuality at New York Medical College, says:

"Children who come from divorced families are much more vulnerable. We know statistically that one of the factors leading to earlier sexual contact is a broken home—specifically, a home in which the father is not present. The father is still, even in our culture, the authoritarian and the disciplinarian, and the traditional importance of that role has not diminished. When that particular control is gone from the home, there tends to be much more sexual activity on the part of the children.

"I have found that the girl who feels that she must go looking for love outside her home at a younger age participates in sex not because she has a stronger sex drive owing to hormonal changes, but because she has a desperate need to prove that she is lovable. She's looking for a human contact and reassurance she can't find within her family."

Children of divorced parents are compelled to grow up fast. The pain and anger which almost always precede the separation; the feeling of having lost both parents when the tie between them breaks; and the constriction, diminution, and preoccupation afterward which isolate children temporarily from whichever parent they live with—usually the mother—all conspire to produce a self-consciousness that is based not on early maturation, but on simple animal wariness. Long before the split, they develop a preternatural sensitivity to the complicated currents of feeling between their parents because they can't take the stability of the family for granted anymore. The parental relationship, no longer the unconscious ground of their existence, has become a source of worry. Many children try to manage their fears by developing their manipulative powers, often playing one parent off against the other, sometimes even pretending to have taken charge of the family's destiny.

One boy, John, said, "Actually, I was the one who initiated the divorce, when I was twelve. My father wasn't around the house too much because he was out making the bread and butter, of course, and he had a lot of extracurricular relationships besides. So did my mother—it was just a question of who had more. They were coming one right after the other, so I finally said, 'Why don't you both get a divorce?' I was caught in the middle, you see. My mother would come to me and want to know what my father had been up to, and my father would come and ask, 'What's your mother been doing, who's she seeing?'

"I just felt, 'Why all of a sudden do I have to become the parent?' So to make things easier, I said to them, 'Why don't you two get a divorce? That would be the best thing because you know it just isn't working this way.' At first, my father wanted to keep the relationship as it was because he was hung up on the idea of the family unit and having to stay together no matter what, although my mother really didn't care. She hated my father by that time, and it was clear that it wasn't ever going to work again. So after about a year, with a few separations first and sort of dragging it out, they got a divorce."

Once the new family arrangement is settled, the pressures change their shape but not their intensity. If single parents of young children are young themselves, failure of the marriage means starting over, this time encumbered by dependents. This responsibility can add direction and drive to a young parent's efforts to start a new life, but it also usually means strains that cannot fail to affect the children.

A young divorced mother typically has to start from scratch in three of the most important areas of her life: home, work, love. She has to settle herself and her children in a new home, mobilize her ambitions toward a career—or a more demanding career. Most divorced mothers, even if they receive child support, have to assume responsibility for a large share of the family's income—and battle the loneliness and the sense of social isolation which almost always threaten at first to overwhelm her.

Very likely she will soon set about finding a new husband, or take a lover, or at least look for some male companionship, however transient. This means an atmosphere of heightened sexual tension that the children breathe, too. Dr. Alan Jong, Chief of Child Psychiatry at New York's Metropolitan Hospital Center, feels that "when parents are divorced and the mother has custody of the children and is living with a man, unquestionably this has an effect on the child. Children find it very stimulating, whether or not the mother has a lover stay overnight—certainly if he lives with them. How the child responds depends on how intense a degree of sexuality he or she is exposed to."

Dr. Sadock agrees: "It means trouble and complications in a one-parent household when there is sexual performance. When the children see the parent with a variety of lovers, it naturally undermines the parent's position when he or she tells them to wait or practice restraint themselves. It's very difficult for young children—they're getting conflicting messages, and the younger they are the more difficult it is for them to comprehend."

Shannon, fourteen, living in New York with her divorced mother, feels that the main message she's receiving is neglect:

"I find it's just a little bit hard, with my mother dating and going out and sleeping around a lot. I don't mind her sleeping around so much, that's her business, but what I do mind is that she's never home. She's always calling me after dinner to say that she's either working late or staying over at some guy's house, or maybe she's invited somebody to come over and stay at our house with us.

"I don't know which is worse, the loneliness when she's gone, or having some strange man always intruding into the house and keeping me from being able to spend any time alone with my mom. I don't remember the last time we spent a day or even an evening together.

"My mother is very pretty. She's in her late forties, I guess, and she leads a very active social life. She tells me that most of the men she goes out with are her business contacts, and that she really ought to be going out even more than she does but resists because of me. But it seems to me I'm on my own most of the time, and it makes me sad."

This feeling of desertion is the most primary and urgent source of anxiety in a child. The younger the child, the more devastating the sense of helplessness and the anger; but, as Shannon makes clear, it can be a misery even to an adolescent. Dr. Jules Bemporad of the Harvard University School of Medicine thinks that the disturbance to the child living with a single parent, especially a mother who takes one or several lovers and sleeps with them at home, arises mainly from the child's sense of loss, and that the sexual stimulation is comparatively unimportant.

"If the parent is discreet and is not blatantly having relations in front of the child or involving the child in it in any way, I don't see any problem at all. I think the problem is not one of sex so much as loyalty or fear of the loss of love on the part of the child. I once saw a little girl who had witnessed through the bedroom door her mother having intercourse with a number of men. They lived in an apartment which had glass doors, with the child on one side and the mother on the other and only a sort of flimsy curtain separating them, which the child could look through.

"When the grandparents found out about this, they were horrified and brought her in for psychiatric evaluation. But I soon found that what actually bothered the child was being put in this room by herself when the paramours came over to see the mother. She had absolutely no understanding of what was going on sexually—or perhaps she did but repressed it. In any event, she certainly didn't think that these men were doing anything violent to her mother, she didn't see them as treating her in a hostile way, which is how many children interpret the moaning and the appearance of struggle in sexual intercourse. This child did not see it that way at all; the sex itself had no effect on her whatever. Her big complaint was simply of being kept alone in this room without her mother. The sense of abandonment was acute—she was extremely angry."

Even when it is obvious that the children are acting out sexually in response to the parent's example, the importance of anger at the mother's withdrawal from them can hardly be overstressed as a cause. But there are also other factors: A child who feels she has lost her mother as a nurturing and protective figure will sometimes try to appropriate those powers by imitating her mother's sexual behavior. The elements of identification and competition can also be strongly present, particularly if the mother encourages the child—as many mothers now do— by talking openly about her adult sexual attitudes. Shannon again shows how a mixture of resentment, emulation, and rivalry can provoke sexual acting out well before there could possibly be any mature sexual feelings:

"My mom is very open about what she does, and she's taught me a lot. She tells me a lot of the things she does with guys, and I hear about who are the better lovers and which lovers are really yecchy, and all about multiple orgasms and everything. Sometimes I feel uncomfortable listening to her and think it's all kind of strange, but I guess I'm getting used to it.

"I don't even know what she's looking for, whether she wants to marry again or is having such a ball in New York that she just wants to keep on with it. Anyway, she tells me it's important not to get pregnant and gives me advice about how not to, but otherwise she says it's all great fun and that I should be able to enjoy everything, including having intercourse. In fact, sometimes I have the feeling I might even have been a bit of a disappointment to her, being such a slow beginner. As of right now, I guess you could say that technically I'm still a virgin—but only technically.

"Last year at camp when I was thirteen, I had an affair with a marvelous lover who ran the camp and was thirty-five years old. We really fell in love head over heels, but he couldn't enter me. I was just too small—or he was just too big. We tried four or five times, but there was absolutely no way he could get into me. You see, I haven't started having periods yet, and even though I do have breasts, they're really very small. Many people have told me that I look much younger than my age. But we did everything else—we had oral sex and masturbation —and I found, just like my mother told me, that I can have orgasms very easily. I don't have multiple orgasms—I'm not even sure what that means—but I know I can get off with a man.

"The camp director last summer was not the first man that I had been involved with. I had tried before with one of my older brother's friends, who's about twenty-one. This was two years ago when I was still twelve, and he couldn't get into me either. I guess boys over twenty have larger penises than kids of fourteen, or even fifteen or sixteen.

"But it doesn't stop me from enjoying sex, and I certainly believe, from everything these guys have said, that I give them as much pleasure back. It makes me feel very grown-up to be with a real man, and I'm very flattered that they choose me. It's very exciting, and I feel I'm no longer a kid but that I'm being taken seriously."

Being taken seriously, to Shannon, means being able to compete with her mother for the attention of men, in which path she is being led—even pushed—by her mother's insistence and example together with her own need to fill the void of her mother's absence—not to mention her father's. (He is living with someone else in another city, and she sees him only a few times a year.) But there are ambivalences:

"I regard myself as a very sensual person, and I like men to be sensual and charming and sweet to me, and treat me like a lady. I don't think that the fact that I just turned fourteen should in any way mean that I shouldn't be treated like a woman.

"Right now there is another man, one of my teachers. He's forty-four years old, and he likes me a lot—really a lot. We've had lunch a few times, and he's talked to me; but just last week, after we had lunch, I was walking home and I realized that I really don't want to get involved with him. I think I've had enough for a while, I just want to get my head together now. It takes a lot out of me to have a lover that old, it really does. Of course, I can't let my mother know how old my lovers are, since some of the guys she goes with are younger than she is and younger than mine.

"I'll see what happens. If the attraction becomes really strong and if we find ourselves really liking each other a lot, maybe we'll end up being lovers. Actually, I don't know if I ever want to get married. I enjoy life, and I think I want to really try to be a somebody in the arts. I don't think I'll have time to have babies, and it doesn't particularly strike me as thrilling, getting married, living with one person and spending the rest of my life with him.

"I must admit sometimes I'm lonely, but I don't know if I

could trust any one person either. Look at my mother and father—they keep going out with different people, always trying to find the one who's going to turn out to be special, but they haven't found them yet, and they're much older than me and know a lot more what to look for. So I think I'm going to use my energy in my career and really try to get somewhere myself."

Shannon's life-style and precocious amorous adventures place her in the pseudosophisticated avant-garde group of early adolescents. Like others pushed too early, she has had to "sink or swim." There is a subtle competitive pressure from her mother which this child is responding to. One can feel the pressure Shannon is under. Nothing can relax, and emotions which in an adult may flow joyously race frantically in this child, with a continual free-floating anxiety. With all the "love" affairs, she has never experienced a sense of comfort, peace, or trust. She is driven to ever more outlandish affairs and ventures. By having sexual relations with men older than her father, she unconsciously negates the roles of her parents by pretending she is a peer and not a dependent. For all practical purposes, the parents have abandoned their parenting role. The fact of intergenerational sex was brought into this child's life by her parents' inviting her into their bedrooms; the mother with her boyfriends, and the father with his girl friends.

Shannon was overstimulated at much too early an age and responds now primarily to the secrecy, the danger of discovery, the ostensibly forbidden quality, and to hostility, rather than love. In this case the parents' exhibitionism provoked the fiercely competitive reaction we see in Shannon now.

Sometimes a mother's example can be a deterrent, and her urgings provoke a reaction. The sexual restlessness and striving so characteristic of the 1970's is nowhere more evident than in the tendency of so many mothers to enlist their daughters in the endless search for self-fulfillment under the guise of "sharing." Even without the disturbances of divorce, mothers often feel a great urge to participate vicariously in the sexual discoveries of their adolescent children—daughters in particular—perhaps so as to recapture the sense of freshness and freedom. This need can be so strong that the mother sometimes even is instrumental in initiating her own child's sexual experiences, a practice which has become more common with the prevalence of the belief that any sex is better than none, and you can't have too much of a good thing or start it too soon. The daughter, however, seldom fails to understand the real meaning behind such maneuvers. We saw something of this dynamic between Shannon and her mother. Here is another case—Joy, aged fifteen:

"I live outside Chicago with my parents and my brother. My father is in the glass business; he has a large factory that makes mirrors and all kinds of glass. He seems to really like his business and absolutely adores my mother. She's a very pretty woman, much younger than he is, about fifteen years younger, and she gets almost anything she wants. She dresses really well and always attracts a lot of attention whenever they go out together.

"My parents are very liberal people. They're both well-educated—my father has a master's degree in business administration, and my mother has a bachelor's in English. They really are good parents, and I can talk to them about a lot of things. For example, when I was in sixth grade and some of the kids started using pot, I asked my mother about it. We discussed it, and she told me that if I wanted to try it because my friends were, that was okay, but I should be careful not to get hooked on it— she didn't know that you can't get hooked on pot.

"But I also found that when I started to talk to her about sex, she began to get just a little uptight, as if she was almost sorry to hear that I was getting interested in it. When I was in fifth grade, I remember making out with a little boy and my mother coming across us and giving me a bit of a lecture. But later she came around to where she told me that if I did decide I wanted to do anything, I should go and get a diaphragm, and that in fact she'd take me to the doctor herself.

"I was twelve then but already on the Pill. I've managed so far to keep it hidden from her. I don't know why I didn't tell her about it, but I guess it was because she wanted so much to be a part of what I was doing, I felt a little crowded. She'd want to go with me every time to the gynecologist, and I felt I ought to have my own gynecologist. I was starting to get very uncomfortable with her knowing everything and probing into everything I was doing. I hate to say it, but in some ways I think she was getting off on hearing what I do. I was lucky— I have a girl friend whose father is a doctor and he gives her pills, so she just gets me an extra supply.

"I don't feel guilty at all about sex. My mother is always telling me how okay it is, and that I should go ahead and do it, and then tell her all about it. I enjoy it but I don't tell her anything. I personally find that the boys in my grade are a little too young for me. I prefer boys who are much older—at least sixteen or seventeen, and if they're eighteen, that's terrific—I really like college boys. I've been away on a couple of weekends to college dorms, and it's so much nicer to be able to spend a whole weekend with a guy you really like than just see him for a couple of hours in the evening.

"For my twelfth birthday, I asked to be allowed to go to an X-rated movie. It took a little pressure, but in the end my parents agreed, although my father refused to go along. I went with my mother, and I must say that I felt a little uncomfortable. It was pretty strange to see some of the stuff that was going down on the screen, though I'd heard about it all and done some of the things myself. But I wasn't prepared for my mother really getting heavy into talking about all the different things like oral sex, anal sex, sex in all kinds of various positions. She seemed not only to know a lot, she seemed to feel this tremendous pressure to tell me all about it—to 'share it' with me, as she calls it. I guess she talks like that because for a little while before she got married, she was a social worker. I go crazy with that expression, but I think all in all she really is a very good mother. For instance, if I got pregnant, I'm sure I could come to her and she'd help me get an abortion.

"I'm being careful, but you never know. My boyfriend is just beautiful. We've been going together for the last year and a half, and we talk about everything there is in life and all the things we hope and plan to do. My mom likes him very much. I think she suspects there's probably something going on between us, but somehow I don't want to give her the satisfaction of going to her gynecologist to get a diaphragm. I don't need another guy who's going to be an informant to my parents and tell them everything that's happening inside of me. It's bad enough my mother knows everything that's happening outside of me. But not quite everything."

Joy is trying to balance her need for her mother's attention and care against a disquieting awareness that the interest has an edge to it, that it's a little too eager, and that it comes from some need of her mother's which Joy senses has nothing to do with protecting her. Joy's mother seems to have a loving concern for a growing daughter mixed up with an avid curiosity about her daughter's developing sexuality—or at least this is how Joy sees it—and she is trying to make use of the first without succumbing to the second.

The mothers of teenage daughters no less than the daughters themselves, it seems, must learn to juggle the conflicting emotions of identification, rivalry, and envy as they live through this moment in their children's lives which is so close to their own memories and yet from which they have moved so far. It's hard to say whether this urge to "share" the experiences of their children is a recent phenomenon or whether it has always been present in a subliminal way. It is certainly true that young, educated, middle-class mothers are no longer content to submerge their sexuality in motherhood, and that increasing numbers of women are articulating a discontent with the repressiveness of their upbringing and seeing in the supposed freedom and openness of the new generation a possibility of self-renewal.

And there is no doubt that, regardless of the permissiveness or strictness of the home environment, children everywhere are speaking far more freely of things which a generation ago would only have been whispered about, and that, to some extent, children are influencing their parents. Dr. Jong says, "I still see a tremendous amount of anxiety in children about intercourse and heavy sex in general, but there is also a great new freedom in talking about it that I didn't see ten years ago.

"Sex is very open now, at least verbally. Whatever children are going through, with divorce and parents remarrying or living with a series of new people, the kids talk about it all much more openly. The overstimulation that they would have had to suffer alone in the past they can talk about now, too, even to the parent—and, of course, this can turn into a discussion that might become quite titillating to both the child and the parent.

"For instance, a child will now tell me quite readily, 'My mother is having an affair with Mr. X.' A decade ago this would have been something I would have had to ferret out. I would have sensed a powerful stimulation, with the child's behavior showing that there were other forces at work that he or she was trying to repress. I probably would have found it out in more derivative ways; it might have emerged in dreams, nightmares, or fantasies. Perhaps I'd even try to get the information from the parents. But now the child will very openly and calmly discuss it all.

"In spite of that, however, I find that children still harbor the same misconceptions and fears about sex that they always have. They may talk more and ask more questions, but the old anxieties are still there. Above all, they still fear abandonment, especially if the parent is out all the time dating other people. Today children venture closer to the parental bedroom not so much because they are interested in their parents' sexual activity, but really much more out of loneliness. Casual dating and having a number of partners may accentuate the child's fear of losing his mother or father, and what then happens is that these fears may pull the child into the bedroom earlier. Of course, the forbiddenness of it also affects children. It is forbidden, therefore it stimulates. With many more working mothers, particularly in divorced families, I see many children who are deserted, lonely, and frightened of being abandoned. They need someone to take care of them and to be with them emotionally."

A new pattern of reciprocal tensions between parent and pubescent child is emerging, particularly following separation from the other parent. The sense of sexual strain, particularly in the mother, communicates itself to the child, who feels a premature need to confront this loaded issue. The mother's conflicts give it an attraction to the child, who then attempts to resolve his or her mother's problems by acting them out.

When the mother has brought a lover to live with her children, the tensions are heightened still further. If the children are young, it is often the lover who is responsible for their sexual initiation. A number of factors contribute to this. Already stimulated by his affair with the mother, the lover may find the continual presence of a curious, questioning child who is hungry for attention and affection to be the additional stimulus that breaks down whatever inhibition he may feel in regard to the child's age and innocence. Initiating the child can also be a way of asserting dominance within the family, especially if he also resists taking real responsibility for the child by marrying the mother. He may even be titillated by the opportunity, through seduction of the child, to attack his rival, the father—although this motive, where it exists, is usually quite unconscious and probably is related to unresolved conflicts with his own father.

Here is Shannon again. Late in her interview, after she had begun to feel comfortable talking about herself, she abruptly said, "There's something that I guess I've never told anyone. I feel funny even telling you about it now. It happened when I was much younger, about ten or eleven. My mother's boyfriend used to massage my back. That doesn't sound like much. Still, I knew that it was wrong, but I didn't want to do anything to stop it.

"He would come over when he knew my mother wasn't going to be home, even though we had started doing this when she was around. I would kind of pull my clothes off or take them off, and he would massage my back. It felt great, it really felt good. You see, when we came to New York from Missouri, my mother was out so much pursuing her career and building up her professional image in the community that very often in the evening he'd get back several hours before she did, and sometimes even when she wasn't coming home at all, he'd come over anyway to keep me company. Nothing ever went beyond that with him—he would just massage my back and touch me, but I loved it. When I got to be about twelve, I realized that maybe I shouldn't be doing this thing with him. About that time I started to get turned off by him anyway, so I put a stop to it. Luckily, soon after that my mother broke up with him.

"But I found out that this was really a terrific way of getting off, when he'd fondle me and touch my crotch, and I was able to have orgasm. I was very quiet, so he wouldn't notice. And, you know, I didn't have to do anything back to him at all. I just lay there and let him do all these nice things to me. We never even talked about it, we never said we loved each other or anything like that; in fact, it was weird, we didn't really say anything at all while this was going on.

"It's funny how it all began. One night my mother was making dinner in the kitchen while he was watching television in my bedroom, sitting on the bed. I came in and lay down just to take a nap, you know, and before I knew it he laid his hands on my back and then slid them down my pants. I felt it, but I made out that I was sleeping. It felt good—he was drunk but very gentle.

"After that, when my mother was out for the evening and I would be in the other room while he was watching television in the living room, then I'd come in. He'd be smoking pot, and he would slowly start to stroke my back. Sometimes he'd drive me to school in the mornings, and on the way we would stop in a wooded area near our house. We'd smoke and get turned on a little, then he'd massage my back and touch my crotch. Actually, he wouldn't just touch my back, he would also stroke my legs, and I would lie across his lap while he was fondling me. I knew it was wrong, and I was always afraid we'd get caught, but I really liked it, it felt just wonderful. Also, I felt that since I wasn't doing anything to him, that made it okay.

"But I knew that if my mother found out about it she would kill me. She used to say that she really loved him. If she ever knew about what we were doing, she'd die. I used to worry about it a lot because if she married him, then he would be my stepfather, and it wouldn't be right to do things like that with your stepfather. He was about twenty-nine, a lot younger than my mother—fifteen or sixteen years younger.

"You know, now that I think about it, it really was a very strange scene. But what makes it even crazier is that when I was about eight or nine, my mother had a different lover, and he also used to stroke me and sit me on his lap, and give me back massages, and this felt good, too. But at the time I really had to totally deny what was going on. I couldn't handle it then, I was too young. Anyway, it only happened a couple of times. But with the other guy it felt even nicer, and it went on for a couple of years."

This contemporary version of the classic triangle may be far more common than is generally supposed. This family pattern of busy working mother, lover with time on his hands, and lonely child more often than not lends itself to some sexual play behind the mother's back. The need to deceive her accounts for some of the air of sophistication we see in girls like Shannon; there is also a strong element of fearful pleasure at paying the mother back for her neglect.

Most of the experts agree that the major changes over the last decade have taken place among girls. The sexual revolution and the women's movement are part of the same trend toward heightened expectations, consciousness, and activity in every sphere of life and in women of all ages. Dr. Robert Gould, Associate Director of the Family Life Division of New York's Metropolitan Hospital Center, says, "The sexual revolution owes more to contraception and being able to avoid pregnancy on demand than any other factor. That, together with the women's movement and the drive for equality, the attack on the double standard, has made the most significant impact on the lives of children.

"It's always been accepted that men can have sex without condemnation, but never women. And this is the aspect that has changed. Now women—and by this time it's moved down to young girls—can have sex freely without fear of censure or sanctions. The girls have been freed."

They have been freed to experiment and to act out very

much as boys always have, but because they mature a little earlier, their sexual play has a purposefulness and, sometimes, consequences which boys their age sometimes find difficult to deal with, especially when coupled with a new aggressiveness. Most girls who are sexually active today will tell you that they like sex because it feels good, and only as an afterthought say that they "really like the guy a lot," too. It's the boys who talk about love, who feel revulsion for sex with a girl they have no deep feeling for. Mark, remembering his first sexual experience at thirteen (he is now fifteen), said,

"We were waiting to go to a movie one Saturday, and this girl came walking by. A couple of guys were playing ball in the park across the street, and they called out, 'Hey, Sexy,' you know, derogatory, very normal sixteen-year-olds, yelling over to her like assholes. She was saying, 'Get away from me, kiddies,' stuff like that—she was about nineteen—and they yelled back, 'How about a good time?' She says to them, 'I'm too good for you, you couldn't hack it,' kidding around, so I said to her, 'Oh, would you like to go to a movie?' She was very attractive, and I didn't look thirteen. She wanted some pot, so I got some from my brother and we just hung out, we didn't go to the movie.

"A couple of my friends made sure she found out how old I was, and that really freaked her out. She said I didn't look that young, and then she said, 'You know, I really think it would be great to do it with a guy your age.' 'Really,' I said. A couple more of my friends overheard this and started coming over. She said, 'You know I'm propositioning you?' 'No shit!' I said. I really didn't want to do it with this girl. For some reason, something just told me you shouldn't do it, but these guys were all saying, 'Oh, my God, this girl just propositioned Mark!' So they talked me into it. They really talked me into it. I wanted to do it slightly, but it was mostly the curiosity or being able to say, 'Wow, you did it, Mark, you're a man, wow.'

"She didn't live in the city, I couldn't go home with her, so we did it in the park on the grass at night in a secluded area.

It was okay, but I don't think I enjoyed it as much as if I'd loved her. That time I sort of wanted to do it anyway, but since then I've had sex with girls I had totally no feelings for, and I might as well have been screwing a cow. Then it's like, what's the difference? It's just there. Buy one of those fifty-dollar blow-up dolls with a vibrator. I'm serious. That's the way it is. There has to be love in it or some kind of feeling—not necessarily love, but some kind of feeling that you have for the girl. As a matter of fact, it has to be pretty close to love for it to be anything at all. That's the way I feel about it, anyway."

When a girl gets pregnant, the boy finds it even harder to stay in control of the situation than she does. We have seen something of the troubles of teenage mothers. For boys, who are almost never ready to assume responsibility for either the girl or her baby, it can mean genuine desperation. Karl, who had a close call, won't soon forget it:

"I met Lisa about three years ago, when I was twelve and she was eleven. She was my first girl, and it really was kind of unreal, it felt so strange going into another person's body. I was always afraid I would hurt her, but she encouraged me, so I didn't feel guilty.

"We must have been absolutely stupid because the first year we didn't use anything. Lisa hadn't got her periods yet, and after she started, she went on the Pill; but we didn't realize that the first month a girl starts taking the Pill she isn't protected, and, lo and behold, she got pregnant.

"When she told me, it was a shock, but what really bothered me was that she didn't tell me right away. She waited about a week and then bought one of those do-it-yourself tests you can get in the drugstore—she's always been very good in science. And it came out that she was pregnant. But she still didn't want to tell me, so she took some money from her house and went and got an exam at a medical laboratory under a false name. Sure enough, that also came back that she was pregnant.

"Well, we talked about it for a long time, and I told her that I really loved her and that I would be glad to take some money out of my bank account to help pay for the abortion. She was very upset. She thanked me but said she didn't know what to do. Then I *really* got scared. 'Don't tell me you're thinking of having the baby?' I asked her. She sat there for a little while, then said probably not but she wanted time to think about it.

"The next couple of days I was really scared out of my mind. I thought I'd go crazy. I called her every day, but she wouldn't talk to me. Finally, at the end of the week, we met, and she told me she had decided to have the abortion. She found a clinic through one of her girl friends, and I went with her. I brought along three hundred dollars, which was all I could sneak out of my bank account, and she got another two hundred dollars.

"When it was over, I got a cab and brought her back to my house—my parents were out. She rested for the afternoon while we played music and relaxed. She was crying quite a bit—not from pain, she said, but from feeling that she had actually had a baby inside her. Well, don't think that didn't blow my mind because here what she was talking about was my baby, too. I really can't find it possible, even now at fifteen, to think of myself as a father, but I guess biologically that's the way it happens.

"What was flashing through my mind was that if she did have the baby, I would have had to quit school, go to high school at night, and somehow, somewhere, get an apartment to take care of her and stay with her. I mean, if she had wanted me to marry her then, I would have. We've only talked about marriage sort of in passing, and I don't know if she's going to be the girl that I marry. I just don't know. I know I love her very much now, but I don't know if that's enough, to plan to build a whole life with somebody just because I love them at fifteen.

"I know I've got a lot of growing up to do. There's so many things that I want to do in life. It's not that I don't love Lisa. I imagine I *will* get married someday, and I really want to have kids, but this would have knocked off my whole life. It would have taken a big chunk out of all the dreams I had.

"From then on you can bet your ass we've been more careful.

We never do anything unless she has her diaphragm and jelly. It took her a couple of months to get over the shock and be able to have intercourse again, but we really are very careful now, and while we're still quite close, we've mellowed a lot. Boy, that experience really made me grow up. I mean, sex can be fun, but unless you're responsible, it can really destroy you."

For a boy who has gotten a girl pregnant, the future suddenly becomes uncertain. Considering the panic most of these boys feel, and with good reason, a surprising number of them do come through and stick by both the girl and the baby if she decides to go ahead and have it.

Following are some representative self-portraits of a sexually active boy and girl. They were chosen not because they were especially "typical," but because neither presented any acute psychological distress and because both were far above average in intelligence and were ambitious and self-directed. I was interested in exploring the consciousness of middle-class children who have accumulated a certain amount of sexual experience at a relatively young age and who are also functioning well in other aspects of their lives.

Dina

"My name is Dina and I was thirteen last June. I live in a suburb of New York, where I've lived all my life. I live with my mom and dad in our own house. I get along with both of them pretty well, but I'm a little closer to my mom because my dad is kind of uptight. My parents are really old—my mother is forty-seven and my father is fifty-two.

"I am in eighth grade and an honor student. I'm friendly with a lot of different kids in school, and we're all into different things. As far as my social life goes, my mother knows about my boyfriends, though she doesn't know what I'm into or what I do. She's really quite straight, so I generally try to avoid saying much about what I do because I know that would upset her. Like she wouldn't be too wild about me smoking, and I don't think she would really like the drinking that I do, although maybe she wouldn't mind too much because I don't drive.

"My mother kind of prides herself on that cliché that we have a 'good mother-daughter relationship.' But I feel lucky that I have good friends who care about me, who I can talk to if I get into any kind of trouble or need help. You can always go to friends to talk about problems that you couldn't with your mother. Also, the advice she'd give might not be the right advice for me. Most of the time I work out the problems myself because I know what's best for me.

"My father is nice, we joke around, but we're not close at all. He's proud of me, of how well I do in school and all that, but he doesn't know anything at all about my social life, and of course I wouldn't tell him. He's a doctor, so he's out of the house a lot, although he isn't working as much as he used to. He's cut his work down by about half after he had a heart attack.

"My parents go away a lot. They know that I feel sure enough and secure enough with myself to stay home alone and take care of myself, so they go away most weekends. When they're away, then I really have much more freedom. I can come back when I have to, whether it's late at night, or if I'm staying overnight, by nine or ten o'clock in the morning. I can also take cabs, but a lot of my friends drive and have cars, so I get rides most of the places I go.

"I get a pretty good allowance, about twenty dollars a week plus occasional extras. I used to buy my lunch at school, but I found it was too expensive and I bring it from home now. I don't really have to save anything, though. I usually can get a few dollars extra if I want, and of course for shopping they give me whatever I need. For the most part, I use my money to go to parties and movies and to help party in my friends' houses. The parties are where a lot of my friends really get drugged up and drunk—many of them take speed and some take acid—but for the most part, they're good kids, and everybody just smokes and enjoys themselves.

"I think personally that the people who take acid and stuff

like that don't really have their heads together. It seems to be big in my town, but I don't think much of the kids who do it. I don't think they're really big people. But pot and booze are okay—I myself just drink, and I'll smoke pot once in a while when I'm with friends or whenever I have a chance. Last year I went for four months straight without partying, and that was the longest I'd ever gone without, but lately I've been back into it again, and now it's been about three months straight, partying every weekend. That's just during school; in the summer we were partying every day for weeks on end.

"I started smoking when I was in sixth grade. Besides pot, I also smoke cigarettes. In the beginning, when I wasn't too together, I was hanging out with kind of a fast crowd—they were very druggy, wasted-out people. Now I look at them and I feel that they're shallow. I mean, all they're interested in is getting drunk and sex.

"I began having heavy sex about a year and a half ago, just before my twelfth birthday. It was with a boy who I really liked; we also had intercourse. I must have been pretty foolish because the first few months I didn't use anything. Then my boyfriend, who is about five years older than me, told me we had to use something, and I got scared, too, and started buying Conceptrol and other foam things so I could use it when I needed to without having to worry about carrying a diaphragm around or taking the Pill—I'm against the Pill.

"I'm not seeing this guy anymore, although he was good for me. I felt that the next guy was, too; we slept together a few times and it was good. But if it's somebody I really like and feel comfortable with, and feel that I could maybe even love, then that's really terrific—that's the best. I can't honestly say that I loved the last two guys I went with, but they were good people and it felt good. I don't think I have to love somebody as long as he's a good person and has got a good head and is coming from the right direction—then I would sleep with him. Frankly, I hope he comes along soon because I'm getting horny.

"To me sex is a way of showing my emotions and feelings and of getting closer to a person. Whatever that takes, that's what I feel and that's what I do. The first few times that I did things like oral sex, which was before I had intercourse, I did it just because it was expected. Now I would only do it if I liked the guy that I was with and if I really wanted to. I find it easier to have an orgasm if someone touches me, or if I have oral sex done to me. I must say that I really do enjoy sex. I enjoy it a lot, a lot, a lot.

"I usually go with a number of different guys, and what we do depends on how I feel about the one I'm with. Sometimes we go out and make out and have sex right that night; other times we wait awhile, and with some guys I don't do it at all. But I must say that with most, I do end up having a kind of heavy sex. Exactly what we do depends on my mood and who the person is and how he comes across to me.

"Do I feel guilty? No, not at all because I feel it's something I want to do; it's big, and I enjoy it, and I feel that I'm a liberated person. If I enjoy it and it feels right for me, then I do it —why not? If you go into something knowing what you want to get out of it, then you should go ahead and do it, it's okay.

"I've never masturbated. I feel nice in different positions when I lie in bed, but I've never actually masturbated. I don't really feel the need to—I have enough boyfriends, and I get plenty of sexual satisfaction from the guys that I'm with.

"I'm kind of advanced, so I've gotten into a special program in school. I would like to go to college and then on to medical school and become a doctor like my father. I really enjoy school. To me sex isn't any hindrance as far as grades and classes are concerned. In fact, it makes me feel better, and I'm able to relax and get through without most of the hassle the other kids have to go through. I think I understand myself, and my parents don't hassle me. They give me enough space so I can do what I want because they know I can handle it.

"The relationship that meant the most to me was one that I had last summer. We only spent about three weeks together, but I learned a lot from it. When I met him, he was very independent—not shy, just kind of slightly aloof—but he was very innocent. He hadn't ever had sex before, and he was two years older than me—I was twelve and he was fourteen. I really loved teaching him. It was beautiful.

"I learned an awful lot about people, about myself, and even about boys from him, and I love him for this. I learned about the head trips that people play on each other, and about gays, and that if you really matter you have to come first for yourself and think a lot about yourself—things like that.

"It's strange, even though I consider myself to be liberated and think I do what I want to do, I'm actually never the one who starts anything or initiates: It's the boy who really has to initiate. Somehow I feel more comfortable with that.

"Mostly I'm very happy with my life. I think I'd like to cut down a little bit on the booze, but it's not really interfering with my life. I use it mostly on weekends and just occasionally during the week. It makes me feel good, it relaxes me. I enjoy what I do with guys, so I think I've kind of got things pretty much together. I enjoy the life that I have. I feel some restlessness, I'd like to try some new experiences, and I hope to see a lot more of the world."

John

John, the boy who "initiated" his parents' divorce, is now living with a friend, near his mother in New York, while his two younger sisters are with their father in Los Angeles.

"I have a very good relationship with her—better than a lot of people have with their mothers, I think. I find it harder to be open with my feelings with my father because he knows a lot of the things I do—he's very smart. Whatever I do behind his back he knows, but there's some conflict, and sitting down and talking about it is very hard.

"The main problem with my mother is that she's very upset because she doesn't have my two sisters with her. I've been the only loyal one who stuck by her and tried to help her and pull her through. At this point right now, I don't need a mother or a father. They're just getting in my way. My father doesn't see that, but my mother does, and she thinks I can take care of myself. I'm pretty much on my own anyway, but my major problem is trying to keep her head together.

"I've been forced to make decisions that I don't think a kid should have to make. If you're put in that position, fine, make the decision; but it ruined my sisters. They were too young to know if they wanted to go with my mother or my father, and it was very heavy, especially with a three-thousand-mile distance.

. "I first got interested in girls when I was about seven, but I didn't have a real relationship until I was about ten. She was older than me, thirteen. It was strange because I was still in a very boyish stage, and I was quite violent and hyperkinetic as a child. I used to beat her up in front of people, but when we were alone it was a different story. At that time I just thought it was all fun and there was really nothing to it. You know, you can still go on playing with each other at that age, even after you've had sex.

"My first serious relationship was with a much older woman. She was twenty-six and I was thirteen, but she thought I was fifteen. It was in the summer in New Hampshire. She was an artist, and she really loved me. We were very serious. I loved her a great deal, too. I couldn't believe anything so big could happen to me. But it was just a summer romance because when I went back to L.A., where we were living then, she gave me her address, and my father did an awful thing. He found this address that had a very weird poem written on it which implied certain things, and my father became very angry and burned it in front of my face. And right there, when he did that, that was it. I never, ever saw her again, never talked to her again. I still think about her once in a while. I hate to make comparisons, but sometimes I do it subconsciously, and I remember her and how she would feel about this or that, compared with people I've met since her.

"That year I was in the seventh grade, and after that there was a period when I was very much into myself. I was very hurt at not being able to see my girl friend in New Hampshire anymore, and I wasn't interested in women too much. I would go out, but I was just in it for the social function part. Then I met a new girl from Indonesia. We had a very sincere attraction for each other, and our relationship went on for about two years.

"I was thirteen, and this was the first time it was sort of based on sex. I mean, she had an incredible mind and she was very soft-spoken and so forth, but we were in bed all the time. Every weekend and all weekend, Friday afternoon until Sunday evening. Usually we'd be at my house. By that time my mother and father were divorced, and my mother allowed me to have females spend the night because she didn't want me going out and doing it somewhere else. So there was never any problem about where to go.

"It ended when I moved to New York and she went to college in Massachusetts—she was three years older than I was. I thought we'd be able to see each other on weekends, but she needs sexual relations quite often—I don't know why—and she sort of fell in love with a few other people up there. For the next four months, it sort of destroyed me.

"After that there was nothing really heavy until tenth grade. That girl, Linda, was only two years older than I was, but she took me for a ride for about six months. My mother and I were living in New York, and she wanted to get out. She couldn't take it anymore. But I had to finish school. I wasn't going to leave just because she felt like it, so Linda decided that I could move in with her family. At the time, we were just distant friends. Then it became sort of brotherly, sisterly, and then the inevitable happened. We went away for the weekend up to my mother's house in New Hampshire, and that's where we fell in love.

"When we came back to the city, her parents didn't enjoy the fact that we were seeing each other, although we were trying to cover it up the best we could. But it got to the point where they threw me out of the house. Then she decided she wanted to move out, too, so we took an apartment together. That worked out for a while until she became very difficult. She's probably the most unique girl I've ever known. She's very average Upper East Side in some ways, but she's also super-intelligent, smart as a whip. I guess I figured it was a challenge of some sort, but pretty soon she became the very loud female and I became the submissive male. I didn't know why she was being so difficult over the most trivial things, so I just told her to shut up. Sometimes *I* got very violent.

"It was sort of like being married. In the beginning we had a fantastic relationship. There was a deep concern for each other and a protection—we were both out on our own for the first time. But she couldn't handle it. I mean, I was ready to settle down for a long relationship, but she wasn't after a while.

"That was when the fighting began. It was like a very weird catalyst—after a while we sort of needed it. Fighting with each other relieved our aggressions, I guess. But then I just couldn't stand it anymore, and there came one point this summer in L.A. when I pushed it too far. I've never hit a female before in my life, but I went for her throat and almost killed her. After that we totally broke it off.

"Now I've decided that since I'm going to try to do two years of school in one, combine eleventh and twelfth grades, I don't want diversions. I'm not getting involved with a female or anybody else who's just going to destroy that. I'm seeing another girl now. It's a good relationship. It's not as closely wound as the last one, it's a little freer and easier, and I don't have to take on any burdens of worrying too much about her or myself.

"It's different from the others because, well, she's not a virgin and she is a virgin, and we're trying to work at it, but it's pretty hard because she's small, she's very petite. But it's not important for me always necessarily to have intercourse. That's not all there is to a relationship. To me there's a big difference between making love and fucking someone. I have fucked people and gotten nothing out of it. I mean, I might as well be on the toilet, jerking off. Making love's a different thing.

"I don't believe in extracurricular activity in a relationship either. I'm really very much against that. That's supposed to be the new way of handling things—if you really love this person, you'll love whatever they do—which I think is such bullshit. I think that sex is sort of sacred. Even though it's fun, it's sacred. If I were going out with somebody and she went off and had sexual relationships with other people, I would hate that. There would be something lost there definitely. I was guilty of it once, only once, and I tried to forget it very fast. I felt like a shithead afterward.

"I've had free run over my life for about a year now. Before that I had a bunch of responsibilities to take care of, but I've basically been my own person for a long time now. That's the way I like it. I don't like being dependent on too many people. Since I've been out of a family structure for four years, I don't care to go back into one. I'm living with a friend now who's like a big brother to me, and that's all the family I need.

"I may go to college next summer, maybe part time, I don't know. It all depends on where my head is at when the time comes. I've been playing drums since I was about three, and playing piano since I was nine, and writing music since I was ten. That's what I really want to do, write music.

"There was a time when I was very introverted and didn't care about other people at all. I was very by myself, and that's the way I liked it. I didn't want people seeing me. I liked being the mastermind in my studio and coming out only for dinner and going to the bathroom. But I've always been in a position where finding friends or being around people wasn't hard, and I can be extroverted if I want to. I'm shy, but after the initial plunge, I can be very loud and rambunctious.

"I can sit down and have a decent conversation with anybody, just as long as they're over ten years old. Young children I don't know much. I want to have kids, though. I have to carry on my last name, and I'm the only one who can do it. I'll get married when I'm ready to. I don't feel in any big hurry about it, but I don't feel I'll necessarily want to wait a long time either. I'm not going to go out there and plan it scientifically, with the girl having to have this or that kind of genes so we can have a certain kind of child. I'm going to wait until the right time. For now, I don't want to tie myself down."

Margaret Ferris, thirty-eight, is a divorced mother whose two teenage children, Julie, fifteen, and Michael, seventeen, live with her and her current lover, Larry, in Texas. Margaret is a filmmaker who began working while she was still married to the children's father, Dan, a businessman. Since the divorce eleven years ago, she has built a home for her children and a career for herself that has made her largely independent, although Dan still does contribute some child support.

Because Margaret and her children may well represent the typical middle-class nuclear-family structure of the 1970's, I talked to them about the difficulties and the pleasures of their life together since the divorce.

MARGARET: I come from outside Chicago, and I see tremendous differences between the way I was raised and the way my children are growing up. When I was a child, my parents put a heavy emphasis on denial under the guise of protection. I don't mean just sexual denial, but every kind. You shouldn't have a car, you shouldn't stay over at a friend's house, you couldn't even have friends in—anything they could use to exert control. I don't think my parents were particularly happy people. They deprived and denied themselves, too, and just passed it on to my brother and me.

With my own children, I don't feel I've been denied much as a mother. I've led my life pretty much as I've chosen to. Their father and I have been separated for eleven years, and since then I've been able to live my life on my own terms. I don't see my children's lives as in any way competitive with mine. I don't feel I'm sacrificing anything that's important to me, and I don't think they've been denied anything that they needed. I don't feel they have to find their happiness through me either. Their lives seem to me much more parallel to mine than mine was to my parents'.

The children were quite young when I separated—Michael

was six and Julie was only four. The marriage was a bad one from the start; we spent most of our time together arguing. We were unhappy long enough, their father and I, but there was still a lot of resentment when the break finally came. And the pressure of our unhappiness was let out on the children, especially Julie. My husband used to discharge all his bad temper on her.

JULIE: I have a very excellent memory, unfortunately, of what life was like before my parents got divorced. It was really hell. What my father wanted to do to my mother, he did to me. He would assault me verbally when he was angry at her. He would pick on very trivial things to be angry over, and he would kick me around verbally, and occasionally he'd even slap me around. It wasn't child abuse or anything that bad; I didn't feel abused, but I knew that he was very angry. The tension in the air was so heavy you could cut it with a knife.

So many times I used to ask Mommy, 'Why don't you and Daddy split, you fight so much?' but I didn't realize that when they actually did, I would feel responsible. I felt very guilty when they divorced; I felt very bad. Even though they split when I was about five, I didn't get over it until I was about twelve or thirteen.

MICHAEL: The way I remember the separation—I was about seven and in the first grade—it wasn't traumatic or anything, like you hear from other kids whose parents get divorced. I saw it coming, and I didn't mind it that much; my sister seemed to get much more upset about it. Even now I can see that it was really the best thing for them.

MARGARET: During the period right after Dan left, I didn't date at all. I was working too hard, for one thing. I had to support myself and the kids—their father doesn't give us much—and of course I had to do something with myself anyway. So Julie and Michael were left on their own at an early age. I think now that was a big mistake, but I can't see how I could have avoided it.

JULIE: My mother had to get established and find herself, you know. She can't just sit around. But while she was going through all this, Michael and I basically had to take care of ourselves, and we did it together. It really screwed me over. I don't know if I really, truly felt abandoned, but I certainly felt left.

MARGARET: The first relationship I had after Dan was with a married writer, whom I adored. He came into our lives like a wonderful gift, and the children adored him, too. He had never had any kids of his own, and he used to come over to our house four evenings a week. Of course, he didn't sleep overnight because I didn't want the children to know that we had a sexual relationship, although they felt no resentment toward him whatever—they loved him as much as I did.

It's hard to explain to a five-year-old and a seven-year-old what the hell is going on. We started talking about sex maybe a year later, but only because they figured it all out themselves.

JULIE: I think I discovered sex when I noticed my brother, that he was different. I had also kind of heard about it from other kids, and I put two and two together.

MICHAEL: Julie and I used to wrestle a lot and fight, but since I'm stronger she always used to end up on the bottom, which she didn't like, so she would scream. She was always very good at that. We spent a lot of time alone in the house together, and we'd make up games. Julie and I are really close, but we don't talk much about it. It's just, you know, we know that we're there. I don't think kids do talk much about that.

MARGARET: Joe and I did get caught by my son—not in the act, but it was very obvious and Michael was very shocked and upset. I didn't discuss it because *he* wouldn't. That was when I decided I'd better tell him what the hell was going on altogether with life, and that was when I found out that he had already been talking about sex with his friends. It wasn't any big secret.

MICHAEL: I learned all about sex from my mother when I was about nine. She took us to the park, sat us down, and started explaining everything. The way she told us, she seemed to be saying that it was something good.

My mother was always very open about sex. I mean, if I had

any questions I would ask her, but usually I have no questions, so I don't often go asking her. I don't have to because besides telling us about it, my mother gave us a number of books about sex to read.

MARGARET: Joe was with us for five years. When he left I was devastated, and so were the children. At that point I went into therapy. It was terribly hard on them because not only did they lose Joe, they lost me, too, at the same time. I was really out to lunch for months; I guess I'd have to say that emotionally I had abandoned the children. As a result they had, and still have, a good deal of anger.

JULIE: During the time when I was between eight and ten, things were totally fucked up. My mother was in the process of going through a nervous breakdown—it really was very rough. She was working through it all, too. She had to, and I guess all in all that was the worst time.

I started masturbating when I was about six, touching myself, and from then on I was able to have orgasms. By the time I was seven or eight, I was doing it fairly regularly, with some pretty active fantasies.

When I was younger, I used to be very affectionate with my mother's boyfriend, Joe. I would sit on his lap, and there was a lot of hugging and holding and fondling me—affection, I guess. This is what may have turned me on so that I started masturbating at such an early age—anyway, it was about then that I figured out about masturbation and how to do it, and I've been doing it ever since.

MICHAEL: I used to like the guys my mother went with after my parents split. People are always asking how did it feel, but I liked them. I was very friendly with Joe, and he was very nice to me. You see, Joe was a very electric, charismatic kind of person, and my father was never electric and never had any charisma.

Joe was never affectionate with me. At night when he left, he would come into our bedroom on his way out and say good night to me and then take twenty minutes saying good night to Julie. I would be dismissed in one second, but he would somehow always have stuff to whisper about and share with Julie. I was kind of jealous because I thought there was something special they were saying to each other; it sounded like very stored-up, intimate conversations. I guess that was when he was, you know, kind of being affectionate and touching her.

MARGARET: Julie tried suicide a couple of times at the age of eleven, which was about the time she started using drugs. Her suicide gestures involved slashing her wrists. Now she is much better, but she went through some very bad times. She was thrown out of school on a drug charge; they found her with marijuana, and this exclusive private school dropped her. She really had a difficult time. Luckily we found a good therapist for her. She spent two years in therapy, and it helped her tremendously.

MICHAEL: I never was in that kind of trouble, but I did have a kind of serious incident once that I had to come to my mother with, although not right away. It was when I was about seven and I was going to one of those after-school play centers. It was an expensive deal where they pick up kids after school at three o'clock and keep them for two or three hours, then bring them home when their parents have returned, about six. Julie used to go there, too, but this place separated boys from girls, so she was in another group.

One of the counselors there tried to molest me. He used to take us out as a group—we would go to a swimming pool—and he started, you know, to come on to me, but I wasn't receptive at all. What happened was he took me to the pool—somehow he got me there alone—and then we took a shower together without any clothes on, but he didn't try anything with me. Afterward, he brought me over to his apartment and asked me to take all my clothes off, which I did. He took pictures of me, nude, and then he brought me back.

He was always trying to do things like carrying the kids and hugging the boys. He was interested in coming on to me more, but my mother wouldn't let him. She said that she always sensed that he was probably a faggot and had to be watched. She never let him take me swimming alone again.

JULIE: I never really smoked pot in school; I smoked it at home or at friends' houses. I began smoking pot in sixth grade when a girl friend of mine found some old stuff that belonged to my mother. We decided after we smoked our first joint that we liked it, and that's how I started on pot. I smoked a lot for a while, and then for a year of two, I didn't smoke at all. I just had no desire to anymore—it made me feel insecure and paranoid.

My brother started smoking much later. He only began about two years ago, and meanwhile I had moved into heavy drugs like LSD, mushrooms, peyote, and mescaline. Now I've decided to go organic; I use mescaline but not LSD. How many trips I've taken with LSD, don't even ask. I can't keep count of them, but a lot, a lot, for a period of about three years

As a matter of fact, most of the kids in my school smoke pot or something. If I were to think of the ones who don't use pot or mescaline or acid, I would have to say it's maybe only ten percent. A lot of kids trip on acid. They think it's groovy, but they don't know the dangers.

MICHAEL: I probably spend more time with our father now than Julie does. I really used to look forward to being with him. Every time we had a vacation, I'd go up and spend two weeks at a time with him at his place in the country. He'd go off to work, and I'd kind of keep myself busy during the day and wait for him to come home.

When I was younger, I never told my mother that I preferred to be with him. I was afraid she might get upset; I only told her last year. I love her, but I thought that she might get bothered by the fact that I really used to enjoy being around my father. Finally, I expressed it to her last year, and she seemed to take it okay.

MARGARET: I think our lives might have been different if I'd been a housewife. My ex-husband is now living with a woman who *is* a housewife. She is very concerned as a mother; in fact, she reminds me of my parents. She's now doing to my kids, when they go up to visit, what my parents did to my brother and me. She's enormously protective, and, even though she and her children live with my husband in a house he owns, he still sleeps on the couch downstairs so her children shouldn't think they're having sex—although they're in their teens, and she and Dan have been living together for seven years. Of course, my children think this is the greatest piece of hypocrisy that ever came down the ramp.

JULIE: This woman, Caroline, that my father is living with is the type that has a giant redwood up her ass. She's very uptight—you can't really talk to her at all. I feel I'm completely liberated, but she lives in a small town and has two obnoxious kids, and she doesn't understand that I smoke pot and all. She has a hard time understanding that I am not ten years old. She is generally disapproving, and sits back and tells me that whatever I do is just not good enough.

I must say, though, that in spite of that, I like her. I am fond of her because she makes my father happy. That's why I find a space in my heart for her because my father being happy is important to me.

MICHAEL: My mother has now been living for the last three years or so with this other man, Larry, who is terrific, he's really very nice. I not only don't mind having another male in the house, I'm glad about it. For a long time, I felt the female atmosphere was getting too heavy, so it's nice to have him here.

JULIE: I never had very much of a social life until fairly recently. I did have a boyfriend in first grade, but boys always seemed to be afraid of me because I was loud and obnoxious. Then in sixth grade I had another boyfriend who I fooled around with a little bit, but I wasn't ready to do anything heavy, so we didn't make out much. He wanted to, but I didn't. And then he died shortly after that. So it was rejection all the way down the line—my father had left me, my mother's boyfriend left me, and now he died on me, too.

I guess you might say that I started making out seriously in seventh grade, when I was about twelve. My favorite friend is Kim, she is like a blood sister to me, and we would make out together with her boyfriend—things like oral sex, masturbation.

The three of us would join in, and it was beautiful.

I have a boyfriend now who really likes me a lot, and the fact that finally someone appreciates me for what I am just freaks the shit out of me. Before, I was never acknowledged by guys at all. I thought it was because I didn't have tits or anything, and because I was underdeveloped.

MARGARET: This weekend Julie is going away with her young man friend, even though she's only fifteen and he's eighteen. As far as I know, she's still a virgin. We've talked about it—in fact, we made all the preparations to get her ready for the weekend just in case she decides to have relations with him. You see, Julie is kind of a late bloomer, and this may be a problem. But I've discussed everything with her, including my abortions, and about a year ago I had an ectopic pregnancy which I almost died from, and of course the children knew all about that.

I'm going to take Julie to a gynecologist soon so she can be fitted for a diaphragm. All of her friends seem to have them already. In my era all the smart girls had their own cars, now they have their own diaphragms; but I guess it's much better for young girls than the Pill.

JULIE: It's not that Robert and I haven't done anything yet—we've done just about everything else. I like being eaten by him—I can really get off that way—and I find it beautiful to have oral sex with him, and even to let him come like that while I'm going down on him. Intercourse is the only thing I haven't done yet, and that's just because I haven't yet got a diaphragm. Most of my friends have them. . . .

MARGARET: I not only talk about sex with Julie, but also with her friends. I find that many of them come to me for advice because they can't talk about it to their own parents.

I would personally have preferred it if my children had waited, but if they aren't going to, I would much rather see to it that they're protected while they're still single and young, keep them safe until they get married. I'm very much concerned that they shouldn't marry at nineteen or twenty, the way I did and my parents did. When you've been through two generations of miserable, rotten marriages, you don't want to see your children marrying too early. I hope to see them do a great many things with their lives and be able to marry later.

MICHAEL: The very first time I had intercourse, I was fifteen and the girl was fifteen, too, and she was a virgin. We used contraception—that is, I used condoms. My mother found out shortly afterward and started asking me about it—she just wanted to make sure that I was using something. She wasn't angry or anything, but she was kind of concerned. She didn't want me to get the girl pregnant and told me to be careful.

I didn't feel guilty about it at all. I knew what to do, and she also knew. I have felt guilty since then, but only because she was able to have an orgasm only once or twice while we were having intercourse.

MARGARET: Michael and Anne, his girl friend, were having troubles, and one day Michael came to me in anger and said that adolescence and sex just didn't go together. I told him, "I guess what it is, you really want a good friend, but what you're doing implies a lot more than that; it involves more feelings and passions, and you aren't too comfortable having sex because you know it means a great deal more. It's really that your emotions aren't fixed yet. At the age of sixteen, you know that it's not forever."

I think they're concerned about that "forever." Virtually all their friends come from disoriented or disrupted homes. Michael and Anne broke up, then became friends, broke up again, and I think they're back together now.

I feel pretty close to both my kids. I even know all about drugs, what they're taking, and where they get it. Besides marijuana, they've taken hashish, peyote, and LSD. When my son took LSD last summer, I had a fit. I got Larry to speak to him. He knows more about drugs than I do.

I used to smoke a little grass, but as soon as the kids started taking drugs, I lost all interest in it. I really object to the way drugs alter your mind. When Michael took the LSD, I could feel myself behaving for the first and only time the way my parents did about sex, screaming and raving. Most of these kids have absolutely no idea what the stuff they take can do to them. They all use uppers and downers and Quaaludes, but the latest drug in fashion is peyote.

I think the kids like living with Larry. I've been careful about that—even right after the divorce I never dated much. And I didn't want people trudging in and out of my life that way in any case; it was our house and our life.

Sometimes I'm concerned whether I'm able to give the kids all I want to. I've read that the quality, the loving time you spend with the children, is more important than the quantity, but I know the kids would definitely prefer that I was around more.

You know, with all the aggravation and heartache, I wouldn't trade places with anyone or do any of it differently. I love being a mother. It's one of the joys of my life.

MICHAEL: Someday I'm going to be married and have children of my own, and I wouldn't do it any differently than the way I had it, the way that I was raised. I think my mother did a terrific job with us. My sister had a different life, and she might not feel the same, but I feel very happy.

JULIE: Since Larry's been here, my mother seems much calmer and easier to get along with. She is very open with us; she shares things and tells us a great deal. I feel very badly about the time when she wasn't around while she was working so hard and having a nervous breakdown, but she really tries hard for us, and things are much better now.

If I were a parent, I would want my child to be very honest with me and be able to speak to me even if they differed with me. I don't feel that they have to lie to me. I wouldn't want my kids to be afraid of reality.

Though perhaps more dramatic, the central dynamics of this family are similar to those of many a struggling single parent who is overwhelmed, tries to cope with the multiple roles, and misses some important cues. Both these children express love for their mother who cares and is there for them; yet, like all children, they have a need to have what they want when they want it. They know, for example, that Mother must spend much time in the office in her role as breadwinner, and though they intellectually understand it, they emotionally reject the perceived abandonment. This now places Margaret in a bind, and she is damned if she does give up all for them, or fits them into a life that has other demanding priorities, and they are not always first.

The obvious mistake of leaving the children to be with her lover, who used his position of trust for personal prurient gain, is sadly more widespread than most would like to acknowledge. We heard stories of a similar nature repeatedly. Julie did not tell her mother of the man's seductive activities in molesting her, as she wanted to protect Mother from the guilt of having permitted this to happen because she was away. Yet the guilt was too overwhelming to be borne alone for long. So, characteristically, when she reached puberty, she tried to hurt herself seriously and perhaps even die because of the intense conflict of emotions. When children are questioned about this possible danger of death, a frequent answer is something to the effect that the others will be better off without them. The guilt of having been involved, even passively, in a forbidden act competes with the masochistic pleasure and secrecy of having experienced a taboo pleasure. While the child struggles with the fear of the hurt Mother would feel "if she knew," she also feels overwhelmed with keeping a secret of such magnitude from her. When this is coupled with the anger of Mother having permitted this, or caused it by her need to be at work, the result may be a deadly one.

Single parents need more than others to be certain of whom they entrust their children to. Children of divorce are more vulnerable to begin with. They already feel abandoned, and they do not need the feeling of now being exposed to temptation or danger. From these stories one can see why all experts in the field agree that the child from a one-parent family is at risk in terms of every social ill affecting children and adolescents. Above all, parents cannot afford to dismiss sexual danger with the mistaken "Oh, he/she is too young." Younger children need love *and* protection perhaps in even greater measure. An enlightened parent who cares and is effective remains in the most needed role—as parent and not as friend.

Chapter 11

THE FAMILY AND SOCIETY

Throughout this book I have examined changes in the sexual behavior of children and changes in the relationship between parents and children, particularly in the transmission of sexual information and attitudes across the generation gap. It is perhaps appropriate at this time to back up and look at the traditional Western view of the family to see just how far we have strayed from it. An understanding of how the family as an institution existed up until our parents' time might be helpful in evaluating where we stand now and where we may be headed.

We are indebted to Prof. Louis Lieberman, sociologist, for a thorough description and analysis of the original functions of the family. They are: sexual gratification, reproduction, economic, education, recreation, religious and social-psychologic:

> By sexual gratification and reproduction, it was meant that children were supposed to be born only within a legitimate and socially recognized family structure. Birth out of this structure, i.e., birth out of wedlock, was not recognized as legitimate and the mother and child subjected to much abuse and ostracism. Related to this, sex was permitted only between husband and wife, for the purpose of reproduction and not pleasure, at least not for women. By the economic function of the family we meant that the family was producer of the goods for consumption. The

family produced its own clothing; most of its own food; most of its own furniture.

In this sense, the family was nearly economically self-sufficient, producing its own tools and housing and so forth.

By education we meant that the role of teaching the child the basic skills of work and housekeeping, as well as the rudiments of social behavior, and the primary socialization skills, was usually carried out by the family.

By recreation, we meant that the main locus of diversion was to be within the family; games, the singing of songs, perhaps the playing of musical instruments, family walks, visiting family friends, etc.

By the religious function of the family, we meant the legitimacy of the family in transmitting religious values to its offspring, to give a religious identity and religious education to its children and to act as an agency through which many of the religious norms of the society were to be carried out. In addition, many other religious activities such as ceremonies and rituals were frequently carried out within the family.

By social-psychologic we meant that the parents were the protectors of the children, especially the father who protected the entire family from physical danger. The father also gave status identity to the family by virtue of the various positions *he* occupied in society and the parents were expected to provide for almost all of the physical, social and psychological needs of the children and of each other.*

Dr. Lieberman concludes, "Today, these functions are a mere shadow of their past. The increasing pace of urbanization has resulted in their modification and weakening to such a degree that there is some speculation about the viability of the traditional family structure as a permanent social institution."* One by one, Prof. Lieberman ticks off the gradual elimination of these traditional functions of the family:

One, the family has become, in our modern technological economy, a consumer rather than a producing unit.

Two, women have joined the labor force in increasing numbers since the 1940's. (According to the American Council of Life Insurance, by 1979, 30.1 million children had working mothers. Half of the children in two-parent families have working mothers, while 60 percent of the children in single-parent families have mothers who work.*)

Three, we have a vast educational system into which children are thrust as early as age two-and-a-half.

Four, there is an increase in leisure time for all family members which, due to the mobility of modern society, is spent mostly outside the home.

Five, family religious activities have, in general, diminished or at least become perfunctory.

As for sexual ties between parents, Lieberman points out that sexual relations outside marriage are increasingly being accepted. And in the social-psychologic functions—parents as protectors —the family has been supplanted by a range of agencies and professionals, from the police to the psychotherapist.

When all is said and done, Dr. Lieberman says we are left with merely the bare bones of an institution:

> We have only some functions which *may* be best carried out in a stable and permanent social relationship, i.e. sexual gratification of family members. But is the traditional nuclear family *structure* really the best for society *and* the individual?
>
> Of main concern . . . is that as functions are modified or eliminated for a social institution, there is a tendency for the structure to be modified to accommodate these changes. If this does not occur, and there is an increase in the discontinuity between structure and function, then there should be an increase in the internal stresses of that system.*

As discussed in the first chapter of this book, the contemporary family is also undergoing pressure from the sexual revolution and the women's movement. The evidence—a 50 percent divorce rate—shows that American men and women are not entirely satisfied with their marriages.* Their search for alternative arrangements, either within marriage or without, has profound implications for the family structure and for the changes it will undergo in the future.

Too often parents detach themselves from the family in an attempt to recapture their lost youth; they are not functioning as parents but rather as competitive older siblings. Dr. Helm Stierlin comments on the void developing between parents and children:

> Nowadays the parent and offspring generations live often in different experiential worlds. How then do they communicate with each other? The answer is, with difficulty. Children who become victims of almost any of the perils besetting childhood all report one thing . . . "My parents don't understand me." *

Parents preoccupied with their own quests may not respond to children's needs to be protected, to communicate, to share. The frustration children feel may take many forms, one of the most extreme of which is running away from home. "By running away, we found, an adolescent often delivers the decisive proof that his parents, contrary to what they might think, are really powerless to control him," says Dr. Stierlin.*

As I pointed out in this book's chapter on runaways, children who take this action may as often be fleeing for safety as they are searching for adventure or freedom. Dr. Stierlin describes the dynamics of three types of pathological family scenarios which may produce runaways. His descriptions offer further insight into the runaway phenomenon and also relate that issue to the disintegration of the family.

The first type is "bound-up" families. Here parents and children cannot separate to develop as individuals. In this setting the child becomes locked into a "family ghetto." The child receives excessive gratification through the family so that he or she becomes confused about individual needs. The child's desire to split from the family generates so much guilt that attempts to flee probably will fail. These children usually return to the parental orbit soon, sometimes in a matter of hours. They may develop a pattern of running and returning, as though tethered to parents.

The second type of family is the one in which children are treated as expendable commodities, as nuisances. Parents neglect and reject their children, who are forced to develop a negative autonomy. These children, when they leave, become "casual runaways," comparable to those designated in this book as "walkaway children." They may develop a pattern of forming sexual alliances and then leaving their sexual partners at their convenience, in much the same way as their parents dispensed with them.

Children in the third family type are called "delegates" of their parents. Parents here "delegate" their children with incompatible missions. For example, the parents may encourage the use of drugs and seductively share sexual confidences with a child (as we saw in several cases in the chapter entitled "Family Sex Games") while simultaneously pressuring the child to study for the ministry, as though to redeem the family. These children, when they break from home, are called "crisis runaways." Their flight was caused by mounting and conflicting pressures. Although they return home often, they will flee again whenever the conflicts become intolerable.

That families are free to develop such pathological interactions may be a result of their isolation and insulation in today's society. In earlier times, families were large social orders with ties to relatives who lived nearby and who exerted a certain amount of behavioral control on members. The community, which consisted of sets of extended families, was organized so that members sought approval from it as well. The family was the institution through which values were transmitted from generation to generation with community approbation.

But for the "Now Generation," such continuity and accountability are irrelevant. Each new family struggles to develop its own life-style, its own beliefs and practices. It is primarily, as

Dr. Lieberman pointed out, an emotional unit—one which, by invoking its right to privacy, has to some extent withdrawn from the community. Dr. Edward Shorter, historian, put it succinctly in his discussion of the fragile state of marriage:

> This new instability is the result of replacing property first with sentiment and then with sex as the bond between man and wife. It also results from the corresponding shearing away of the traditional couple's ties with the community, kin and lineage. Formerly, the expectations that these surrounding institutions had of a couple served to keep the partners together throughout life, perhaps (in fact almost certainly) not happy, yet integrated within a firm social order. But then the couple terminated its associations with these outside groups and strolled off into the dusk holding hands. . . . *

Separation from the community is a price society pays for romantic love and spontaneity, Dr. Shorter seems to be saying. The couple is separated not only from dictates imposed by a larger group of people, but also from interaction with members of that group.

Thus, the definition of parenthood is now left for each couple to "work out." With parental roles being so unsettled and so dependent upon "self-discovery," it is no wonder that children, too, stress their needs to find and express themselves. Such children are unlikely to accept their parents' values, and certainly not without criticizing them first. Sensitive to the dynamics at work in peers' families, in families on television and in movies, children may become aware that there is no one established value system to conform to. Why, of all value systems then, should they accept their parents'?

Once alienated from parental values, children become much more vulnerable to peer pressures. In Sheila and Michael Cole's review of Uri Bronfenbrenner's book, *Two Worlds of Childhood: U.S. and U.S.S.R.*, they talked about parents abdicating responsibility for their children: "Who then is raising our kids? The answer is hardly comforting. To a large extent children are brought up among and by other children of the same age." *

The child culture is often one which involves its own kind of conformity—a conformity to whatever is *au courant*. Dr. John Wilms points this out in relation to sexual mores: "Sexual liberation is often a cultural mandate, and as such is sometimes actually more confining than it is liberating." * And he adds, "Another strain secondary to sexual liberation may follow the realization that 'doing your own thing' may in fact be more felt as doing the 'thing' of some other person or agency." *

Ever younger children feel they should be doing "their thing" without being certain of just what it is. The lack of structure presented by parents, and the conflicting signals they pick up from peers, may lead to constant experimentation, which produces its own casualties. Dr. Jacob Chwast characterizes this process in a 1976 paper when he says, "If other times earned such sobriquets as the age of anxiety or the age of alienation, the past decade surely qualifies as the age of acting out. . . . Nothing is private nor is anyone sacrosanct anymore. At all levels throughout the U.S., the cultural restraints have been let down and sanctions lifted." *

What becomes apparent as those sanctions are lifted is that the family is failing to nurture, teach, and protect its young. Children increasingly are finding themselves bereft of standards to which they might cling in a society which is changing so rapidly that the changes are noticeable not over a decade, but over a period of a year or two. Since values are chiefly derived from the home and from parental example, the loss of the family's authority has created a frightening moral void for our children.

As Dr. Lieberman warned, we are going to have to make some changes in the family if we are to revitalize its roles. Furthermore, we are going to have to change our attitudes toward sex and sexual roles if we are to prevent sexual exploitation of our children. Until recently, it was common for families to encourage little boys to be more aggressive and competitive than little girls. This is an example of an attitude which must be altered. Gloria Steinem, in an article about child pornography, examines the repercussions when such attitudes are perpetrated:

> In fact it [child pornography] is neither sexual nor a perversion. It is one logical, inevitable result of raising boys to believe they must control or conquer others as a measure of manhood, and producing men who may continue to believe that success or even functioning—in sex as in other areas of life—depends on subservience, surrender, or some clear tribute to their superiority.*

She also points out that consumers of child pornography are overwhelmingly middle- and upper-class, middle-aged white males who "seem to be of a group most likely to have been raised to expect power and authority." *

The consumers of child pornography, of course, represent only a small group within the middle class, and their appetite for pornography cannot simply be attributed to their having been raised within that socioeconomic group. But it is from that same background that the adults of today—parents such as those we met in the last chapter—come, bringing higher social and material aspirations than ever before. They enter adulthood with extravagant expectations, they are brutally competitive, and they punish themselves mercilessly for their inevitable failures in the ceaseless search for fulfillment. The consequences are now appearing in the second generation, as psychologists become all too familier with the effects on the children who are being sacrificed to this anxious pursuit of self-realization.

Parental insecurity affects children in many, often contradictory ways, both directly and indirectly. One common pattern swings between neglect or indifference (disguised as an enlightened permissiveness) and intolerant demands for social or academic achievement because the parent conceives of the child alternately as a projection of self-contempt and as a fresh source of ego gratification. This is nothing new; parents have always seen in their children the image of their despised or idealized selves, or both together at once. But when the parental ego is small and frail and continually menaced, pressure on the child to compensate for the mother's or the father's sense of inadequacy can become too intense to bear—especially since with increasing frequency the pressure assumes a sexual form. We have seen how often girls are used by their mothers as surrogates for their own sexual fantasies; and by fathers as sexual objects who won't talk back or make embarrassing comparisons with other men.

Premature sexual demands on a child can be highly destructive, as is shown throughout the book. Even the family, often unwittingly, joins society in misusing children sexually. In 85 percent of cases of sexual molestation, the culprit is known to the child. It may be a teacher, scout leader, or family member. The remarkable increase in the number of runaways and of child prostitutes, as well as other related phenomena, is of such frightening proportions as to have provoked extensive media coverage in addition to numerous government investigations. These phenomena have been shown repeatedly to be direct consequences of deteriorating family life either because the family, although intact, has itself become a source of danger or because the home has literally disintegrated and left the parents unwilling or unable to mobilize themselves to care for their children, who then are essentially abandoned.

Much of the discussion about the effects of early sexual stimulation centers around the question of the sexual partner. Most—although not all—authorities agree that sexual experimentation among children the same age is normal, healthy, and perhaps even to be encouraged, though it should never be forced. They also agree that nothing but harm can come to a child from sexual involvement with an adult. Their only argument in these cases is over the extent and duration of the damage.

Dr. James Comer, Professor of Child Psychiatry at Yale University, believes that "when a child has sexual experience with an adult there is always the element of exploitation and abuse, while with peers it could be exploration and curiosity. It can be very disorienting for kids to be involved with adults, overstimulating, even overwhelming. What can happen is that the child becomes preoccupied with sexuality, or sexual expression, and fails to develop in other ways. Certainly it will also affect a child's ability to relate to other people. However, the immediate consequences center around the guilt the child feels at the time; if guilt is not present, then there will probably be no anxiety over the act."

Dr. Judianne Densen-Gerber is more emphatic: "There is really no healthy sexual activity that can occur at all between a child and an adult—I can't stress that strongly enough. The enormous discrepancy between the two partners in terms of their size, their power, their ability to negotiate the system and their experience makes it impossible. If you take for example a sixty-pound child pinned under a 270-pound man who is forcing his penis down her throat, how can you possibly call that a healthy sexual relationship—even if Daddy gives her a quarter afterward and tells her she has been a good girl?"

Dr. Toby Bieber of Bellevue Hospital states the long-term danger when she says, "Our own clinical experience has been that when fathers seduce their daughters, are openly sexual with them and have intercourse, the girls become schizophrenic."

However, a consensus of mental health experts is that sex play by children with other children definitely is a part of normal, healthy development. Dr. Edward Greenwood, consultant for the Children's Division of The Menninger Clinic, Topeka, Kansas, maintains, "In general, I feel that early sexual activity—if we're talking about the exploratory activity that all children engage in before they become adults, investigating their bodies to see how they work and so on—is an educational thing. To say that it's bad is to deny children an essential part of their growth. In other words, it's exploitative if it's with adults, but positive, if it's exploratory, with their peers. That's part of growing up. Boys will masturbate together, examine each other, try to find out how to do it and what happens, and compare notes about what they think they're doing with girls—all this is part of learning about oneself and the world."

But here also, strength and support from the family are essential. Dr. Bieber says, "Sexual activity among children is basically positive; I don't believe that there are any negative aspects. They aren't crazy, they know what's good for them. But I must add that many elements in our culture tend to push kids into things that they really aren't prepared for, and this is especially true when, as so often happens, the family is fractured—and I don't mean coming apart, I mean *fractured*. I see many parents who are simply incapable of guiding their children in any way. However, a child coming from a strong, healthy family will have a sexuality that is integrated just as any other function will be integrated. When there is strength in the family, the child will grow up with a minimum of anxiety and will be as responsible about sex as he or she is about any other function of body or life."

Dr. Densen-Gerber, however, feels that early sexual experience even with other children interferes with normal development: "Certainly the trend toward acceptance of one's body, including one's genitals, as an integral part of one's self just like having a nose and two feet, is a good thing. But lowering the age of sexual intercourse is something else because sex carries with it commitment and relationship and a whole cadre of feelings that I do not believe young children are ready for. I think fooling around with other kids is fine, but when it comes to integrating sensations and emotions and really understanding what sexuality is all about, they simply can't yet manage it.

"To me the emotional aspect of sex is crucial, and human sexuality must be considered in all its ramifications—physical, emotional, intellectual, and spiritual. And trying to reconcile all of these when a child is capable only of the physical is highly damaging to the child's ability to experience full sexuality later on."

Given the primacy of the family in determining early values and behavior, how important are such secondary factors as the influence of other children and the suggestive impact of the media? Lyrics to pop songs have attained an explicitness startling to adults; how they affect the children who are their most avid consumers is difficult to assess. And when a significant proportion, even a majority, of the other children in a seventh-grade class have crossed the frontier of sexual intercourse, how strong an inducement is this to the rest of the children who without this influence might not have thought about it at all?

Dr. Greenwood believes that "more and more children are being influenced by their peers rather than their parents. In other words, more outside influence is being brought to bear on the rearing of children than ever before. Our children, along with the rest of us, are saturated with messages from the media, and in many ways these replace information and attitudes they would have received from their parents a generation ago. This is the world we're now living in, and it's simply a fact of life we've got to recognize."

Dr. Comer says, "There is certainly a greater problem now than before with early exposure. Children are exposed too soon to sexual stimulation; even though their bodies may be ready, their heads aren't, which means that sex becomes something to be handled only in a mechanical way. First, we had the problem of repression, now it's the opposite." And the result is a kind of deadening of response later, as children move from adolescence into adulthood.

"Songs and television are part of this early exposure, putting pressure on children to perform way before their time. But I find that if a child comes from a home which permits him to develop at his own rate, which supports and encourages him in long-range goals and gives him time and breathing space, then no matter what happens at school or what he hears on television, he's not going to get involved in early sexuality."

Dr. Densen-Gerber adds, "The most important thing is for the child to respect the parents—and I don't mean obey, I mean in the sense of admiring, liking, and feeling that the parent is a good person. Without that respect, and if parents don't offer a strong model, then the peer groups take over and tend to dominate, and the peer groups are profoundly affected by the media.

"For example, my children go to schools that are heavily laden with drugs, but they don't use them, and it's because we believe deeply, and have convinced our children in long talks about it, that drugs are dangerous and bad. Now my children are also exposed to a great deal of promiscuity in school, but we explained to them that we didn't believe sexual intercourse was a good idea until they were in college—certainly not before the age of eighteen—and I don't think they would consider it as a possibility because they respect our judgment. We've never said, 'Oh, my God, you've had relations, you'll burn in hell,' but we *have* said, 'Until you're eighteen or nineteen, you don't do this.'

"Children today have been tremendously sensitized to sexuality, to drugs, and to acting out in all kinds of ways, but if the family is respected, then values come first; if not, then the child will respond to peer pressure."

But even among young children, all sexual acts do not carry an equal significance, she believes: "The kind of masturbatory digital manipulation that kids generally go in for doesn't make much difference and isn't particularly harmful; this kind of masturbatory activity among peers is okay, I think. What *is* destructive is for young girls to be penetrated. The only thing comparable for boys is being anally sodomized. I see terrible damage resulting from being penetrated too young. It seems that one can't bear the invasion of one's inner territory until one is truly ready for an adult love relationship. This is why I think the age of consent laws should not be lower than eighteen or nineteen—because you need to be at least that old before you're emotionally prepared for intercourse."

In the absence of a strongly supportive family, many children will succumb to the tensions of a sexualized environment not only before they are ready to deal with the demands of a sexual relationship, but also before they feel the least desire for it. This is begining to be true of boys as well as girls. Says Dr. Bieber, "One effect of the sexual revolution you don't hear so much about is the fact that before, only the more mature and assertive boys had contact with girls and made out with them. The more timid boys just didn't show up, and they didn't have to. Now it's harder for them to avoid this kind of activity even if they want to. The girls are going after them, seeking them out. The shyer boys used to be able to postpone sex quite easily; now many of them are coming to it prematurely—for them.

"But I find that in general children are ready when they do it. When they're not ready, they don't do it—if left to their own devices."

Dr. Densen-Gerber has observed that some children find ways of instinctively keeping sexual tension within manageable bounds, such as by recourse to what she calls the "pack phenomenon." "I often see the youngest kids organizing themselves in groups; for example, five girls and six or seven boys. They travel in a pack. They have pack intimacy, but they don't seem to go in for one-to-one intimacy, not even emotionally. They don't permit pairing off. I think this is a way of resisting the emotional pressure that they couldn't otherwise tolerate because of all the other strains they're subjected to at that age."

What advice do the experts offer parents who need to know how best to help their children negotiate this difficult passage in today's sexually overstimulated world—whether the stress originates in the world outside or, unavoidably sometimes, in the home itself? How can we best support our children's right to explore their sexuality at their own rate without either repressing them or pushing them too fast?

Dr. Greenwood warns that "sometimes parents try to be too sophisticated in dealing with their children, by which I mean sharing adult sexual knowledge and attitudes with them too soon, wanting to make sure they know it all before they really ask for it. Parents in their efforts to be liberal often overeducate, and they may be giving their children material they're not yet ready to cope with."

Dr. Comer believes that "parents should help their children appreciate their sexuality, and should not deny their right to express themselves, but at the same time should encourage them as well in their right to say no. Children are goal-oriented and task-oriented; they feel urgently that they have things to accomplish in life. Given half a chance, their sexual expression can be modified, channeled into other activities until they reach the level of maturity where they can handle their emotions more effectively."

Dr. Densen-Gerber feels that "first of all, there must be real communication and mutual respect between husband and wife, and an atmosphere in which sex is considered a healthy, accepted activity, even though it may be inappropriate at certain ages and between certain people. If the home provides an environment of acceptance of sexuality without embarrassment, together with a capacity to say that certain behavior is prohibited, for whatever reason, then the children will listen. But parents must be willing to sit down and talk these things over with their children." *

And what about the increasingly familiar single-parent home in which the mother or father is trying to raise the children alone and at the same time carry on a social life of his or her own? "I'm convinced," says Dr. Densen-Gerber, "that it is very traumatic for the children actually to be confronted with the sexual activity of divorced parents, and I am adamant that parents should never bring their present lovers onto the scene. Their new romances should be conducted away from the home because the child will always see the parent taking on a new lover as competition with or rejection of the other parent. I think that for the sake of the children, discretion after divorce is absolutely essential."

Dr. Greenwood believes that "one of the most complicated and difficult aspects of family life today is the situation of the divorced parent, but it must be faced. It begins before the divorce, when the children first became aware that relations between their mother and father are not good. They can't help hearing what's going on, and inevitably they take sides.

"After the divorce, when the parent they live with starts going out with other people, it affects the children deeply. For many this is very frightening. A boy tends to grow up comforted by the thought that sometime his mother will truly belong to him as a love object, and now he's forced to realize that others are more desirable to her than he is. The same thing, of course, holds true for little girls and their fathers."

The only way to deal with these problems, it is generally agreed, is by talking about them openly, giving expression to painful feelings as far as possible, respecting privacy, too, but always making sure the children trust and believe that although the parents may divorce each other, they will never divorce their children.

Children are more afraid of abandonment than of any other single threat. Sexual acting out, as we have seen, is very often a response to that fear. But abandonment, as the child sees it, can be both more and less than a literal broken home. We abandon our children also when, hoping to make "friends" of them, we renounce our responsibilities as models and as lawgivers. This is a betrayal that children feel acutely because no need is stronger to a growing child than the sense of boundaries and limits. The child experiences them as love, as the support given from without which makes possible an inner freedom. If this book has accomplished nothing else, I hope it has encouraged parents in their impulse to express this form of love.

Changes in the traditional family structure have paralleled upheavals in society, upheavals which have permitted children's sexual exploitation to become a growth industry in the past decade. Although the United States is one of the most advanced societies in the world today, with a sophisticated medical and psychiatric establishment and a responsive, representative form of government, it has as yet been unable to combat this exploitation and to protect the children who are its victims. The second half of the twentieth century has seen more social revolutions than most, and they seem to come with increasing frequency. Traditions in America, which are new compared with those of European countries, for example, now do not even have the time to become recognized as codes of behavior before they are outmoded. We have moved from ritual or codified norms of behavior to anarchy. The chaos is exemplified in the current expression "Do your own thing."

Time-Life Books published a book in 1968 called *Sex in the Sixties*, which states:

The nineteenth century frantically insisted on propriety precisely because it felt its real faith and ethics were fast disappearing. While it feared nudity like the plague, Victorian puritanism had the effect of an all covering gown that only inflamed the imagination. By stridently insisting on suppressing the sex instinct in everything, the age betrayed the fact that it really saw that instinct in everything. So too with Sigmund Freud, Victorianism's most perfect rebel. Freudian psychology in its popularized version became one of the chief forces that combined against Victorian puritanism. Gradually the belief spread that repression not license was the great evil, and that sexual matters belonged in the realm of science, not morals. A second force was the new woman, who swept aside the Victorian double standard. Women claimed not only the right to work and to vote, but siding with Galen, the even more important right to pleasure.

The 1960's and 1970's have been a successful stage for the women's liberation movement and for the consciousness-raising development of feminism.

Medical technology affects morality as well. With rapid improvements in contraception from the condom to the diaphragm, from the IUD to the Pill, there is further emphasis on sex for pleasure. While this has lessened inhibitions about sex, responsible sexuality is still the exception, not the rule. Certainly pregnancy and childbearing have moved lower and lower on the list of priorities of young people growing up in the United States. There are not enough parents available to serve as successful role models because they, too, are "doing their own thing" and finding themselves. The award-winning movie *Kramer vs. Kramer* poignantly portrays the conflict in both parental roles, especially the mothering role. The difficulty of being a nurturing mother and a fulfilled individual, judging by the crowds at the box office, seems a particularly timely problem. However, these are not the only social revolutions that have affected the family.

Gay liberation has gone even further in advocating alternate sexual and family life-styles. Some radical lesbian groups advocate raising children without men and outside of marriage. This in theory would make men quite dispensable. Such groups seriously question the viability of the heterosexual family structure. Children born during the chaos of the 1960's and 1970's certainly face serious challenges to the concept of family they are a part of.

In today's society, children are not always desired as an expression of love. There are those who propose to manipulate them for political needs. Although in early societies children were conceived and, especially male children, valued for the work they could do on the family farm, they were nonetheless born and raised within the constellation of a family. They were needed but they were also appreciated. In the turmoil of recent social change and the accompanying devaluation of the family, there should be little surprise that the children, who have been lost in the shuffle, become victims. An array of groups in society have attempted to assume control over children's lives. One of the more outlandish groups is the Rene Guyon Society, which has as its motto, "Sex by eight, or it's too late." In Denmark groups like these have succeeded in revoking the age of consent laws. They are attempting to do the same thing here in the United States.

The extensive nationwide use of hallucinogenic drugs has affected children even more than adults. Drugs produce confusion in states of consciousness, especially for children. Among younger, less developed children this is most serious. In interviews I conducted, every child, preadolescent or adolescent, who was involved in producing pornographic films and pictures said that he or she worked while drugged. They also claimed that often the introduction to pornography would come during drug-filled parties, when someone would take pictures and then offer them money for more. Only too frequently a child's refusal would result in severe beatings or, occasionally, death.

In general, even among the wider population of children, the younger the child is, the more likely drugs have been an

introductory transition to promiscuous sexual activity or commercial sex. Especially among children between eight and thirteen, the combination of drugs, sex, and violence is a deadly one.
Fully 97 percent of the thousands of children interviewed in the
course of researching this book who are promiscuous—who engage in casual sex without emotion—were regular users of hallucinogenic drugs. And 88 percent of sexually active children
below fifteen use drugs. It is an overwhelming experience to
hear pregnant thirteen- and fourteen-year-olds say, with all the
innocence of childhood, that they came out of a drug-induced
fog of nonawareness one day and found themselves pregnant.
It is even more distressing when eleven- and twelve-year-olds
say that they became pregnant after having had only one menstrual period or no period at all.

The greater danger here is that this is not yet the end of the
cycle. The babies of these children have, for the most part, real
problems of physical survival. The neglect by the mothers of
their own nutritional needs, their heavy drug, cigarette, and
alcohol use as well as their extensive sexual action, seriously
endangers these fetuses. Thus, the problem is a double one; not
only are the ages of the children used in the adult sex market
lower, but the well-being and safety of the babies they give
birth to are at risk.

One of society's newest liberation movements in the late
1970's is the child liberation movement. It became a serious issue
in 1978. This growing movement concerns itself with the separation of children from families which are unfit to take care
of them and/or are abusive. Those children who feel oppressed
at home can now legally separate from their parents in several
states. But who will care for them? As of 1980 the only legislation to care for almost one million children who run away
annually is the Runaway Youth Act. Nationally, there are only
250 centers for millions of these children. The agencies which
are needed to care properly for children who leave their parents' homes don't exist, and there are no new laws contemplated
to care for these children. In fact, the only federally funded
project for juvenile prostitution, the Metropolitan Adolescent

Resource Center (M.A.R.C.) in New York City, terminated when its funds were permitted to run out in mid-1979.

There is a necessity for a national realization that all children need help. While there are literally thousands of adult programs, funded by a host of governmental agencies, for alcohol, drug, and sex offenders, the only federally funded project to research the rehabilitation of juvenile prostitutes, M.A.R.C., was in existence for less than two years. There is a need for programs to educate parents and for laws to stop child abusers.

The laws on the books now are not being used effectively to halt child abuse and punish sex abusers. Dr. William Prendergast, the director of the New Jersey Rehabilitation Center for sex offenders, states that while one in twelve adult rape cases results in an arrest, only one in 200 childhood rapes results in arrest. What happens to those few after they are arrested is even more upsetting. Sergeant John Johnstone of the New York State Police did a two-and-a-half-year study from 1977 through 1979 in an upstate New York county. His results show that less than 4 percent of the few who are arrested for child sex abuse spend any time at all in jail. *All* the rest are either dismissed, go to conference, or are referred to social agencies.

As more research studies have been published, it has become appallingly clear that this is indeed not the exception but the national pattern. Dr. Jennifer James, in a study in Seattle, Washington, showed that even when cases of child sex abuse were reported to physicians by families, less than one third of all physicians reported these cases to the authorities or any social agency.* The message is clear—no one wants to get involved.

Father Bruce Ritter, Director of Under 21 and Covenant House in New York City, warns, "In other words, the availability breeds the appetite." And he adds, "Our experience is that the toughest kids to reach are the twelve-, thirteen-, and fourteen-year-old children once they are into the child-sexploitation system. They have no understanding of the consequences."

In most states, prosecution of juvenile sex offenders is very difficult for many technical and legal reasons. Many states still require corroboration. In California, as well as in some other states, a child over fourteen is considered an accomplice. The laws, in general, range from being obstructive to permitting exploitation. Father Ritter, testifying before the Senate Select Committee on Crime, on November 14, 1977, said:

> The problem is extremely acute for those over 16, since the law simultaneously permits a child to emancipate himself and then effectively disenfranchises that child. For the most part he cannot get the medical help he needs, cannot easily qualify for public assistance, cannot enter into contracts, cannot find a decent job. Children are free to wander the streets panhandling, exploiting and being exploited, no one seems willing, either to accept clear responsibility for the thousands of children over 15 who stand outside the jurisdiction of Family Court, of Criminal Court, and in a large part, the Child Welfare System. . . . Parents are effectively helpless too. Since it is manifestly not in the best interests of the child or the public to permit this to happen, some office, some court, some jurisdiction must be given the clear responsibility. Our systems have gotten too quickly out of date. We operate on a principle, seemingly, of caveat puer; let the child beware.

He says bluntly what most in the field have found: "I think that our political and judicial systems and our law enforcement agencies have demonstrated quite amply their unwillingness and inability to deal effectively with the problem."

Even tough, experienced police officers feel the pressure to rescue children from a life of sexual exploitation. I have found that in almost all instances where there is a specialized squad or unit to deal with children and the dangers they face on the streets, it has been started by pressure from the lower ranks—by the patrolmen themselves. This is true of the Juvenile Division, Sexually Exploited Child Unit, of the Los Angeles Police Department, headed by Sergeant Lloyd Martin. He says:

"Almost all law enforcement agencies, the Los Angeles Police Department included, prior to the establishment of this unit would only handle cases when Mom or Dad brought the little girl or boy down and said, 'This is what happened to me.' The victim I deal with now is the real victim, the runaway him- or herself, the broken-home situation itself directly. The child may not even realize that he is a victim. The sexually exploited child is often a noncomplaining, willing victim. These children don't complain to the police department. They don't complain to their parents, and therefore there are no reports, no statistics to back up how many children are actually sexually exploited."

To start the juvenile unit in Los Angeles, Sergeant Martin compiled a book that documented the problems of child sex abuse in Los Angeles. In October, 1976, the unit began to function independently on a temporary basis with the understanding that it would have to prove its value to justify its continued existence. By working seventeen- and eighteen-hour days, Sergeant Martin and the other nine men in the squad rolled up an impressive number of arrests and reports on juvenile sex crimes. For some months it remained a temporary unit until the residents of Los Angeles heard about its work on the television show *60 Minutes*, and read about it in *Time* magazine. Many listeners enthusiastically wrote in and voiced their support for the group. Finally, after much public pressure, the unit became permanent on July 1, 1977. At this time there is no other city in the United States with a comparable juvenile vice unit.

In New York, Robert Meltzer, Director of Project Contact, an outreach program, believes that much of today's social disorganization is an outgrowth of the dislocations during the Vietnam years. He says, "There are more kids now seeking the option to split from their families because many other kids have done it before, and they have seen it. Prior to the war, there wasn't that kind of experience. We have at times had to buy kids out of the pimp system and negotiate with the pimps with cartons of cigarettes. While there is no set price on girls being liberated from the pimps, there is a 'steerage' fee for young boys, who collect two hundred dollars for steering their young girl friends to pimps. There is also a fee for a girl who gives up her baby, especially if the baby is white, and the fee, until recently, in the East Village was four hundred dollars."

The Time-Life book, *Sex in the Sixties*, states: "The rebels of the sixties have parents with only the tattered remnants of a code expressed for many of them." Children now get contradictory messages from society. For example, mental health professionals are concerned about the introduction of a bill in San Francisco to "demystify" homosexual sex practices in the schools. This teaching of homosexual sex education is already taking place in some of the suburbs around San Francisco. It begins in fourth grade when children learn how to achieve "gay orgasm."

Ira Riess, a respected sociologist, wrote in the 1960's about "permissiveness with affection." What he meant was: (1) Morals are a private affair; (2) being in love justifies premarital sex and, perhaps by implication, extramarital sex; and (3) nothing really is wrong as long as nobody "gets hurt."

The extensive and growing abuse of ever younger children characterizes today's sexual exploitation business. Whereas parents during the sixties worried about their seventeen- and nineteen-year-olds, and in the seventies about their fourteen- and sixteen-year-olds, today the pornographic industries are producing kiddie porn using children as young as six years of age. There is a whole genre of films and pornographic visual aids that focus on children between six and ten years old. We seem, as a society, to be moving from protecting our children to allowing their exploitation. We are abandoning our children in the same way as the parent who has renounced his or her responsibilities as model and lawgiver.

Dr. Densen-Gerber's view that our society hates its children finds an echo in Father Ritter when he testified before the House Subcommittee on Select Education, May 31, 1977:

> The horror stories are literally endless. Our society has permitted to develop an enormous sex industry that we seem powerless to do anything about. Under the protection of the First Amendment we are witnessing an almost anything goes explosion of exploitation and abuse that is

destroying thousands of young people every year. Our political leaders, our law enforcement agencies, the Judiciary blame each other and point accusatory fingers elsewhere.

Chapter 12

SUMMING UP

The sexual revolution has brought about an upheaval in society that is changing the character of the American experience. And it is our children who are the most profoundly affected by this upheaval. Concerned parents must confront the contradictions between their generation and this one, they must realize the effect these contradictions are having on their children, and they must assert themselves as parents and as citizens to ensure that their children have the right to be children.

Each of the problems discussed in this book plays a role in the tragedy, "Death of Innocence," that is being enacted in the country today. It is time now to examine the implications of these problems, to see where we are now and where we may be going.

The sharp increase in the incidence of venereal disease and the astounding number of teenage and even preteenage pregnancies in the past decade are proof that relaxed standards for adolescent sexual behavior can have tragic results. Our new morality tells children that they do not need the justification of love to have sex. In fact, love is frowned upon by avant-garde children as being unsophisticated. The "in" thing is to be "cool," and to do "it." However, our new morality has not created institutions to educate children about basic bodily functions. Adolescents who believe that they will not get pregnant if they stand up immediately after intercourse are victims of this contradiction in society. While they follow the dictates of the new morality on the one hand, they are not educated to cope with the results of that morality on the other. The result is, of course, that they become pregnant.

Their pregnancy then places a whole new set of stresses on the family. Parents who are used to thinking of their children as children must suddenly look at them as harbingers of a new age. They feel out of step and probably even more bewildered than before at the role of the traditional family in modern society. A further disintegration of family structure is the almost inevitable result.

The child mothers themselves are in an equally confusing position. Their own families are unable to help them, and society seems unwilling to help them. If they decide to continue their education, they will embark on a difficult path that few will be able to complete. Teenage pregnancy is a severe problem for the family and for the teenager; and it seems inevitable that the child, the offspring in a sense of the new morality, will suffer most in the end.

The response of adult family members to the sexual revolution is a part of the exploitation of children. Often children are no longer allowed to enjoy a period of latency, a period of childhood removed from adult demands of sexuality. Now their parents are "finding themselves," and in some cases that means either directly exposing their children to sexual experiences or indirectly making their children the victims of their own confusion.

Children are helpless victims in family sex games and in the all-too-frequent occurrence of incest. They become entangled in their parents' complex of sexual needs, needs that often surface in response to the sexual revolution outside of the family. Children involved in these situations feel helpless and guilty; they become trapped in exercises of power and submission. Adult sexual fantasies are increasingly encouraged, and increasingly children are the objects which fulfill these fantasies.

Such children have little recourse. It is extremely difficult for them to talk about their experiences with outsiders. And unless they leave home altogether, it is almost impossible for them to escape from such situations. Trained counselors are able, after much work, to help children articulate their anxieties. Sadly, society has not yet recognized the severity and extent of family sex games and incest, so patient long-term help is generally not available to children who need it.

Those children who leave their homes, who become runaways, are even worse off. On the street they are prey to a whole host of exploitative elements. And, as we have discussed in previous chapters, society is simply not equipped to help runaways effectively. They tend to slip into the cracks between the jurisdictions of legal and social welfare organizations. Because of the confusion, often both sides find that their hands are tied.

In families where one or both parents feels the need to "find him or herself," children are always the victims. In the movie *Kramer vs. Kramer*, the mother of a young boy decides that she must leave her child in order to fulfill herself. She has chosen to abandon her son, to abrogate her responsibility toward him, in response to a vague and undefined craving. Rather than search for meaning in a life that includes her child, she has decided to cast him out, then begin her search. The insistent refrain of the women's consciousness-raising movement today tends to support her. But, as always, the child is left with no societal advocate and no societal solution.

The response of adults to the sexual revolution has created a whole host of problems for today's children. The adult view of children has changed. Children are no longer innocent, goes the refrain among certain segments of society, but are objects to be exploited. We are now able to assess the implications of this adult exploitation. Institutions devoted to sexual exploitation of children that are economically viable and socially recognized, though not countenanced, are springing up all over the country. Groups devoted to the rights of pedophiles, companies producing kiddie porn, cross-country networks created to take advantage of vulnerable runaways, are all flourishing. They will continue to flourish unless parents and society can take quick and effective action.

Parents must recognize that pedophiliac groups who speak of the rights of children to receive love are really lobbying for their own legal rights to exploit children.

Companies that produce pornographic films and pictures and then defend their right to do so by citing freedom of speech are not only perverting the intent of the First Amendment, they are ignoring one of the most basic, humanistic rights of man—the right not to be exploited. If their superficial parroting of the First Amendment is allowed as a justification for their continued existence, then this society is in danger of losing one of the most basic tenets of its faith.

The pimps and entrepreneurs who exploit the runaways all over the country are part of a subculture that has always existed. But the people they are exploiting are younger adolescents who are too confused and powerless to protect themselves. If society abrogates its responsibility to protect its most vulnerable members, then it is denying one of its most important functions.

In all these cases, it is society which must take action. However, society has been sadly delinquent in doing so. This is partly due to the confusion that has resulted from the sexual revolution. It is also partly a consequence of an increasingly sexualized society which is seeking release from its own frustrations. However, it is time for us all to examine what we as a society and what we as parents can do to protect the rights of our children, or we risk losing touch with the most basic precepts of our notion of freedom. There is no freedom in license.

Society must create more institutions to rescue children from lives of sexual exploitation. The Los Angeles juvenile vice unit is the only one of its kind in the country. New York City has the only runaway squad. There should be comparable units in every major city. An educated public can bring pressure on authorities to create such units.

There are few public or private groups to help the huge population of runaways in the country. More are needed.

And, perhaps most important, society must approach incidents of child sexual exploitation in a more coherent way. Just last summer a New York State Supreme Court judge ruled that a Queens teacher accused of dealing in child pornography could not be deprived of his pension. Although more than 1,000 photographs, slides, and films of young boys in nude and semi-nude poses were found in this man's apartment, although he was accused by the school chancellor of "betraying his trust," and although the judge himself characterized the defendant as "a person of low and depraved morals," this teacher will receive a state-subsidized pension. All agree that he betrayed society, but society was unable to deny him his pension.

As parents, our job is equally important. We must realize that it is no longer enough to be a worried or an anxious parent. We must be educated, knowledgeable parents with the determination to care for our children whether or not it is socially popular. Reaching out and giving care to children, as well as providing them with healthy role models, are the most important parental responsibilities.

The issue of legalities such as joint custody, so much discussed today, is minor. What must be assumed by all parents, married, separated or divorced, is joint responsibility. It can be shown in tangible form by caring adults. Being there for the child is the beginning. Parents often need support themselves. The traditional parent organizations such as P.T.A.'s and church groups need to be energized to become catalysts for effective action. Examples of parent effectiveness can be seen in the record of parent groups who have affected television programming and commercials directed at children.

Parent power for the benefit of children can shield children and permit them to grow to a healthy adulthood.

The schools, along with other societal institutions, have failed our children. The policy of acting *in loco parentis* has been abandoned and *laissez-faire* now rules the day. It is ironic that often it is the students who will call in the police to a school, and not the authorities, in cases of drug abuse or sexual exploitation. Parents should activate the P.T.A.'s as effective in-

SUMMING UP / 339

struments for child care, and should change the concept of "guidance counseling," since as of today, it neither guides nor counsels. Creating program cards for academic subjects is not as vital as supervision of safety and welfare. Effective preparation for life can be aided by enlightened parent-school cooperation.

Clearly, the situation now is chaotic. The sexual revolution has produced a myriad of victims, almost all of them children. Adults, families, and society are unable and unwilling to protect them. The implications are staggering.

A crippled generation is growing up. Many in this generation will hardly be able to function themselves, let alone become contributing members of society.

And society itself, in its failure to cope with these problems, has lost sight of the humanistic, philosophical, and legal tenets on which it is based. We must reach back to these tenets and protect the weak and helpless. We must remember our basic responsibility to guard against the exploitation of one member of society by another. And this call to action is doubly urgent because it is the children of our society who are the victims. They are the most helpless members of society and, more important, they are the future. If they are crippled because of our inability to act, then the future is very bleak indeed.

Father Ritter concluded his testimony on the sexual exploitation of children with words that every concerned parent would do well to read carefully. He said:

> The time for pious rhetoric and expressions of concern is long past. We need appropriate, effective action. I doubt that the voters of this country will be satisfied with less for much longer. We are wallowing in unspeakable filth and we wring our hands about the First Amendment. More importantly our children are being daily used and exploited and sometimes being killed while we stand around helplessly. Is it wrong to be outraged? Did we not see this coming long ago? Has outrage become too un-

sophisticated for us? Are we incapable of saying very simply that this is wrong and we will not tolerate it any longer? For God's sake, gentlemen, and for the sake of the children, do something about it!

APPENDIX

Table 1

Dating and age—by Group
"At what age did you have your first date?"

	8 to 17 year olds			20-21 year olds
Age at First Date	Sexually Inactive	Sexually Average	Sexually Active	20+
8, 9	3.4%	5 %	6.5%	0 %
10, 11, 12	23.2%	29.5%	33 %	10.6%
13, 14	29.3%	41.5%	57 %	44 %
15, 16	24.1%	13 %	3.5%	44 %
17	20 %	11 %	0 %	1.4%

Table 2

Unchaperoned party and age—by Group
"Age at first unchaperoned party?"

	8 to 17 year olds			20-21 year olds
Age	Sexually Inactive	Sexually Average	Sexually Active	20+
8, 9	0%	0%	4%	0%
10, 11, 12	26%	33%	34%	14%
13, 14	24%	32%	32%	29%
15, 16	18%	14%	30%	37%
17	7%	9%	0%	20%
Not Yet	25%	12%	0%	0%

Table 3

Smoking and age—by Group
"If you smoke, at what age did you start?"

| | 8 to 17 year olds | | | 20-21 year olds |
Age	Sexually Inactive	Sexually Average	Sexually Active	20+
8, 9	0 %	2 %	18.7%	0 %
10, 11, 12	11 %	16 %	32.4%	14.4%
13, 14	10.2%	16.2%	7 %	19.7%
15, 16	15.7%	7.9%	17.7%	21 %
17	3.7%	0 %	.2%	5.3%
Not yet	59.4%	57.9%	24 %	39.6%

Table 4

Saturday night curfew—by Group
"What is your Saturday night curfew?"

| | 8 to 17 year olds | | | 20-21 year olds |
Age	Sexually Inactive	Sexually Average	Sexually Active	20+
10 P.M.	6%	3 %	0%	0 %
11 P.M.	10%	6.6%	3%	0 %
Midnight to 1 A.M.	18%	10.6%	5%	1.3%
2 A.M.	26%	24 %	25%	8 %
4 A.M.	19%	18 %	18%	4 %
No curfew	21%	37.8%	49%	86.7%

Table 5

Parents waiting up—by Age
"Do your parents wait up for you?"

Ages	Yes
10-12	100 %
13	86.8%
14	61.4%
15	44.4%
16	43.4%
17	37.5%
20+	8 %

Table 5A

Parents waiting up—by Group
"Do your parents wait up for you?"

| | 8 to 17 year olds | | | 20-21 year olds |
	Sexually Inactive	*Sexually Average*	*Sexually Active*	*20+*
Yes	45.3%	41%	17.6%	20.4%
No	54.7%	59%	82.4%	79.6%

Table 6

Marriage age—by Group
"The ideal age for me to marry is _____"

| *Ideal Marriage Age* | 8 to 17 year olds | | | 20-21 year olds |
	Sexually Inactive	*Sexually Average*	*Sexually Active*	*20+*
16-17	2 %	1.4%	9.6%	0 %
20-23	56.7%	45.3%	39.3%	21.2%
24-27	27.3%	38.4%	22.9%	25.6%
28-35	13.5%	11.5%	15.2%	2.1%
Undecided	.5%	3.4%	13 %	51.1%

Table 7

Importance of marriage—by Age
"In my opinion marriage is _____"

Subject's Age	*Very Important*	*Important*	*Not Important*
10-12	31.6%	68.4%	0 %
13-14	39.8%	43.2%	17 %
15-16	31 %	49.5%	19.5%
17	30.3%	49.7%	20 %
20	37.5%	25 %	37.5%

Table 8

Attitude toward politics—by Group
"Politics is very important, important, not important."

	Sexually Inactive	Sexually Average	Sexually Active
Very Important	37.8%	22.8%	35.3%
Important	56.9%	53.5%	41.2%
Not Important	5.3%	23.7%	23.5%

Table 8A

Attitude toward politics—by Age
"Politics is very important, important, not important."

Age	Very Important	Important	Not Important
11-12	30 %	58 %	12 %
13-14	17 %	62 %	21 %
15-16	20 %	54.5%	25.5%
17	28.9%	51.3%	19.8%
20	27.6%	63.2%	9.2%

Table 9

Attitude toward values—by Group
"I feel that values are changing _____"

	8 to 17 year olds			20-21 year olds
	Sexually Inactive	Sexually Average	Sexually Active	20+
Too Rapidly	19 %	30.3%	57.1%	14.5%
Rapidly	67.2%	54.6%	35.7%	71.1%
Slowly	12.1%	12.3%	5.9%	13.2%
Not at all	1.7%	2.8%	1.3%	1.2%

Table 10

Attitude toward dating and values—by Group
"People I date have to be _____"

| Trait | 8 to 17 year olds | | | 20-21 year olds |
	Sexually Inactive	Sexually Average	Sexually Active	20+
Religion	6%	2.5%	0%	0 %
Sex	0%	3 %	9%	8 %
Money	0%	0 %	14%	1.4%
Intelligence	17%	13.8%	7%	12.9%
Looks	14%	25 %	21%	6.8%
Sense of humor	2%	2.3%	0%	2.7%
Other Superlative *	52%	41.3%	28%	60 %
Personality	9%	12.1%	21%	8.2%

* Note: "Other Superlative" includes: wonderful, fabulous, great, wow, super, etc.

BIBLIOGRAPHY

Adler, R. P. *Research on the Effects of T.V. Advertising on Children.* Washington, D. C.: National Science Foundation, 1978.

Balswick, J., and D. Ward. *Strong Men and Virtuous Women: A Content Analysis of Sex Role Stereotypes.* Meeting of the Southern Sociological Society, Atlanta, Ga., 1977.

Bandura, A. *Aggression: A Social Learning Analysis.* Englewood Cliffs, N.J.: Prentice-Hall, 1973.

Beigel, Hugo G. "The Innocent Child," *Sex in the Childhood Years.* New York: Sexology, 1970.

Berman, Louis A., and Dennis R. Jensen. "Father Daughter Interactions and the Sexual Development of the Adopted Girl." *Psychotherapy: Research & Practice*, Fall, 1973, Vol. 10 (3), pp. 253–255.

Boles, Jacqueline, and Charlotte Tatro. *The New Male Model, Androgyny or Traditional?* Paper presented at the American Psychiatric Association national convention, May, 1978.

Brown, Joe David. *Sex in the Sixties.* New York: Time-Life Books, 1968.

Browning, D., and B. Boatman. *Incest, Children at Risk.* Paper presented at the American Psychiatric Association national convention, May, 1978.

Chwast, Jacob. *Psychotherapy of Disadvantaged Acting-Out Youths.* Paper presented at the Twelfth National Scientific Meeting of the Association for the Advancement of Psychotherapy, May 9, 1976.

Cole, Sheila, and Michael Cole. Review of *Two Worlds of Childhood, U.S. and U.S.S.R.*, by Uri Bronfenbrenner. *Psychology Today*, July, 1970.

Collins, W. A. "The Effect of Temporal Separation Between Motivation, Aggression and Consequences: A Developmental Study." *De-*

velopmental Psychology, 1973, 8, pp. 215–221.

Collins, W. A., T. Berndt, and V. Hess. "Observational Learning of Motives and Consequences for Television Aggression: A Developmental Study." Child Development, 1974, 45, pp. 799–802.

Corder-Bolz, Charles, and S. O'Bryant. "Teacher vs. Program." Journal of Communication, 1978, 28, (1), pp. 97–103.

Daven, J., J. F. O'Connor, and R. Briggs. "The Consequences of Imitative Behavior in Children, the 'Evel Knievel Syndrome.'" Pediatrics, 1976, 57, pp. 418–419.

Drabman, R. S., and M. H. Thomas. "Does T.V. Violence Breed Indifference?" Journal of Communication, 1975, 25, (4), pp. 86–89.

Drabman, R. S., and M. H. Thomas. "Does Watching Violence on Television Cause Apathy?" Pediatrics, 1976, 57, pp. 329–331.

Dudar, Helen. "America Discovers Child Pornography." Ms., August, 1977, pp. 45–47.

Dwelley, Amy. "Sex Interests of the Pre-School Child," The Childhood Years. New York: Sexology, 1970.

Friedrich, L. K., and A. H. Stein. "Aggressive and Prosocial Television Programs and the Natural Behavior of Pre-School Children." Monographs of the Society for Research in Child Development, 1973, 38, (4, serial no. 51).

Freud, S. The Origins of Psychoanalysis: Letters to Wilhelm Fliess, Drafts and Notes (1887–1902). London: Imago Publishing Co., Ltd., 1954.

Freud, S. Some General Remarks on Hysterical Attacks, standard ed., 1909, 9. London: Hogarth Press, pp. 229–234.

Freud, S. "Three Contributions to the Theory of Sex," trans. A. A. Brill. Nervous and Mental Disease Monographs. New York: Johnson Reprint Corp., 1930.

Freuh, T., and P. E. McGhee. "Traditional Sex-Role Development and Amount of Time Spent Watching Television." Developmental Psychology, 1975, 11, p. 109.

Gadberry, Sharon, and Mary Schneider. Effects of Parental Restrictions on T.V. Viewing. Paper presented at the American Psychological Association national convention, September, 1978.

Galst, Joanne P. Young Children's Snack Choices: Is Television An Influencing Factor? Paper presented at the American Psychological Association national convention, September, 1979.

Galst, Joanne P., and Mary A. White. "The Unhealthy Persuaders: The Reinforcing Value of Television and Children's Purchase-Influencing

Attempts at the Supermarket." *Child Development*, 1976, *47*, pp. 1089–1096.

Gilberg, Arnold L. *Gender Specific Therapy Problems in Male Youths.* Paper presented at the American Psychiatric Association national convention, May, 1978.

Glueck, B. "Pedophilia," Slovenko, R. (ed.), *Sexual Behavior and the Law.* Springfield, Ill.: Chas. Thomas, 1965, pp. 539–562.

Goodwin, Jean, Mary Simms, and Robert Bergman. *Hysterical Seizures, a Sequel to Incest.* Paper presented at the American Psychiatric Association national convention, May, 1979.

Greenson, R. "Disidentifying from Mother." *The International Journal of Psychoanalysis*, 1968, *49*, pp. 370–373.

Horton, Robert W., and David A. Santagrossi. *Mitigating the Impact of Televised Violence Through Concurrent Adult Commentary.* Paper presented at the American Psychological Association national convention, August, 1978.

James, Jennifer, and William Womack. "Physician Reporting of Child Sex Abuse." *Journal of the American Medical Association*, September 8, 1978.

Jersild, A. T., and F. B. Holmes. "Children's Fears." *Child Development Monographs*, 1935, no. 20.

Johnson, A., and S. A. Szurek. "The Genesis of Anti-Social Acting Out in Children and Adults." *Psychoanalytic Quarterly*, XXI, 1952, pp. 323–343.

Kaufman, I., A. Peck, and C. Taguiri. "The Family Constellation and Overt Incestuous Relations Between Fathers and Daughters." *American Journal of Orthopsychiatry*, 1954, *24*, pp. 266–279.

Kinkead, Gwen. "The Family Secret." *Boston Magazine*, October, 1972, pp. 100–105.

Kolb, L., and A. Johnson. "Etiology of Overt Homosexuality, and the Need for Therapeutic Modification." *Psychoanalytic Quarterly*, XXIV, 1955, pp. 506–515.

Komerovsky, Mirra. *Dilemmas of Masculinity: A Study of College Youth.* New York: Norton, 1976.

Laing, R. D., and A. Esterson. *Sanity, Madness and the Family.* New York: Viking Press, 1964.

Leifer, A. D., and D. F. Roberts. "Children's Response to Television Violence." *Television, Social Behavior, and Social Learning*, eds.

J. P. Murray, E. A. Rubinstein, and G. A. Comstock. Washington, D.C.: U.S. Government Printing Office, 1972.

Liebert, Robert M., and R. A. Baron. "Some Immediate Effects of Televised Violence on Children's Behavior." *Developmental Psychology*, 1972, 6, pp. 469–475.

Liebert, R. M., and N. S. Schwartz. "Effects of Mass Media." *Annual Review of Psychology*, 1977, 28, pp. 141–173.

Litin, E. M., M. Giffin, and M. Johnson. "Parental Influences in Unusual Sexual Behavior in Children." *Psychoanalytic Quarterly*, 1956, 25, pp. 37–55.

Maccoby, E. E., and C. N. Jackson. *The Psychology of Sex Differences.* Calif.: Stanford University Press, 1974.

Mead, Margaret, at Third Annual National Conference on Child Abuse and Neglect. *Daily News*, April 18, 1978.

Mony, J., and A. Ehredt. *Man and Woman, Boy and Girl: The Differentiation and Dimorphism of Gender Identity from Conception to Maturity.* Baltimore: Johns Hopkins University Press, 1972.

Nielsen, A. C. *The Television Audience.* Chicago: Nielsen Co., 1975.

Offer, J. B., and David Offer. *Sexuality in Adolescent Males.* Paper presented at the American Psychiatric Association national convention, May, 1976.

Orel, H. "Investigations of Incest in Vienna." *Beitr. Z. Gerichtl. Med.*, 1932, 12, pp. 107–122.

Father Ritter's testimony before the Senate Select Committee, November 4, 1977; and the House Subcommittee on Select Education, May 31, 1977.

Rosenbaum, Maj-Britt. *Gender Specific Therapy Problems in Female Youths.* Paper presented at the American Psychiatric Association national convention, 1978.

Rosenfeld, Alvin, R. Nadelson, et al. "Incest and the Sexual Abuse of Children." *Journal of the American Academy of Child Psychiatry*, 1977, 16, pp. 334–346.

Rosenfeld, Alvin A. "Sexual Misuse and the Family." *Victimology, an International Journal*, 1977, 2, pp. 226–235.

Rosenfeld, Alvin A. "The Clinical Management of Incest and Sexual Abuse of Children." *Journal of the American Medical Association*, October 19, 1979, vol. 242, no. 16.

Rosenfeld, A. A., Carole Smith, A. W. O'Reilly, Wenda Brewster, and D. K. Haarvies. *The Primal Scene: A Study on Incidence.* Paper presented at the American Psychiatric Association national convention, May, 1980.

"Runaway Youth." *Annual Report on Activities Conducted to Implement the Runaway Youth Act.* Washington, D.C.: Department of H.E.W. Office of Human Development Services Administration for Children, Youth and Families, Youth Development Bureau, 1978.

Scheffe, H. *The Analysis of Variance.* New York: John Wiley, 1959.

Schramm, W., J. Lyle, and E. G. Parker. *Television in the Lives of Our Children.* Calif.: Stanford University Press, 1961.

Schultz, Le Roy G. Speech on incest at The First National Conference on the Sexual Abuse of Children, in Washington, D.C., as reported in *The New York Times*, December 3, 1979.

Shorter, Edwin. *The Making of the Modern Family.* New York: Basic Books, 1977.

Silverman, L. T., J. N. Sprafkin, and Eli A. Rubinstein. *Sex on Television: A Content Analysis of the 1977 Season.* American Psychological Association national convention, August, 1977.

Stein, A., and L. Friedrich. "Television Content and Young Children's Behavior." *Television and Social Behavior (Vol. 2)*, eds. J. P. Murray, E. A. Rubinstein, and G. A. Comstock. Washington, D.C.: U.S. Government Printing Office, 1972.

Steinem, Gloria. "Pornography—Not Sex but the Obscene Use of Power." *Ms.*, August, 1977, pp. 43–44.

Stierlin, Helm. *On the Therapy of Adolescent Runaways.* Paper presented at the American Psychiatric Association national convention, May, 1974.

Stoller, R. "Passing and the Continuum of Gender Identity." *Sexual Inversion*, ed. J. Marmor. New York: Basic Books, 1965.

Szurels, S. A. "The Genesis of Anti-Social Acting Out in Children and Adults." *Psychoanalytic Quarterly*, XXII, 1953, pp. 475–496.

Tavris, C., and C. Offir. *The Longest War: Sex Differences in Perspective.* New York: Harcourt Brace Jovanovich, Inc., 1977.

Thomas, M. H., and R. S. Drabman. "Effects of Television Violence on Expectations of Others' Aggression." *Personality and Social Psychology Bulletin*, 1978, 4, pp. 73–76.

Tuddenham, R. D. "Studies in Reputation, Sex and Grade Differences in School Children's Evaluation of Their Peers, The Diagnosis of Social Adjustment." *Psychological Monographs*, 1952, 66, no. 333.

Walling, J. I. "The Effect of Parental Interaction on Learning from Television." *Communication Education*, 1976, 25, (1), pp. 16–25.

Weinberg, S. K. *Incest Behavior.* New York: Citadel Press, 1955.

Wesley, F., and C. Wesley. *Sex Role Psychology.* New York: Human Services Press, 1977.

White, Mary A., and Barbara Sandberg. *The Reinforcement and Modeling of Sex vs. Education on Prime-Time Television, Watched by School Age Children.* American Psychological Association national convention, September, 1978.

Wilms, John. "New Strains on Youth Due to Sexual Liberation." *Medical Aspects of Human Sexuality*, August, 1978, pp. 45–54.

INDEX

353

GOLDEN GATE SEMINARY LIBRARY